Learning Desire

Learning Desire

Perspectives on Pedagogy, Culture, and the Unsaid

edited by

Sharon Todd

ROUTLEDGE
New York & London

Published in 1997 by
Routledge
29 West 35th Street
New York, NY 10001

Published in Great Britain in 1997 by
Routledge
11 New Fetter Lane
London EC4P 4EE

Copyright © 1997 by Routledge
Printed in the United States of America
Design: Jack Donner

Shoshana Felman's "Psychoanalysis and Education: Teaching Terminable and Interminable" was first published in *Yale French Studies* 63 (1982) and is reprinted by permission.

Judith P. Robertson's "Fantasy's Confines: Popular Culture and the Education of the Female Primary-School Teacher" is a slightly altered version of an article that appears in *Canadian Journal of Education, Revue canadienne de l'éducation*. Reprinted with permission.

Laurie Finke's "Knowledge as Bait: Feminism, Voice and the Pedagogical Unconscious" first appeared in *College English* (January 1993). Copyright 1993 by the National Council of Teachers of English. Reprinted with permission.

An earlier version of Helen Harper's "Disturbing Identity and Desire: Adolescent Girls and Wild Words" appears in *JCT: An Interdisciplinary Journal of Curriculum Studies* (Winter 1996) and is reprinted with permission.

Library of Congress Cataloging-in-Publication Data

Learning desire: perspectives on pedagogy, culture, and the unsaid /
    edited by Sharon Todd.
        p.   cm.
    Includes bibliographical references and index.
    ISBN 0–415–91766–2. — ISBN 0–415–91767–0 (pbk.)
    1. Critical pedagogy.   2. Desire.   3. Feminism and education.   4. Teacher-
student relationships.   5. Learning, psychology of.   I. Todd, Sharon, 1962–   .
LC196.L43   1997
370.11'5—dc21
                                                                    97–11238
                                                                    CIP

They will hear with a third ear
what is said here between the lines
—and even what is left unsaid

—Theodor Reik,
Listening With the Third Ear

Contents

Acknowledgments

Putting this book together has been quite a learning experience for me and would not have been possible without the financial support of the Social Sciences and Humanities Research Council of Canada and the cooperation and assistance of a number of people. First and foremost, of course, I would like to thank the contributors. Each one of them embraced this project with an enthusiasm and a sense of commitment that continually kept me on my toes. Without their willingness to voice their struggles, this volume would have remained but a dream. I also wish to recognize the work of Claudia Eppert, which, due to unfortunate circumstances, did not make it into this collection; it is sorely missed. Thanks also to a number of people at Routledge—both past and present—who put on the editorial hat at various stages of this project. To Jayne Fargnoli, who took an interest in this book from the start, and to Anne Sanow, who did much to guide a neophyte through the labyrinths of the publishing business. An especially warm thanks to Alex Mummery, who was tremendously patient with my every query. I also benefited from the experience and advice of Ratna Ghosh at the initial stages of the project. Roger Simon was more than helpful in putting me in contact with a number of people and was a source of encouragement when this book was but a nascent idea. Henry Giroux generously offered his advice and support along the way. Finally, my loving thanks to Stan Nemiroff, with whom I have "learned" a great deal—especially about desire.

Acknowledgments

Introduction

Desiring Desire in Rethinking Pedagogy

SHARON TODD

What does "learning desire" mean? Educators often speak of wanting to "instill" the love of learning in their students; we want students to desire learning, to yearn, long, and develop an insatiable appetite for knowledge. In so doing, we express, perhaps inadvertently, the paradoxical notion that desire *can* be taught and learned and that desire is *necessary* for learning to occur. As transformative educators, in particular, we are also concerned with developing and engaging a desire to act on our knowledge in order to effect social change. Thus, there is an intangible, ineffable quality to our goal, for the kind of desire we aim to teach is about love, passion, and commitment. This is what constitutes, in part, the unsaid in our educational encounters. We struggle to teach what seems to be the unteachable, the limits of knowability. Indeed, educators acknowledge daily that the scene of education, the scene of learning, is fraught with tensions, pleasures, fears, and ambivalences that are connected to the kind of subject matter being taught, to teacher-student interaction, and to the images and representations that shape how we think about education. So if our goal is to develop the desire *for* learning and to engage the desire *in* learning, we must seriously ask ourselves, How do we think about desire? What does it have to do with the affective dimensions connected to learning, particularly transformative learning?

The importance of desire for education has a long history. From Plato's emphasis on Eros to Aristotle's famous dictum "All men by nature desire to know," the classical notion of education, indeed of learning, has been deeply intertwined with the (unsaid) desire for knowledge. It is a desire that has been consistently associated with love: the love of wisdom that takes delight in seeking knowledge simply because we experience its absence. Knowledge holds the promise of fulfillment, but only for those who, like Plato's philosophers, place themselves in a position of "feeling want," of longing for that which they feel a lack. That is, recognition or belief in lack, absence, or ignorance is prerequisite to any search for knowledge, wisdom, or enlightenment. Thus, in a curious twist, education may become that which instills the very want, the very love, it proposes to satiate; it "creates" desire as it offers the means for its gratification.

Indeed, this impulse is engraved in the erotic relations between teachers and students as embodied subjects; the relation between love and knowledge in classical education is performed through a homoerotic, pederastic teacher-student economy. It is an economy in which the "teacher" is invested with the authority to "instill" desire—or at least the belief in the necessity for such desire. As Jane Gallop suggests:

> Pederasty is undoubtedly a useful paradigm for classic Western pedagogy. A greater man penetrates a lesser man with his knowledge. The student is an empty receptacle for the phallus; the teacher is the phallic fullness of knowledge.... This structure and its sexual dynamic are explicit in [the Marquis de] Sade. The student is an innocent, empty receptacle, lacking his own desires, having desires "introduced to him by the teacher."[1]

Gallop draws our attention here to the libidinal economy that not only structures learning relations but informs the very way education itself has been thought. It is important to note that it is not the naming of a singular individual's desire for pederasty that is at issue here; rather, it is the organizing fantasy (or what Luce Irigaray would call the morphology) of traditional educational discourse that is phallic, pederastic, and penetrating insofar as education is seen to be about "instilling" the love for knowledge or "depositing" the desire for lifelong learning. Calling attention to the place that desire occupies in our paradigmatic thinking enables us to reinterrogate that place, to question how we theorize and analyze "learning" desires in order to fulfill them and how our theories and practices are involved in a particular libidinal economy and social imaginary.

For instance, the above-mentioned student-as-empty-receptacle motif echoes the banking model of education that Paulo Freire has critiqued.[2] The model is familiar: the teacher is supposed to fill up the student with knowledge, acquire the desires of the teacher, and display those knowledge/desires back to the teacher, untouched, unsullied, uncontaminated as it were, by the student's own thinking, desires, and ways of knowing. Education becomes a "necrophilic" "exercise in domination," where the "educator's role is to regulate the way the world 'enters into' the students."[3] Here, the teacher-student dynamic is structured by an imaginary that deems "natural" relations that are one-directional, penetrative, and incisive: the teacher enters the student, deposits the seed of learning, disseminates knowledge.[4]

If we look to the transformative model Freire proposes as a counterpart, what happens to the "banking" dynamic of desire? Shifting toward a new term of "teacher-student with student-teacher,"[5] Freire advocates that education is about the practice of freedom and bringing to consciousness the conditions that shape students' places in the world. Teacher-students and student-teachers are involved in a dialogic process in which knowledge leads to reflective, deliberative action. This conception of knowledge production refuses the traditional association of knowledge with the factual "filling up" of the student. Instead, as knowledge is "produced" (and not deposited), the terms of desire thus shift from the erotic framing of the teacher-student relationship as penetrative to a more lateral view of desire as an exchange of mutuality, of fluidity. The position of "teacher-student with student-teacher" suggests a reconfiguration of the place of desire in the pedagogical encounter. But what should this reconfiguration look like?

Any response to this question requires examining some of the more recent influences that have shaped issues in and for transformative pedagogy since Freire's "seminal" text. I note here four influences that highlight the significance of desire for transformative pedagogy and that have contributed to how and why this volume has been created.

First, the post-structural turn in the discourses, research, and practice of transformative education has had enormous impact upon how we think about education.[6] In insisting upon the nature of the subject as simultaneously contingent, multiply determined, and constantly shifting, poststructuralism has occasioned awareness of the place of indeterminacy in thinking about oppression, identity, and social location, which earlier, more stable views of subjectivity did not account for. That is, how do social subjects *avoid* becoming automatons, mere victims of oppression? How can social agency be understood in terms of (*re*)*shaping* meaning? Those social categories of fixed locations or standpoints that rely upon overly romanticized views of experience—be they according to race, class, gender, sexuality, or ethnicity—have limited ability to explain the more complex relations between power, pleasure, pain, systems of meaning, and general affect that confound any easy equation between knowledge and agency. In some measure, therefore, discourses on transformative pedagogy have drawn particularly upon feminist, critical, and postcolonial appropriations of poststructuralism, and postmodernism more generally, in order to trouble the seeming stasis at the heart of this equation.[7] That is, they have been concerned with maintaining a balance between how subjects are "inscribed," and yet they refuse such inscriptions as potential agents of social change. Moving away, then, from essentialized views of oppression and subjecthood, pedagogy may be rethought as a process that gets tangled up in the nexus of social relations where identification, fantasy, and desire begin to emerge as pressing concerns within the field of the social.

Second, in drawing upon and becoming embedded within the vast literature in the field of cultural studies, transformative pedagogy has fielded broader pedagogical questions. That is, transformative pedagogy has opened itself to working with psychoanalytic and postcolonial, as well as poststructural, categories of analysis to explore the meaning of cultural differences, nonessentialized views of the subject, and the negotiation of identities with popular cultural forms.[8] Rather than simply referencing schooling practices, questions are posed as to how we "learn" our culture and our place within it; how identities and communities are negotiated through complex systems of representation; and how meaning is framed within dominant social codes as well as struggled over and created anew. Through rigorous examination of our specific pedagogical encounters with film, literature, television, photography, advertisement, popular media, and religious institutions as well as schooling practices, we may begin to understand how we come to champion certain values, galvanize our communities, form conceptions of our selves, and forge "points of connection" with others.[9] It is through a process of learning that we become speakers, listeners, agents, citizens, workers, and members of neighborhoods, families, and communities. We learn social norms and learn how to resist those norms. We learn how to survive in circumstances beyond our control and how to alter those circumstances in order to survive. How individual agents, then, desire against the grain of dominant representations, languages, and meanings becomes central to the workings of pedagogy.

Third, considerations of teacher-student interaction as performative have had enormous impact upon how we think about teaching and learning.[10] These considerations disrupt the sense that education is or can be transparent in its assumptions, goals, and practices and ask us to seriously consider what is at stake psychically and socially in our pedagogical encounters.[11] Focusing on performativity places a greater focus on pedagogy as a symbolic and cultural practice through which subjects are racialized, genderized, sexualized, and ethnicized. It is not merely that subjects occupy a standpoint (such as black-woman-bisexual-Jewish) that has pedagogical implications but that the formation of such possibilities of social positioning is fundamentally a pedagogical process. Moreover, the meanings of these symbolic and cultural prac- tices are not neutral, overdetermining, or entirely conscious. Thus, if we think about our classroom interactions as instances of pedagogy broadly conceived, then we need to develop tools for "reading" or "interpreting" meaning in what we do (or not do), say (or not say), and represent (or not represent). How we "perform" as learners and teachers constitutes the terms through which we en- gage and indeed produce desire.

Last, a growing emphasis has been placed on eros, sexuality, and emotion in teaching and learning encounters. That is, some educators and theorists are concerned to articulate the goals of social transformation—often in terms of antiracism and feminism—together with the affective investments produced in our learning encounters, broadly conceived. Expressing issues ranging from transference[12] to identification,[13] from sexual harassment[14] to vulnerability,[15] and from the erotic exchange between teachers and students[16] to that between students,[17] educators attempt to demonstrate that affect is not simply an indi- vidual or idiosyncratic feature of pedagogical life but is structurally opera- tional in what gets learned, by whom, and how. Hence, this literature is central in formulating what desire has to "do" with pedagogy.

The emphases and questions enabled by all four of these areas have led to the creation of this volume. Focusing on one of many possible entry points into the pedagogical labyrinth (where it is difficult to discern the lines divid- ing knowledge, relations of power, social and cultural differences, and in- terpsychical interaction), the essays presented here struggle to make sense out of desire, its relation *to* learning, its relation *in* learning. They attempt to ad- dress the question posed earlier: what should a reconfiguration of desire look like for transformative pedagogy?

Clearly, the libidinal structuring of the banking model of education is not suitable; desire would premise itself on what Erica McWilliam (this volume) calls a "missionary position," the phallic penetration that offers (the hope of) completeness and fulfillment, the teacher who "introduces" knowledge and desire (in)to the student within a "top-down" logic. The call for self-reflection and social transformation would not be supported by such a unidirectional economy. But, does the answer lie in conceiving desire as a "flowing" out of the student, by contrast? Can a reconfiguration of desire simply be rendered through an opposing trajectory? Or can desire be rendered as neither linear nor directional? Given the multiple discourses currently informing transfor- mative pedagogical discourse, and given that the general goal of transforma- tive practice is to effect social change, it would seem that the shape, or morphology, of desire is something that must resist definite parameters and be open to constant amendment. A reconfiguration of desire for transformative pedagogy would need to be flexible in addressing itself to the particularities of a learning situation and would not be rendered a priori in terms of either an entering or an exiting current.

However, in their attempt to theorize desire, each of the essays here inevitably enacts a tension and reveals contradictory desires. Each author *does* attempt to sketch the contours of desire, seeking to name desire for a reading audience, seeking to represent that which has been inadequately represented. But if, as Cornelius Castoriadis notes, desire is not that which is unrepresented but is simply not representable, what does this say about our attempts here to "name" it, "communicate" it, "represent" it, or at least "work" with some notion of it?[18] How do we reconfigure desire and affect as part of a transformative libidinal economy, and how are these reconfigurations themselves part of that economy?

In "desiring desire" in rethinking pedagogy, the essays perform at the limits of representation, seeking to fix and articulate, however provisionally, that most slippery of terms and to claim its significance for pedagogical theory and action. In this sense, theorizing or writing about desire reveals something akin to a penetrative impulse, to the classical position of love and knowledge that is founded on a recognition of lack. For even as we struggle to reconfigure desire otherwise, we are also trying to fill a void, to instruct readers, to "insert" our views into a larger body of pedagogical discourse. Particularly since the text assumes—at least in the case of these essays—an underlying commitment and "belief" in the words spoken and written, this kind of desire appears to me inescapable. In addition, it is inescapable because one of the purposes of educating—and writing essays—turns on the possibility that one can move beyond the familiar and can thereby "instill" in students—and readers—the desire to do so as well.

However, even with this said, there is another important side to this tension. I am not suggesting here that the penetrative, pederastic, phallic desire is (or should be) the only desire structuring the educational enterprise, nor is it (nor should it be) the sole position at stake in our pedagogical encounters. Making desire contingent upon lack alone—even from a position of love—does not speak to the multivalent ways desire can be understood as a productive, creative, and sometimes—as Rebecca Martusewicz notes in this volume—violent aspect of our encounters. Nor does positing an opposing trajectory of desire founded on a strategy of the nonphallic, or indeed the "feminine," solve all our problems. Rather, it is important to read the essays here *through* their tension, for they portray the often times conflicting desires at the heart of the pedagogical encounter itself between what is said (what we say we want) and how we say it (the affective and psychical investments embedded therein; what is left unsaid). On the one hand, the tension between the desire that frames our *writing* about desire (the penetrative impulse of the argument) and, on the other hand, the desire *of which* we write (the specific configurations of desire offered in the content of the argument) should not be thought of as something that can be entirely surmountable through recourse to a different style or mode of writing.[19] It exists as a tension precisely because desire lies outside of symbolization. We can never make the pedagogy of the argument reflect the pedagogy advocated, particularly as we write about desire. To insist that we can suggests the very transparency of desire these essays are seeking to challenge. A more fruitful way of looking at the tension might be to ask ourselves, following Gayatri Spivak's line of thought: what strategic purpose can the content of our writing serve as it performs the tensions brought about by the act of writing itself? And in the context of this book, what does learning desire signal about the unsaid *for* transformative pedagogy and about the unsaid *in* transformative pedagogy?

In assuming that schooling practices are instances of pedagogy broadly conceived, this volume asserts that the line between what we "learn" in school and what we "learn" outside school cannot always be so easily drawn. Teachers and students are always far more than the sum of their schooling performances. Indeed, the profound concern in education with sexual harassment, sexual relations, and fraternization between teachers and students speaks to this recognition: there is something more to pedagogy than the spoken word; there is something about desire operating within, through, and between our teaching and learning bodies.

In fact, my own concern with the unsaid dimensions of pedagogy partially grew out of an intense personal dilemma. As a student, I confronted the emotional storm and subsequent breaking of the sexual taboo with a male professor. Then, it was a source both of bitter shame and ecstatic transgression, of guilt and fulfillment. But this relationship was not only about sex between two people, nor was it about predatory teacherly power versus student victimization; rather it involved complex issues of recognition, passion, knowledge, embodiedness, longing, reminiscences, and understandings of self and other, which constantly shifted the terms of desire itself. Most important it was about how these multivalent aspects of desire were negotiated through the institution of the university, through the protocols of gender that shape (hetero)sexual expression, through the already existing codification of such teacher-student relations as that which must remain unspeakable. Having listened to and read about numerous encounters between teachers and students—concerning not only sexual affairs but also the repeated importance that affection, aggression, caring, compassion, recognition, anger, pleasure, sensuality, fantasy, and vulnerability carry in those encounters—it seems to me necessary to begin to talk about, as best we can, how we understand and engage desire; for if desire is not about sex alone but is also about these other unsaid issues, what is at stake for teachers and students in transformative education?

Indeed, it is to these other unsaid issues that this volume primarily addresses itself. Although the importance of the relation of desire to sexuality cannot be underestimated in the pedagogical encounter, the essays here offer a multitextured account of desire that refuses an overly facile conflation of desire with sexuality, narrowly defined. Rather, the essays pursue the unsaid, elaborating different notions of desire in order to begin a necessary intervention into its workings in the scene of pedagogy and to initiate dialogue about what we "do" with desire. And although, as stated earlier, each essay may be caught in the tension posed by the desire to represent, to fix, to fill a void (even provisionally), each also exceeds the bounds of this penetrative impulse.

Indeed, as already alluded to, the title of this volume—*Learning Desire*—itself exceeds such bounds, reflecting a certain ambiguity that lies at the heart of pursuing the traces of desire in pedagogy. On the one hand, "learning" as a conjugate of the verb "to learn," signals the possibility that desire is something that we apprehend, produce, or possess—something that develops in conjunction with our surroundings, environment, and communities. Taken rather broadly, "learning desire" suggests that it is through the field of the social that desires are taken up as one's own. When Slavoj Žižek, for example, speaks of the way we act for the purpose of the Other's desire, when we act so that the Other will desire us,[20] we are "learning" to become desirous subjects; that is, we "acquire" the desire to become desirable, to become "subjects of desire," as Derek Briton's essay (this volume) reminds us. The question then becomes, What does this unconscious learning of desire have to do with the commonplace understanding of learning as a conscious act of cognition? This leads to the second reading of *Learning Desire*.

On the other hand, taking "learning" as an adjective in the phrase "learning desire" suggests that there is a type of desire that participates in the act of cognition. Just as "sexual" desire is involved in sexual interaction and "colonial" desire is involved in the economy of colonization,[21] "learning" desire suggests that desire is involved in the process of how we come to know something. In this sense, learning desire speaks to the specific stagings of desire—the longings, wishes, or fantasies—associated with the production of knowledge. In coming to "know" something (or someone), what dynamics of longing inflect that search for understanding? Are our fantasies merely epiphenomenal to our acquiring knowledge, or are they intricately entwined with why we want to know? How do desires "manage" or structure the limits as well as the possibilities for our receptivity to difference, the precondition of learning something new?

Taken together, both of these meanings suggest that learning desire constitutes a double dynamic: desire is both learned and implicated in the learning process. The essays in this volume continually expose the overlap and the discontinuity between these two meanings and constitute a productive intervention into the silences that shroud issues of desire in transformative pedagogy. Building upon, rather than expending with, a notion of critical teaching and learning, the volume explores the ambiguity, the slipperiness, and the intangible quality of what does, can, and, perhaps, should go on in the name of pedagogy. Indeed, each of the following essays struggles to define what desire can mean in the learning context and how desires come to be fashioned through engagement with cultural texts such as films and literature and through the cultural meanings of the performance of teaching and learning itself.

The book has been divided into five parts, each consisting of two essays. The coupling of the papers under each of the headings does not reflect a uniformity of perspective. Rather, the ideas put forth therein echo, pull, tease, and wrestle with one other in exploring their respective topics, and each reveals the tension of writing about the unrepresentable—desire. In part 1, "Desire and Knowledge," Shoshana Felman and Derek Briton both explore the relation between desire and knowledge through Lacanian formulations. Together they raise questions about what it means to "learn" when the conditions of knowledge are premised on a paradoxical "desire not to know." Yet, each reads Jacques Lacan's desire differently. Felman's now-classic essay "Psychoanalysis and Education: Teaching Terminable and Interminable" foregrounds the relation of transference that makes cognition possible—that is, the desire constituted when the teacher (or analyst) is positioned as the "subject presumed to know." Here, she emphasizes the dynamic, intersubjective quality of the pedagogical exchange as unconscious. Briton, by contrast, analyzes his own transferential reading of Lacan in "Learning the Subject of Desire." He shifts Felman's terms of engagement with Lacan, namely the symbolic constitution of the transference, and focuses on the "unanswerable question" that lies at its core. Through his engagement with Slavoj Žižek's interpretations of Lacan, Briton is thus less concerned with the discursive interaction between teacher and student in producing knowledge than with the unknown and unsayable that makes learning and saying possible.

Similarly, part 2, "Desire and Recognition," draws together two essays that grapple with both the limitations and possibilities posed when desire is about "being recognized." Drawing on a study of white women teachers, Judith Robertson, in "Fantasy's Confines: Popular Culture and the Education of the

Female Primary-School Teacher," discusses a particular fantasy that is shared among these women after they watch the film *Stand and Deliver*. Working within a psychoanalytic framework, Robertson's essay reveals that the "dream of love"—of recognition—that organizes the shared fantasy turns on a narcissistic position that does little to move beyond the bounds of the familiar, traditional view of teacher as a nongendered, nonracialized subject. Rebecca Martusewicz utilizes an autobiographical approach to root out the effects of the desire to be recognized. Pushing against a psychoanalytic reading of desire, "Say Me to Me: Desire and Education" draws instead upon the work of René Girard and Gilles Deleuze to analyze the author's own conflict of/in desire. Through the retelling of her own story, Martusewicz reveals the violence that can lie at the heart of such desire and the problematic effects this can have on teaching and learning.

Laurie Finke and Helen Harper position voice as significant to the work of desire in education in part 3, "Desire and Voice." Finke's work, "Knowledge as Bait: Feminism, Voice, and the Pedagogical Unconscious," focuses on the "pedagogical unconscious" to examine how resistance to knowledge operates as a textual practice between teacher and student. She elaborates a notion of authority in which desire is caught up within the unequal relations between teacher and student and argues that this needs to be factored into how "voice" is taken up within feminist teaching practices. Harper centers on analyzing adolescent resistance to feminist poetry. In "Disturbing Identity and Desire: Adolescent Girls and Wild Words," she works with Anna Freud's motif of "developmental disturbances" (which depicts the separation from "home" that adolescents must face) and inquires into the nature of desire and identification at play in the "disruption" of female identity occasioned by girls' reading of the poetry. Here, the girls' voices are not simply heard as "lacking" feminist consciousness but as negotiating their own identities as they confront alternative visions of "heterosexual woman." Both essays reveal the complex ways in which voice and identity are constituted in the encounter with new languages, new others.

In part 4, "Desire and Re-Signification," Gae Mackwood and Kaarina Kailo offer psychoanalytic alternatives to the Freudian-Lacanian model of desire. Both essays suggest ways of "unblocking," and re-signifying desire, the former through a strategy of reading, the latter through a strategy of imagination. Mackwood's essay, "Desire and Encryption: A Theory of Readability," delves into Nicolas Abraham and Maria Torok's notion of desire as encrypted—as that which is "buried and kept secret"—but which nonetheless contributes to a sense of identity that is passed on to others. Mackwood's thesis is that transformative pedagogy must learn to "read" anasemically, that is, to search for desires (such as racist subtexts) encrypted in pedagogical practices, in textbooks, and in literature. Without this reading, these desires risk being passed on to future generations, often with destructive effects. Building upon Jung's conception of active imagination and his views of education, Kailo, in "Integrative Feminist Pedagogy: C. G. Jung and the Politics of Visualization," discusses the importance of politicizing this practice in women's studies classrooms. In this regard, her essay works doubly to re-view Jungian theory in terms that make sense to her feminist teaching practices, while reviewing feminist pedagogy as that which needs to take a closer look at how the imagination can be used as a source of empowerment and transformation. Kailo thus offers practical suggestions for utilizing visualization as a means of unblocking desires that have been "bottled up" under social and cultural pressures.

The final part, "Desire and Bodies," concerns the place and role of the body in transformative teaching and learning. Erica McWilliam's essay "Beyond the Missionary Position: Teacher Desire and Radical Pedagogy" centers pleasure as an important aspect of teaching and suggests ways of rethinking the pedagogical body as a substantive dimension of desire and eroticism. She calls for a "body that matters" to the purpose and performance of radical teaching and suggests that transformative teaching needs to see itself as having a desirous body that is ambiguous as the site of authoritative performance. That is, teaching bodies are pleasured and eroticized in, as well as being central to, the pedagogical encounter. My own essay "Looking at Pedagogy in 3-D: Rethinking Difference, Disparity, and Desire" is concerned with how desire is important for working across, through, and with difference in order to work against the social disparities that structure differences differently. By conceiving of pedagogy as a site where Otherness is "articulated" and desires are forged, I look at the body and gesture, drawing upon Luce Irigaray's work, as that which forms part of the discourse of the classroom. Here, the relation of the body to desire is not so much about pleasure as it is about how a body signifies to an other through an economy of difference and disparity.

In sum, the essays here offer many different conceptions of desire through performing the ever-present tension occasioned by our "saying" the "unsaid." It is hoped that the volume's polyvalency will provoke further consideration of the place, meaning, and implications of desire for transformative pedagogy and that it will strike a chord with many of you who are struggling with the dilemmas, ambiguities, and ambivalences in your own pedagogical encounters, and with your own "penetrative" and "transformative" desires.

NOTES

1. Jane Gallop, "The Immoral Teachers," *Yale French Studies* 63 (1982), 118.
2. Paulo Freire, *Pedagogy of the Oppressed* (New York: Continuum, 1989), chap. 2, *passim*.
3. Ibid., 64, 62.
4. This social imaginary operating in educational encounters is probably familiar to most of us who have attended traditional schools. However, it may be most traumatically illustrated in the residential schools set up by the Canadian government to ensure that First Nations youth would be assimilated into the dominant "white" Western culture. The physical and sexual abuses often suffered in these schools—frequently at the hands of Christian nuns, brothers, and priests—reveal in the most extreme manner the libidinal structuring of these institutions.
5. Freire, *Oppressed*, 67.
6. For a sampling of this literature, see Stephen J. Ball, ed., *Foucault and Education* (London: Routledge, 1990); Deborah Britzman, "The Terrible Problem of Knowing Thyself: Toward a Poststructural Account of Teacher Identity," *JCT* 9, no. 3 (1992); Cleo H. Cherryholmes, *Power and Criticism: Poststructural Investigations in Education* (New York: Teachers College Press, 1988); Henry Giroux, "The Turn Toward Theory," in *Disturbing Pleasures* (New York: Routledge, 1994); Maria-Regina Kecht, ed., *Pedagogy Is Politics: Literary Theory and Critical Teaching* (Urbana: University of Illinois Press, 1992); Patti Lather, *Getting Smart: Feminist Research and Pedagogy with/in the Postmodern* (New York: Routledge, 1991); Rebecca Martusewicz, "Mapping the Terrain of the Post-Modern Subject: Post-Structuralism and the Educated Woman," in *Understanding Curriculum as Phenomenological and Deconstructed Text*, ed. William F. Pinar and William M. Reynolds (New York: Teachers College Press, 1992), 131–58; and various essays in Valerie Walkerdine's *School Girl Fictions* (London: Verso, 1990).
7. Paradigmatic here is the collection of essays, *Postmodernism, Feminism and Cultural Politics*, ed. Henry Giroux (Albany: SUNY, 1991).
8. See, for example, Roger Simon, Henry Giroux, and contributors, *Popular Culture, Schooling and Everyday Life* (South Hadley, Mass.: Bergin and Garvey, 1989); Giroux, *Fugitive Cultures: Race, Violence, and Youth* (New York: Routledge, 1996); Deborah Britzman, "What Is This Thing Called Love," *TABOO* 1 (spring 1995), 65–93; and Claudia Mitchell and Sandra Weber, *Funny You Don't Look Like a Teacher: Interrogating Images of Identity in Popular Culture* (Philadelphia: Falmer Press, 1995).
9. Roger Simon, "Constructing a Global Memory," unpublished paper 1996.
10. See, in particular, the essays in Jane Gallop ed. *Pedagogy: The Question of Impersonation* (Bloomington: Indiana University Press, 1995).
11. Walkerdine writes of the need to engage with the "educational politics of subjectivity, a politics which refuses to split the psychic from the social and attempts to understand the complexity of defence and resistance, and to find ways of dealing with them for teachers and students alike." "Femininity as Performance," in *Schoolgirl Fictions*, 145.
12. See Deborah Britzman and Alice Pitt, "Pedagogy in Transferential Time," *Theory into Practice* 35, no. 2 (spring 1996).
13. Chris Amirault, "Good Teacher, Good Student: Identifications of a Student Teacher," in *Pedagogy*, ed. Gallop, 64–78.
14. Alison Jones, "Desire, Sexual Harassment, and Pedagogy in the University," *Theory into Practice* 35, no. 2 (spring 1996), 102–6.

15. bell hooks, "Passionate Pedagogy: Erotic Student-Faculty Relationships," *Z Magazine* (March 1996), 45–51.
16. bell hooks, "Eros, Eroticism and the Pedagogical Process," in *Teaching to Transgress* (New York: Routledge, 1994), 191–200.
17. Naomi Scheman, "On Waking up One Morning and Discovering We Are Them," in *Pedagogy*, ed. Gallop, 106–16.
18. Cornelius Castoriadis, *The Imaginary Institution of Society*, trans. Kathleen Blamey (Cambridge: MIT Press, 1987), 297.
19. Of course, Luce Irigaray's writing style in such texts as *Marine Lover*, trans. Gillian Gill (New York: Columbia University Press, 1991), *Elemental Passions*, trans. Joanne Collie and Judith Still (New York: Routledge, 1992), and *Speculum* trans. Gillian Gill (Ithaca: Cornell University Press, 1985) certainly displays a different textual desire (as do the texts of writers like Hélène Cixous, Monique Wittig, and Nicole Brossard). However, my point is that insofar as they carry a didactic intent (e.g., to mobilize an alternative mode of discourse), the text also performs pedagogically in its communicative function. Thus the *style* of writing cannot fully overcome the text's authority in a system of meaning; it still proclaims its own importance by virtue of being written, published, and circulated. Similarly, the style of teaching cannot do away with the conditions of institutional authority, but can only work within/against them.
20. Slavoj Žižek, *The Sublime Object of Ideology* (London: Verso, 1989), 106; and for the relation between desire and guilt, see his "Superego by Default," in *Metastases of Enjoyment: Six Essays on Woman and Causality* (London: Verso, 1994).
21. For the use of the term "colonial desire," see Robert J. C. Young's book by that name: *Colonial Desire: Hybridity in Theory, Culture and Race* (London: Routledge, 1995).

Part 1

Desire and Knowledge

1

Psychoanalysis and Education

Teaching Terminable and Interminable

SHOSHANA FELMAN

In memory of Jacques Lacan

> *Meno:* Can you tell me, Socrates, if virtue can be taught? Or is it not teachable but the result of practice, or is it neither of these, but men possess it by nature?
>
> *Socrates:* . . . You must think me happy indeed if you think I know whether virtue can be taught . . . I am so far from knowing whether virtue can be taught or not that I do not even have any knowledge of what virtue itself is.
>
> . . . .
>
> *Meno:* Yes, Socrates, but how do you mean that we do not learn, but that what we call learning is recollection? Can you teach me how this is so?
>
> *Socrates:* . . . Meno, you are a rascal. Here you are asking me to give you my "teaching," I who claim that there is no such thing as teaching, only recollection.
>
> —Plato, *Meno*[1]

THE MEASURE OF A TASK

Socrates, that extraordinary teacher who taught humanity what pedagogy is, and whose name personifies the birth of pedagogics as a science, inaugurates his teaching practice, paradoxically enough, by asserting not just his own ignorance, but the radical impossibility of teaching.

Another extraordinarily effective pedagogue, another one of humanity's great teachers, Freud, repeats, in his own way, the same conviction that teaching is a fundamentally impossible profession. "None of the applications of psychoanalysis," he writes, "has excited so much interest and aroused so many hopes . . . as its use in the theory and practice of education . . .":

> My personal share in this application of psychoanalysis has been very slight. At an early stage I had accepted the *bon mot* which lays it down that there are three impossible professions—educating, healing, and governing—and I was already fully occupied with the second of them.[2]

In a later text—indeed the very last one that he wrote—Freud recapitulates this paradoxical conviction which time and experience seem to have only reinforced, confirmed:

> It almost looks as if analysis were the third of those 'impossible' professions in which one can be sure beforehand of achieving unsatisfying results. The other two, which have been known much longer, are education and government. (Standard, XXIII, 248)

If teaching is impossible—as Freud and Socrates both point out—what are we teachers doing? How should we understand—and carry out—our task? And why is it precisely two of the most effective teachers ever to appear in the intellectual history of mankind, who regard the task of teaching as impossible? Indeed, is not their radical enunciation of the impossibility of teaching itself actively engaged in teaching, itself part of the lesson they bequeath us? And if so, what can be learnt from the fact that it is impossible to teach? What can the impossibility of teaching teach us?

As much as Socrates, Freud has instituted, among other things, a revolutionary pedagogy. It is my contention—which I will here attempt to elucidate and demonstrate—that it is precisely in giving us unprecedented insight into the impossibility of teaching, that psychoanalysis has opened up unprecedented teaching possibilities, renewing both the questions and the practice of education.

This pedagogical renewal was not, however, systematically thought out by Freud himself, or systematically articulated by any of his followers; nor have its thrust and scope been to date fully assimilated or fully grasped, let alone utilized, exploited in the classroom. The only truly different pedagogy to have practically emerged from what might be called the psychoanalytic lesson is the thoroughly original teaching-style of Jacques Lacan, Freud's French disciple and interpreter. If Lacan is, as I would argue, Freud's best student—that is, the most radical effect of the insights of Freud's teaching—perhaps his teaching practice might give us a clue to the newness of the psychoanalytic lesson about lessons, and help us thus define both the actual and, more importantly, the potential contribution of psychoanalysis to pedagogy.

WHAT IS A CRITIQUE OF PEDAGOGY?

Lacan's relationship with pedagogy has, however, been itself—like that of Freud—mostly oversimplified, misunderstood, reduced. The reason for the usual misinterpretations of both Lacan's and Freud's pedagogical contribution lies in a misunderstanding of the critical position taken by psychoanalysis with respect to traditional methods and assumptions of education. Lacan's well-known critique of what he has pejoratively termed "academic discourse" *(le discours universitaire)* situates "the radical vice" in "the transmission of knowledge." "A Master of Arts," writes Lacan ironically, "as well as other titles, protect the secret of a substantialized knowledge."[3] Lacan thus blames "the narrow-minded horizon of pedagogues" for having "reduced" the "strong notion" of "teaching"[4] to a "functional apprenticeship" (E 445).

Whereas Lacan's pedagogical critique is focused on grown-up training—on academic education and the ways it handles and structures knowledge, Freud's pedagogical critique is mainly concerned with children's education and the ways it handles and structures repression. "Let us make ourselves clear," writes Freud, "as to what the first task of education is":

> The child must learn to control his instincts. It is impossible to give him liberty to carry out all his impulses without restriction . . . Accordingly, *education must inhibit, forbid and suppress*[5] and this is abundantly seen in all periods of history. But we have learnt from analysis that precisely this suppression of instincts involves the risk of neurotic illness. . . . Thus education has to find its way between the Scylla of non-interference and the Charybdis of frustration. . . . An optimum must be discovered which will enable education to achieve the most and damage the least. . . . A moment's reflection tells us that hitherto education has fulfilled its task very badly and has done children great damage. (Standard, XXII, 149)

Thus, in its most massive statements and in its polemical pronouncements, psychoanalysis, in Freud as well as Lacan—although with different emphases—is first and foremost *a critique of pedagogy*. The legacy of this critique has been, however, misconstrued and greatly oversimplified, in that the critical stance has been understood—in both Lacan's and Freud's case—as a desire to escape the pedagogical imperative: a desire—whether possible or impossible—to do away with pedagogy altogether. "Psychoanalysis," writes Anna Freud, "whenever it has come into contact with pedagogy, has always expressed the wish to *limit education*. Psychoanalysis has brought before us the quite definite danger arising from education."[6]

The illocutionary force of the psychoanalytical (pedagogical) critique of pedagogy has thus been reduced, either to a simple negativity, or to a simple positivity, of that critique. Those who, in an oversimplification of the Freudian lesson, equate the psychoanalytic critical stance with a simple positivity, give consequently positive advice to educators, in an attempt to conceive of more liberal methods for raising children—methods allowing "to each stage in the child's life the right proportion of instinct-gratification and instinct-restriction."[7] Those who, on the other hand, in an oversimplification of the Lacanian lesson, equate the psychoanalytical critical stance with a simple negativity, see in psychoanalysis "literally an inverse pedagogy": "the analytic process is in effect a kind of reverse pedagogy, which aims at undoing what has been established by education."[8] In the title of a recent book on the relationship of Freud to pedagogy, Freud is thus defined as "The Anti-Pedagogue."[9] This one-sidedly negative interpretation of the relation of psychoanalysis to pedagogy fails to see that every true pedagogue is in effect an anti-pedagogue, not just because every pedagogy has historically emerged as a critique of pedagogy (Socrates: "There's a chance, Meno, that we, you as well as me . . . have been inadequately educated, you by Gorgias, I by Prodicus"[10]), but because, in one way or another, every pedagogy stems from its confrontation with the impossibility of teaching (Socrates: "You see, Meno, that I am not teaching . . . anything, but all I do is question . . ."[11]). The reductive conception of "Freud: The Anti-Pedagogue" thus fails to see that there is no such thing as an anti-pedagogue: an anti-pedagogue is *the* pedagogue par excellence. Such a conception overlooks, indeed, and fails to reckon with, Freud's own stupendous pedagogical performance, and its relevance to his declarations about pedagogy.

The trouble, both with the positivistic and with the negativistic misinterpretations of the psychoanalytical critique of pedagogy, is that they refer exclusively to Lacan's or Freud's explicit *statements* about pedagogy, and thus fail to see the illocutionary force, the didactic function of the *utterance* as opposed to the mere content of the statement. They fail to see, in other words, the pedagogical situation—the pedagogical dynamic in which statements function not as simple truths but as performative speech-*acts*. Invariably, all existing psychoanalytically-inspired theories of pedagogy fail to address the question of the pedagogical speech-act of Freud himself, or of Lacan himself: what can be learnt about pedagogy not just from their theories (which only fragmentarily and indirectly deal with the issue of education) but from their way of *teaching* it, from their own practice as teachers, from their own pedagogical performance.

Lacan refers explicitly to what he calls the psychoanalyst's "mission of teaching" (E 241, N 34 TM[12]), and speaks of his own teaching—the bimonthly seminar he gave for forty years—as a vocation, "a function . . . to which I have truly devoted my entire life" (S-XI, 7, N 1).[13] Unlike Lacan, Freud addresses the issue of teaching more indirectly, rather by refusing to associate his person with it:

But there is one topic which I cannot pass over so easily—*not, however, because I understand particularly much about it* or have contributed very much to it. Quite the contrary: *I have scarcely concerned myself with it at all.* I must mention it because it is so exceedingly important, so rich in hopes for the future, perhaps the most important of all the activities of analysis. What I am thinking of is the application of psychoanalysis to education. (Standard, XXII, 146)

This statement thus promotes pedagogy to the rank of "perhaps the most important of the all the activities of analysis" only on the basis of Freud's denial of his own personal involvement with it. However, this very statement, this very denial is itself engaged in a dramatic pedagogical performance; it itself is part of an imaginary "lecture," significantly written in the form of an academic public address and of a dialogue with students—a pedagogic dialogue imaginarily conducted by a Freud who, in reality terminally ill and having undergone an operation for mouth-cancer, is no longer capable of speech:

My *Introductory Lectures on Psychoanalysis* were delivered . . . in a lecture room of the Vienna Psychiatric Clinic before an audience gathered from all the Faculties of the University. . . .

These new lectures, unlike the former ones, have never been delivered. My age had in the meantime absolved me from the obligation of giving expression to my membership in the University (which was in any case a peripheral one) by delivering lectures; and a surgical operation had made speaking in public impossible for me. If, therefore, I once more take my place in the lecture room during the remarks that follow, it is only by an artifice of the imagination; it may help me not to forget to bear the reader in mind as I enter more deeply into my subject. . . . Like their predecessors, [these lectures] are addressed to the multitude of educated people to whom we may perhaps attribute a benevolent, even though cautious, interest in the characteristics and discoveries of the young science. This time once again it has been my chief aim to make no sacrifice to an appearance of being simple, complete or rounded-off, not to disguise problems and not to deny the existence of gaps and uncertainties. (Standard, XXII, 5–6)

No other such coincidence of fiction and reality, biography and theory, could better dramatize Freud's absolutely fundamental pedagogic gesture. What better image could there be for the pedagogue in spite of himself, the pedagogue in spite of everything—the dying teacher whose imminent death, like that of Socrates, only confirms that he is a born teacher—than this pathetic figure, this living allegory of the speechless speaker, of the teacher's teaching out of—through—the very radical impossibility of teaching?

Pedagogy in psychoanalysis is thus not just a theme: it is a rhetoric. It is not just a statement: it is an utterance. It is not just a meaning: it is action; an action which itself may very well, at times, belie the stated meaning, the didactic thesis, the theoretical assertion. It is essential to become aware of this complexity of the relationship of pedagogy and psychoanalysis, in order to begin to think out what the psychoanalytic teaching about teaching might well be.

Discussing "The Teaching of Psychoanalysis in Universities," Freud writes: "it will be enough if [the student] learns something *about* psychoanalysis and something *from* it" (Standard, XVII, 173). To learn "something *from* psycho-analysis" is a very different thing than to learn "something *about* it": it means that psychoanalysis is not a simple *object* of the teaching, but its *subject*. In his essay "Psychoanalysis and its Teaching," Lacan underlines the same ambigu-ity, the same dynamic complexity, indicating that the true object of psycho-analysis, the object of his teaching, can only be that mode of learning which institutes psychoanalysis itself as subject—as the purveyor of the act of teach-ing. "How can what psychoanalysis teaches us be taught?" he asks (E 439).

As myself both a student of psychoanalysis and a teacher, I would here like to suggest that the lesson to be learnt about pedagogy from psychoanalysis is less that of "the *application* of psychoanalysis to pedagogy" than that of the *implication* of psychoanalysis in pedagogy and of pedagogy in psychoanalysis. Attentive, thus, both to the pedagogical speech-act of Freud and to the teach-ing-practice of Lacan, I would like to address the question of teaching as itself a psychoanalytic question. Reckoning not just with the pedagogical thematics in psychoanalysis, but with the pedagogical rhetoric of psychoanalysis, not just with what psychoanalysis says *about* teachers but with psychoanalysis *itself as teacher*, I will attempt to analyze the ways in which—modifying the con-ception of what *learning* is and of what *teaching* is—psychoanalysis has shifted pedagogy by radically displacing our very modes of intelligibility.

ANALYTICAL APPRENTICESHIP

Freud conceives of the process of a psychoanalytic therapy as a learning process—an apprenticeship whose epistemological validity far exceeds the contingent singularity of the therapeutic situation:

> Psychoanalysis sets out to explain . . . uncanny disorders; it engages in careful
> and laborious investigations . . . until at length it can speak thus to the ego:

> "... A part of the activity of your own mind has been withdrawn from your knowledge and from the command of your will ... you are using one part of your force to fight the other part ... A great deal more must constantly be going on in your mind than can be known to your consciousness. Come, *let yourself be taught* ...! What is in your mind does not coincide with what you are conscious of; whether something is going on in your mind and whether you hear of it, are two different things. In the ordinary way, I will admit, the intelligence which reaches your consciousness is enough for your needs; and *you may cherish the illusion that you learn of all the more important things.* But in some cases, as in that of an instinctual conflict ... your intelligence service breaks down ... In every case, the news that reaches your consciousness is incomplete and often not to be relied on. ... Turn your eyes inward, ... *learn first to know yourself!* ...
>
>   It is thus that *psychoanalysis has sought to educate the ego.* (Standard, XVII, 142–143)

Psychoanalysis is thus a pedagogical experience: as a process which gives access to new knowledge hitherto denied to consciousness, it affords what might be called a lesson in cognition (and in miscognition), an epistemological instruction.

Psychoanalysis institutes, in this way, a unique and radically original mode of learning: original not just in its procedures, but in the fact that it gives access to information unavailable through any other mode of learning—unprecedented information, hitherto *unlearnable.* "We learnt," writes Freud, "a quantity of things which could not have been learnt except through analysis" (Standard, XXII, 147).

This new mode of investigation and of learning has, however, a very different temporality than the conventional linear—cumulative and progressive—temporality of learning, as it has traditionally been conceived by pedagogical theory and practice. Proceeding not through linear progression, but through breakthroughs, leaps, discontinuities, regressions, and deferred action, the analytic learning-process puts indeed in question the traditional pedagogical belief in intellectual perfectibility, the progressistic view of learning as a simple one-way road from ignorance to knowledge.

It is in effect the very concept of both ignorance and knowledge—the understanding of what "to know" and "not to know" may really mean—that psychoanalysis has modified, renewed. And it is precisely the originality of this renewal which is central to Lacan's thought, to Lacan's specific way of understanding the cultural, pedagogical, and epistemological revolution implied by the discovery of the unconscious.

KNOWLEDGE

Western pedagogy can be said to culminate in Hegel's philosophical didacti-
cism: the Hegelian concept of "absolute knowledge"—which for Hegel defines at once the potential aim and the actual end of dialectics, of
philosophy—is in effect what pedagogy has always aimed at as its ideal: the
exhaustion—through methodical investigation—of all there is to know; the
absolute completion—termination—of apprenticeship. Complete and totally
appropriated knowledge will become—in all senses of the word—a mastery.
"In the Hegelian perspective," writes Lacan, "the completed discourse" is "an
instrument of power, the scepter and the property of those who know" (S-II,
91). "What is at stake in absolute knowledge is the fact that discourse closes
back upon itself, that it is entirely in agreement with itself." (S-II, 91).

But the unconscious, in Lacan's conception, is precisely the discovery that
human discourse can by definition never be entirely in agreement with itself,
entirely identical to its knowledge of itself, since as the vehicle of unconscious
knowledge, it is constitutively the material locus of a signifyiing difference
from itself.

What, indeed, is the unconscious, if not a kind of *unmeant knowledge* which
escapes intentionality and meaning, a knowledge which is spoken by the language of the subject (spoken, for instance, by his "slips" or by his dream), but
which the subject cannot recognize, assume as *his*, appropriate; a speaking
knowledge which is nonetheless denied to the speaker's knowledge? In Lacan's own terms, the unconscious is "knowledge which can't tolerate one's
knowing that one knows" (Seminar, Feb. 19, 1974; unpublished). "Analysis
appears on the scene to announce that there is *knowledge which does not know
itself*, knowledge which is supported by the signifier as such" (S-XX, 88). "It is
from a place which differs from any capture by a subject that a knowledge is
surrendered, since that knowledge offers itself only to the subject's slips—to
his misprision" (*Scilicet* I, 38).[14] "The discovery of the unconscious . . . is that
the implications of meaning infinitely exceed the signs manipulated by the individual" (S-II, 150). "As far as signs are concerned, man is always mobilizing
many more of them than he knows" (S-II, 150).

If this is so, there can constitutively be no such thing as absolute knowldge:
absolute knowledge is knowledge that has exhausted its own articulation; but
articulated knowledge is by definition what cannot exhaust its own self-
knowledge. For knowledge to be spoken, linguistically articulated, it would
constitutively have to be supported by the ignorance carried by language, the
ignorance of the *excess of signs* that of necessity its language—its articulation—
"mobilizes." Thus, human knowledge is, by definition, that which is *untotaliz-*

able, that which rules out any possibility of totalizing what it knows or of eradicating its own ignorance.

The epistemological principle of the irreducibility of ignorance which stems from the unconscious, receives an unexpected confirmation from modern science, to which Lacan is equally attentive in his attempt to give the theory of the unconscious its contemporary scientific measure. The scientific a-totality of knowledge is acknowledged by modern mathematics, in set theory (Cantor: "the set of all sets in a universe does not constitute a set"); in contemporary physics, it is the crux of what is known as "the uncertainty principle" of Heisenberg:

> This is what the Heisenberg principle amounts to. When it is possible to locate, to define precisely one of the points of the system, it is impossible to formulate the others. When the place of electrons is discussed . . . it is no longer possible to know anything about . . . their speed. And inversely . . . (S-II, 281)

From the striking and instructive coincidence between the revolutionary findings of psychoanalysis and the new theoretical orientation of modern physics, Lacan derives the following epistemological insight—the following pathbreaking pedagogical principle:

> Until further notice, we can say that *the elements do not answer in the place where they are interrogated.* Or more exactly, as soon as they are interrogated somewhere, it is impossible to grasp them in their totality. (S-II, 281)

IGNORANCE

Ignorance is thus no longer simply *opposed* to knowledge: it is itself a radical condition, an integral part of the very *structure* of knowledge. But what does ignorance consist of, in this new epistemological and pedagogical conception?

If ignorance is to be equated with the a-totality of the unconscious, it can be said to be a kind of forgetting—of forgetfulness: while learning is obviously, among other things, remembering and memorizing ("all learning is recollection," says Socrates), ignorance is linked to what is *not remembered*, what will not be memorized. But what will not be memorized is tied up with repression, with the imperative to forget—the imperative to exclude from consciousness, to not admit to knowledge. Ignorance, in other words, is not a passive state of absence—a simple lack of information: it is an active dynamic of negation, an active refusal of information. Freud writes:

> It is a long superseded idea ... that the patient suffers from a sort of igno-
> rance, and that if one removes this ignorance by giving him information
> (about the causal connection of his illness with his life, about his experi-
> ences in childhood, and so on) he is bound to recover. The pathological fac-
> tor is not his ignorance in itself, but the root of this ignorance in his *inner
> resistances*; it was they who first called this ignorance into being, and they
> still maintain it now. The task of the treatment lies in combating these re-
> sistances. (Standard, XI, 225)

Teaching, like analysis, has to deal not so much with *lack* of knowledge as
with *resistances* to knowledge. Ignorance, suggests Lacan, is a "passion." Inasmuch as traditional pedagogy postulated a desire for knowledge, an analytically informed pedagogy has to reckon with "the passion for ignorance"
(S-XX, 110). Ignorance, in other words is nothing other than a *desire to ignore*:
its nature is less cognitive than performative; as in the case of Sophocles' nuanced representation of the ignorance of Oedipus, it is not a simple lack of information but the incapacity—or the refusal—to acknowledge *one's own
implication* in the information.

The new pedagogical lesson of psychoanalysis is not subsumed, however,
by the revelation of the dynamic nature—and of the irreducibility—of ignorance. The truly revolutionary insight—the truly revolutionary *pedagogy* discovered by Freud—consists in showing the ways in which, however,
irreducible, *ignorance itself can teach us something*—become itself *instructive*.
This is, indeed, the crucial lesson that Lacan has learnt from Freud:

> It is necessary, says Freud, to interpret the phenomenon of doubt as an in-
> tegral part of the message. (S-II, 155)

> The forgetting of the dream is ... itself part of the dream. (S-II, 154)

> The message is not forgotten in just any manner.... A censorship is an in-
> tention. Freud's argumentation properly reverses the burden of the proof—
> "In these elements that you cite in objection to me, the memory lapses and
> the various degradations of the dream, I continue to see a meaning, and
> even an additional meaning. When the phenomenon of forgetting inter-
> venes, it interests me all the more ... *These negative phenomena, I add them
> to the interpretation of the meaning, I recognize that they too have the function
> of a message.* Freud discovers this dimension ... What interests Freud ...
> [is] *the message as an interrupted discourse*, and which insists. (S-II, 153)

The pedagogical question crucial to Lacan's own teaching will thus be:
Where does it resist? Where does a text (or a signifier in a patient's conduct)

precisely make no sense, that is, *resist interpretation*? Where does what I see—and what I read—resist my understanding? Where is the *ignorance*—the resistance to knowledge—located? And what can I thus *learn* from the locus of that ignorance? How can I interpret *out of* the dynamic ignorance I analytically encounter, both in others and in myself? How can I turn ignorance into an instrument of teaching?

> ... Teaching—says Lacan—is something rather problematic. ... As an American poet has pointed out, no one has ever seen a professor who has fallen short of the task because of ignorance. ...
>
> One always knows enough in order to occupy the minutes during which one exposes oneself in the position of one who knows. ...
>
> This makes me think that there is no true teaching other than the teaching which succeeds in provoking in those who listen an insistence—this desire to know which can only emerge when they themselves have *taken the measure of ignorance as such*—of ignorance inasmuch as it is, as such, fertile—in the one who teaches as well. (S-II, 242)

THE USE OF THAT WHICH CANNOT BE EXCHANGED

Teaching, thus, is not the transmission of ready-made knowledge, it is rather the creation of a new *condition* of knowledge—the creation of an original learning-disposition. "What I teach you," says Lacan, "does nothing other than express the *condition* thanks to which what Freud says is possible" (S-II, 368). The lesson, then, does not "teach" Freud: it teaches the "condition" which makes it *possible to learn* Freud—the condition which makes possible Freud's teaching. What is this condition?

In analysis, what sets in motion the psychoanalytical apprenticeship is the peculiar pedagogical structure of the analytic situation. The analysand speaks to the analyst, whom he endows with the authority of the one who possesses knowledge—knowledge of what is precisely lacking in the analysand's own knowledge. The analyst, however, knows nothing of the sort. His only competence, insists Lacan, lies in "what I would call *textual knowledge*, so as to oppose it to the referential notion which only masks it" (*Scilicet* I, 21). Textual knowledge—the very stuff the literature teacher is supposed to deal in—is knowledge of the functioning of language, of symbolic structures, of the signifier, knowledge at once derived from—and directed towards—interpretation.

But such knowledge cannot be acquired (or possessed) once and for all: each case, each text, has its own specific, singular symbolic functioning, and requires thus a different—an original—interpretation. The analysts, says

Lacan, are "those who share this knowledge only at the price, on the condition of their *not being able to exchange it*" (*Scilicet* I, 59). Analytic (textual) knowledge cannot be *exchanged*, it has to be *used*—and used in each case differently, according to the singularity of the case, according to the specificity of the text. Textual (or analytic) knowledge is, in other words, that peculiarly specific knowledge which, unlike any commodity, is subsumed by its use value, having no exchange value whatsoever.[15] Analysis has thus no use for ready-made interpretations, for knowledge given in advance. Lacan insists on "the insistence with which Freud recommends to us to approach each new case as if we had never learnt anything from his first interpretations" (*Scilicet* I, 20). "What the analyst must know," concludes Lacan, "is how to ignore what he knows."

DIALOGIC LEARNING,
OR THE ANALYTICAL STRUCTURE OF INSIGHT

Each case is thus, for the analyst as well as for the patient, a new apprenticeship. "If it's true that our knowledge comes to the rescue of the patient's ignorance, it is not less true that, for our part, we, too, are plunged in ignorance" (S-I, 78). While the analysand is obviously ignorant of his own unconscious, the analyst is doubly ignorant: pedagogically ignorant of his suspended (given) knowledge; actually ignorant of the very knowledge the analysand presumes him to possess of his own (the analysand's) unconscious: knowledge of the very knowledge he—the patient—lacks. In what way does knowledge, then, emerge in and from the analytic situation?

Through the analytic dialogue the analyst, indeed, has first to learn where to situate the ignorance: where his own textual knowledge is *resisted*. It is, however, out of this resistance, out of the patient's active ignorance, out of the patient's speech which says much more than it itself knows, that the analyst will come to *learn the patient's own* unconscious *knowledge*, that knowledge which is inaccessible to itself because it cannot tolerate knowing that it knows; and it is the signifiers of this constitutively a-reflexive knowledge coming from the patient that the analyst *returns* to the patient from his different vantage point, from his non-reflexive, asymmetrical position as an Other. Contrary to the traditional pedagogical dynamic, in which the teacher's question is addressed to an answer from the other—from the student—which is totally reflexive, and expected, "the true Other" says Lacan, "is the Other who gives the answer one does not expect" (S-II, 288). Coming from the Other, knowledge is, by definition, that which comes as a surprise, that which is constitutively the return of a difference:

Teiresias: . . . You are the land's pollution.

Oedipus: How shamelessly you started up this taunt! How do you think you will escape?

Teiresias: . . . I have escaped, the truth is what I cherish and that's my strength.

Oedipus: And who has taught you truth? Not your profession surely!

Teiresias: You have taught me, for you have made me speak against my will.

Oedipus: Speak what? Tell me again that I may *learn* it better.

Teiresias: Did you not understand before or would you provoke me into speaking?

Oedipus: I did not grasp it, not so to call it known. Say it again.

Teiresias: I say you are the murderer of the king whose murderer you seek.[16]

As Teiresias—so as to be able to articulate the truth—must have been "taught" not by "his profession" but *by Oedipus*, so the analyst precisely must be taught by the analysand's unconscious. It is by structurally occupying the position of the analysand's unconscious, and by thus making himself a *student of the patient's knowledge*, that the analyst becomes the patient's teacher—makes the patient learn what would otherwise remain forever inaccessible to him.

For teaching to be realized, for knowledge to be learnt, the position of alterity is therefore indispensable: knowledge is what is already there, but always in the Other. Knowledge, in other words, is not a *substance* but a structural dynamic: it is not *contained* by any individual but comes about out of the mutual apprenticeship between two partially unconscious speeches which both say more than they know. Dialogue is thus the radical condition of learning and of knowledge, the analytically constitutive condition through which ignorance becomes structurally informative; knowledge is essentially, irreducibly dialogic. "No knowledge," writes Lacan, "can be supported or transported by one alone" (*Scilicet* I, 59).

Like the analyst, the teacher, in Lacan's eyes, cannot in turn be, alone, a *master* of the knowledge which he teaches. Lacan transposes the radicality of analytic dialogue—as a newly understood structure of insight—into the pedagogical situation. This is not simply to say that he encourages "exchange" and calls for students' interventions—as many other teachers do. Much more profoundly and radically, he attempts to *learn from the students his own knowledge*. It is the following original pedagogical appeal that he can thus address to the audience of his seminar:

> It seems to me I should quite naturally be the point of convergence of the questions that may occur to you.

Let everybody tell me, in his own way, *his idea of what I am driving at.*
How, for him, is opened up—or closed—or how already he resists, the
question as I pose it . . . (S-II, 242)

This pedagogical approach, which makes no claim to total knowledge, which
does not even claim to be in possesion of its own knowledge, is, of course,
quite different from the usual pedagogical pose of mastery, different from the
image of the self-sufficient, self-possesed proprietor of knowledge, in which
pedagogy has traditionally featured the authoritative figure of the teacher.
This figure of infallible human authority implicitly likened to a God, that is,
both modeled on and guaranteed by divine *omniscience*, is based on an illusion:
the illusion of a consciousness transparent to itself. "It is the case of the unconscious," writes Lacan, "that it abolishes the postulate of the subject presumed to know" (*Scilicet* I, 46).

Abolishing a postulate, however, doesn't mean abolishing an illusion: while
psychoanalysis uncovers the mirage inherent in the function of the subject
presumed to know, it also shows the prestige and the affective charge of that
mirage to be constitutively irreducible, to be indeed most crucial to, deter-
minant of, the emotional dynamic of all discursive human interactions, of all
human relationships founded on sustained interlocution. The psychoanalytical account of the functioning of this dynamic is the most directly pal-
pable, the most explicit lesson psychoanalysis has taught us about teaching.

In a brief and peculiarly introspective essay called "Some Reflections on
Schoolboy Psychology," the already aging Freud nostalgically probes into his
own "schoolboy psychology," the affect of which even time and intellectual
achievements have not entirely extinguished. "As little as ten years ago,"
writes Freud, "you may have had moments at which you suddenly felt quite
young again":

> As you walked through the streets of Vienna—already a grey-beard and
> weighed down by all the cares of family life—you might come unexpectedly
> on some well-preserved, elderly gentleman, and would greet him humbly al-
> most, because you had recognized him as one of your former schoolmasters.
> But afterwards, you would stop and reflect: 'Was that really he? or only some-
> one deceptively like him? How youthful he looks! And how old you yourself
> have grown! . . . *Can it be possible that the men who used to stand for us as types of
> adulthood were so little older than we were?*' (Standard, XIII, 241)

Commenting on "my emotion at meeting my old schoolmaster," Freud goes on to give an analytical account of the emotional dynamic of the pedagogical situation:

> It is hard to decide whether what affected us more . . . was our concern with the sciences that we were taught or with . . . our teachers . . . In many of us *the path to the sciences led only through our teachers.* . . .
>
> We courted them and turned our backs on them, we imagined sympathies and antipathies which probably had no existence . . .
>
> . . . *psychoanalysis has taught us* that the individual's emotional attitudes to other people . . . are . . . established at an unexpectedly early age . . . The people to whom [the child] is in this way fixed are his parents . . . His later acquaintances are . . . obliged to *take over a kind of emotional heritage;* they encounter sympathies and antipathies to the production of which they themselves have contributed little . . .
>
> These men [the teachers] became our *substitute fathers.* That was why, even though they were still quite young, *they struck us as so mature and so unattainably adult.* We *transferred* to them *the respect and expectations attaching to the omniscient father of our childhood,* and then we began to treat them as we treated our own fathers at home. We confronted them with the *ambivalence* that we had acquired in our own families and with its help we struggled with them as we had been in the habit of struggling with our fathers . . . (Standard, XIII, 242–44)

This phenomenon of the compulsive unconscious reproduction of an archaic emotional pattern, which Freud called "transference" and which he saw both as the energetic spring and as the interpretive key to the psychoanalytic situation, is further thought out by Lacan as what accounts for the functioning of authority in general: as essential, thus, not just to any pedagogic situation but to the problematics of knowledge as such. "As soon as there is somewhere a subject presumed to know, there is transference," writes Lacan (S-XI, 210).

Since "transference is the acting out of the reality of the unconscious" (S-XI, 150, 240, N 174, 267), teaching is not a purely cognitive, informative experience, it is also an emotional, erotical experience. "I deemed it necessary," insists Lacan, "to support the idea of transference, as indistinguishable from love, with the formula of the subject presumed to know. I cannot fail to underline the new resonance with which this notion of knowledge is endowed. The person in whom I presume knowledge to exist, thereby acquires my love" (S-XX, 64). "The question of love is thus linked to the question of knowledge" (S-XX, 84). "Transference *is* love . . . I insist: it is loved directed toward, addressed to, knowledge" (*Scilicet* V, 16).

"Of this subject presumed to know, who," asks Lacan, "can believe himself to be entirely invested?—That is not the question. The question, first and foremost, for each subject, is how to situate *the place from which he himself addresses* the subject presumed to know?" (S-XX, 211) Insofar as knowledge is itself *a structure of address*, cognition is always both motivated and obscured by love; theory, both guided and misguided by an implicit transferential strcture.

ANALYTIC PEDAGOGY, OR DIDACTIC PSYCHOANALYSIS: THE INTERMINABLE TASK

In human relationships, sympathies and antipathies usually provoke—and call for—a similar emotional response in the person they are addressed to. Transference on "the subject presumed to know"—the analyst or the teacher—may provoke a counter-transference on the latter's part. The analytic or the pedagogical situation may thus degenerate into an imaginary mirror-game of love and hate, where each of the participants would unconsciously enact past conflicts and emotions, unwarranted by the current situation and disruptive with respect to the real issues, unsettling the topical stakes of analysis or education.

In order to avoid this typical degeneration, Freud conceived of the necessity of a preliminary psychoanalytic training of "the subjects presumed to know," a practical didactic training through their own analysis which, giving them insight into their own transferential structure, would later help them understand the students' or the patient's transferential mechanisms and, more importantly, keep under control their own—avoid being entrapped in counter-transference. "The only appropriate preparation for the profession of educator," suggests Freud, "is a thorough psycho-analytic training . . . The analysis of teachers and educators seems to be a more efficacious prophylactic measure than the analysis of children themselves" (Standard, XXII, 150).

While this preliminary training (which has come to be known as "didactic psychoanalysis") is, however, only a recommendation on Freud's part as far as teachers are concerned, it is an absolute requirement and precondition for the habilitation—and qualification—of the psychoanalyst. In his last and therefore, in a sense, testamentary essay, "Analysis Terminable and Interminable," Freud writes:

> Among the factors which influence the prospects of analytic treatment and add to its difficulties in the same manner as the resistances, must be reck-

oned not only the nature of the patient's ego but the individuality of the analyst.

It cannot be disputed that *analysts . . . have not invariably come up to the standard* of psychical normality *to which they wish to educate their patients.* Opponents of analysis often point to this fact with scorn and use it as an argument to show the uselessness of analytic exertions. We might reject this criticism as making unjustifiable demands. *Analysts are people who have learnt to practice a particular art;* alongside of this, they may be allowed to be *human beings like anyone else.* After all, nobody maintains that a physician is incapable of treating internal diseases if his own internal organs are not sound; on the contrary, it may be argued that there are certain advantages in a man who is himself threatened with tuberculosis specializing in the treatment of persons suffering from that disease. . . .

It is reasonable [however,] . . . to expect of an analyst, as part of his qualifications, a considerable degree of mental normality and correctness. In addition, he must possess some kind of superiority, so that in certain analytic situations he can *act as a model for his patient* and in others *as a teacher.* And finally, we must not forget that the analytic relationship is based on a love of truth—that is, on a recognition of reality—and that it precludes any kind of sham or deceit. . . .

It almost looks as if analysis were the third of those 'impossible' professions . . . *Where is the poor wretch to acquire the ideal qualifications* which he will need in his profession? *The answer is, in an analysis of himself,* with which his preparation for his future activity begins. For practical reasons this analysis can only be short and incomplete. . . . It has accomplished its purpose if it gives the learner a firm conviction of the existence of the unconscious, if it enables him . . . to perceive in himself things which would otherwise be incredible to him, and if it shows him a first example of the technique . . . in analytic work. *This alone would not suffice for his instruction; but we reckon on the stimuli he has received in his own analysis not ceasing when it ends* and *on the process of remodelling the ego continuing* spontaneously in the analysed subject and making use of all subsequent experiences in this newly-acquired sense. This does in fact happen, and *in so far as it happens, it makes the analysed subject qualified to be analyst.* (Standard, XXIII, 247–49)

Nowhere else does Freud describe as keenly *the revolutionary radicality of the very nature of the teaching* to be (practically and theoretically) derived from the originality of the psychoanalytical experience. The analysand is qualified to be an analyst as of the point at which he understands his own analysis to be inherently unfinished, incomplete, as of the point, that is, at which he settles into his own didactic analysis—or his own analytical apprenticeship—as fundamentally interminable. It is, in other words, as of the moment the student recognizes that *learning has no term*, that he can himself become a teacher, assume the position of the teacher. But the position of the teacher is itself the position of *the one who learns*, of the one who *teaches* nothing other than *the way he learns*. The subject of teaching is interminably—a student; the subject of teaching is interminably—a learning. This is the most radical, perhaps the most far-reaching insight psychoanalysis can give us into pedagogy.

Freud pushes this original understanding of what pedagogy is to its logical limit. Speaking of the "defensive" tendency of psychoanalysts "to divert the implications and demands of analysis from themselves (probably by directing them on to other people)"—of the analysts' tendency, that is, "to *withdraw from the critical and corrective influence of analysis*," as well as of the temptation of power threatening them in the very exercise of their profession, Freud enjoins:

> Every analyst should periodically—at intervals of five years or so—submit himself to analysis once more, without feeling ashamed of taking this step. This would mean, then, that not only the therapeutic analysis of patients[17] but *his own analysis would change from a terminable into an interminable task.* (Standard, XXIII, 249)

Of all Freud's followers, Lacan alone has picked up on the radicality of Freud's pedagogical concern with didactic psychoanalysis, not just as a subsidiary technical, pragmatic question (how should analysts be trained?), but as a major theoretical concern, as a major pedagogical investigation crucial to the very innovation, to the very revolutionary core of psychoanalytic insight. The highly peculiar and surprising style of Lacan's own teaching practice is, indeed, an answer to, a follow-up on, Freud's ultimate suggestion—in Lacan's words—"to make psychoanalysis and education (training) collapse into each other" (E 459).

This is the thrust of Lacan's original endeavor both as psychoanalyst and as teacher: "in the field of psychoanalysis," he writes, "what is necessary is the restoration of the identical status of didactic psychoanalysis and of the teaching of psychoanalysis, in their common scientific opening" (E 236).

As a result of this conception, Lacan considers not just the practical analyses which he—as analyst—directs, but his own public teaching, his own seminar—primarily directed towards the (psychoanalytical) training of analysts—as partaking of didactic psychoanalysis, as itself, thus, analytically didactic and didactically analytical, in a new and radical way.

"How can what psychoanalysis teaches us be taught?" (E 439)—Only by continuing, in one's own teaching, one's own interminable didactic analysis. Lacan has willingly transformed himself into the *analysand* of his Seminar[18] so as to teach, precisely, psychoanalysis as teaching, and teaching as psychoanalysis.

Psychoanalysis as teaching, and teaching as psychoanalysis, radically subvert the demarcation-line, the clear-cut opposition between the analyst and the analysand, between the teacher and the student (or the learner)—showing that what counts, in both cases, is precisely the transition, the struggle-filled *passage* from one position to theother. But the passage is itself interminable; it can never be crossed once and for all: "The psychoanalytic act has but to falter slightly, and it is the analyst who becomes the analysand" (*Scilicet* I, 47). Lacan denounces, thus, "the reactionary principle" of the professional belief in "the duality of the one who suffers and the one who cures," in "the opposition between the one who knows and the one who does not know. . . . The most corrupting of comforts is intellectual comfort, just as one's worst corruption is the belief that one is *better*" (E 403).

Lacan's well-known polemical and controversial stance—his *critique of psychoanalysis*—itself partakes, then, of his understanding of the pedagogical imperative of didactic psychoanalysis. Lacan's original endeavor is to submit *the whole discipline of psychoanalysis* to what Freud called "the critical and corrective influence of analysis" (Standard, XXIII, 249). Lacan, in other words, is the first to understand that the psychoanalytic discipline is an unprecedented one in that its teaching does not just reflect upon itself, but turns back upon itself so as to *subvert itself*, and truly *teaches* only insofar as it subverts itself. Psychoanalytic teaching is pedagogically unique in that it is inherently, interminably, self-critical. Lacan's amazing pedagogical performance thus sets forth the unparalleled example of a teaching whose fecundity is tied up, paradoxically enough, with the inexhaustibility—the interminability—of its *self-critical potential.*

From didactic analysis, Lacan derives, indeed, a whole new theoretical (didactic) mode of *self-subversive self-reflection.*

> A question suddenly arises . . . : in the case of the knowledge yielded solely to the subject's mistake, what kind of subject could ever be in a position to know it in advance? (*Scilicet* I, 38)

> Retain at least what this text, which I have tossed out in your direction, bears witness to: my enterprise does not go beyond the act in which it is caught, and, therefore, its only chance lies in its being mistaken. (*Scilicet* I, 41)

> This lesson seems to be one that should not have been forgotten, had not psychoanalysis precisely taught us that it is, as such, forgettable. (E 232)

Always submitting analysis itself to the instruction of an unexpected analytic turn of the screw, to the surprise of an additional reflexive turn, of an additional self-subversive ironic twist, didactic analysis becomes for Lacan what might be called a *style*: a teaching style which has become at once a life-style and a writing-style: "the ironic style of calling into question the very foundations of the discipline" (E 238).

> Any return to Freud founding a teaching worthy of the name will occur only on that pathway where truth ... becomes manifest in the revolutions of culture. That pathway is the only training we can claim to transmit to those who follow us. It is called—a style. (E 458)

Didactic analysis is thus invested by Lacan not simply with the practical, pragmatic value, but with the theoretical significance—the allegorical instruction—of a paradigm: a paradigm, precisely, of the interminability, not just of teaching (learning) and of analyzing (being analyzed), but of the very act of thinking, theorizing: of teaching, analyzing, thinking, theorizing, in such a way as to make of psychoanalysis "what it has never ceased to be: an act that is yet to come" (*Scilicet* I, 9).

TEACHING AS A LITERARY GENRE

Among so many other things, Lacan and Freud thus teach us teaching, teach us—in a radically new way—what it might mean to teach. Their lesson, and their pedagogical performance, profoundly renew at once the meaning and the status of the very act of teaching.

If they are both such extraordinary teachers, it is—I would suggest—because they both are, above all, quite extraordinary learners. In Freud's case, I would argue, the extraordinary teaching stems from Freud's original—unique—position as a student; in Lacan's case, the extraordinary teaching stems from Lacan's original—unique—position as disciple.

"One might feel tempted," writes Freud, "to agree with the philosophers and the psychiatrists and like them, rule out the problem of dream-interpretation as a purely fanciful task. *But I have been taught better*" (Standard, IV, 100).

By whom has Freud been taught—taught better than by "the judgement of the prevalent science of today," better than by the established scholarly authorities of philosophy and psychiatry? Freud has been taught *by dreams* themselves: his own, and those of others; Freud has been taught by his own patients: "*My patients* ... told me their dreams and so *taught me* ... *"* (Standard, VI, 100–101).

Having thus been taught by dreams, as well as by his patients, that—contrary to the established scholarly opinion—dreams do have meaning, Freud is further taught by a literary text:

> This discovery is confirmed by a legend that has come down to us from antiquity. . . .
>
> While the poet . . . brings to light the guilt of Oedipus, he is at the same time compelling us to recognize our own inner minds . . .
>
> Like Oedipus, we live in ignorance of these wishes. . . . and after their revelation, we may all of us well seek to close our eyes to the scenes of our childhood. (Standard, VI, 261–263)

"But I have been taught better." What is unique about Freud's position as a student—as a learner—is that he learns from, or puts in the position of his teacher, the least authoritative sources of information that can be imagined: that he knows how to derive a teaching, or a lesson, from the very unreliability—the very *non-authority*—of literature, of dreams, of patients. For the first time in the history of learning, Freud, in other words, has recourse—scientific recourse—to a knowledge which is not authoritative, which is not that of a master, a knowledge which does not know what it knows, and is thus *not in possession of itself.*

Such, precisely, is the very essence of literary knowledge. "I went to the poets," says Socrates; ". . . I took them some of the most elaborate passages in their own writings, and asked them what was the meaning of them—thinking that they would teach me something. Will you believe me? I am almost ashamed to confess the truth, but I must say that there is hardly a person present who would not have talked better about their poetry than they did themselves. Then I knew that *not by wisdom do poets write poetry, but by a sort of genius or inspiration*; they are like diviners or soothsayers who also *say many fine things, but do not understand the meaning of them.* The poets appeared to me to be much in the same case."[19] From a philosophical perspective, knowledge is mastery—that which is in mastery of its own meaning. Unlike Hegelian philosophy, which *believes it knows all that there is to know*; unlike Socratic (or contemporary post-Nietzschean) philosophy, which *believes it knows it does not know*—literature, for its part, *knows it knows, but does not know the meaning of its knowledge*—does not know *what* it knows.

For the first time, then, Freud gives authority to the instruction—to the teaching—of a knowledge which does not know its own meaning, to a knowledge (that of dreams, of patients, of Greek tragedy) which we might define as literary: knowledge that is not in mastery of itself.

Of all Freud's students and disciples, Lacan alone has understood and emphasized the *radical* significance of Freud's indebtedness to literature: the role played by *literary knowledge* not just in the historical constitution of psychoanalysis, but in the very actuality of the psychoanalytic act, of the psychoanalytic (ongoing) *work* of learning and of teaching. Lacan alone has understood and pointed out the ways in which Freud's teaching—in all senses of the word—is not accidentally, but radically and fundamentally, a *literary* teaching. Speaking of "the training of the analysts of the future," Lacan thus writes:

> One has only to turn the pages of his works for it to become abundantly clear that Freud regarded a study . . . of the resonances . . . of literature and of the significations involved in works of art as necessary to an understanding of the text of our experience. Indeed, Freud himself is a striking instance of his own belief: he derived his inspiration, his ways of thinking and his technical weapons, from just such a study. But he also regarded it as a necessary condition in any teaching of psychoanalysis. (E 435, N 144)

> This [new] technique [of interpretation] would require for its teaching as well as for its learning a profound assimilation of the resources of a language, and especially of those that are concretely realized in its poetic texts. It is well known that Freud was in this position in relation to German literature, which, by virtue of an incomparable translation, can be said to include Shakespeare's plays. Every one of his works bears witness to this, and to the continual recourse he had to it, no less in his technique than in his discovery. (E 295, N 83)

> The psychoanalytic experience has rediscovered in man the imperative of the Word as the law that has formed him in its image. It manipulates the poetic function of language to give to his desire its symbolic mediation. (E 322, N 106)

> Freud had, eminently, this feel for meaning, which accounts for the fact that any of his works, *The Three Caskets*, for instance, gives the reader the impression that it is written by a soothsayer, that it is guided by that kind of meaning which is of the order of poetic inspiration. (S-II, 353)

It is in this sense, among others, that Lacan can be regarded as Freud's best student: Lacan is the sole Freudian who has sought to learn from Freud how to learn Freud: Lacan is "taught" by Freud in much the same way Freud reads *Oedipus the King*, specifically seeking in the text its *literary knowledge*. From Freud as teacher, suggests Lacan, we should learn to derive that kind of *liter-*

ary teaching he himself derived in an unprecedented way from literary texts. Freud's text should thus itself be read as a poetic text:

> ... the notion of the death instinct involves a basic irony, since its meaning has to be sought in the conjunction of two contrary terms: instinct ... being the law that governs ... a cycle of behavior whose goal is the accomplishment of a vital function; and death appearing first of all as the destruction of life....

> This notion must be approached through its resonances in what I shall call *the poetics of the Freudian corpus*, the first way of access to the penetration of its meaing, and the essential dimension, from the origins of the work to the apogee marked in it by this notion, for an understanding of its dialectical repercussions. (E 316–17, N 101–102)

It is here, in conjunction with Lacan's way of relating to Freud's literary teaching and of learning from Freud's literary knowledge, that we touch upon the historical uniqueness of Lacan's position as disciple, and can thus attempt to understand the way in which this pedagogically unique discipleship accounts for Lacan's astounding originality as teacher.

"As Plato pointed out long ago," says Lacan, "it is not at all necessary that the poet know what he is doing, in fact, it is preferable that he not know. That is what gives a primordial value to what he does. We can only bow our heads before it" (Seminar, April 9, 1974, unpublished). Although apparently Lacan seems to espouse Plato's position, his real pedagogical stance is, in more than one way, at the antipodes of that of Plato; and not just because he bows his head to poets, whereas Plato casts them out of the Republic. If Freud himself, indeed, bears witness, in his text, to some poetic—literary—knowledge, it is to the extent that, like the poets, he, too, cannot exhaust the meaning of his text—he too partakes of the poetic ignorance of his own knowledge. Unlike Plato who, from his position as an admiring disciple, reports Socrates; assertion of his ignorance without—it might be assumed—really believing in the *non-ironic truth* of that assertion ("For the hearers," says Socrates "always imagine that I myself possess the wisdom I find wanting in others"[20]), Lacan can be said to be the first disciple in the whole history of pedagogy and of culture who *does indeed believe in the ignorance of his teacher—of his master.* Paradoxically enough, this is why he can be said to be, precisely, Freud's own best student: a student of Freud's own revolutionary way of learning, of Freud's own unique position as theunprecedented student of unauthorized, unmastered knowledge. "The truth of the subject," says Lacan, "even when he is in the position of a master, is not in himself" (S-XI, 10).

[Freud's] texts, to which for the past . . . years I have devoted a two-hour seminar every Wednesday . . . without having covered a quarter of the total, . . . have given me, and those who have attended my seminars, the surprise of genuine discoveries. These discoveries, which range from concepts that have remained unused to clinical details uncovered by our exploration, demonstrate *how far the field investigated by Freud extended beyond the avenues that he left us to tend,* and how little his observation, which sometimes gives an impression of exhaustiveness, was the slave of what he had to demonstrate. Who . . . has not been moved by this research in action, whether in 'The Interpretation of Dreams,' 'The Wolf Man,' or 'Beyond the Pleasure Principle'? (E 404, N 117, TM)

Commenting on *The Interpretation of Dreams,* Lacan situates in Freud's text the discoverer's own transferential structure—Freud's own unconscious structure of address:

What polarizes at that moment Freud's discourse, what organizes the whole of Freud's existence, is the conversation with Fliess. . . . It is in this dialogue that Freud's self-analysis is realized . . . This vast speech addressed to Fliess will later become the whole written work of Freud.

The conversation of Freud with Fliess, this fundamental discourse, which at that moment is unconscious, is the essential dynamic element [of *The Interpretation of Dreams*]. Why is it unconscious at that moment? Because its significance goes far beyond what both of them, as individuals, can consciously apprehend or understand of it at the moment. As individuals, they are nothing other, after all, than two little erudites, who are in the process of exchanging rather weird ideas.

The discovery of the unconscious, in the full dimension with which it is revealed at the very moment of its historical emergence, is that the scope, the implications of meaning go far beyond the signs manipulated by the individual. As far as signs are concerned, man is always mobilizing many more of them than he knows. (S-II, 150)

It is to the extent that Lacan precisely teaches us to read in Freud's text (in its textual excess) the signifiers of Freud's ignorance—his ignorance of his own knowledge—that Lacan can be considered Freud's best reader, as well as the most compelling teacher of the Freudian pedagogical imperative: the imperative to learn from and through the insight which does not know its own meaning, from and through the knowledge which is not entirely in mastery—in possession—of itself.

This unprecedented *literary* lesson, which Lacan derives from Freud's revolutionary way of learning and in the light of which he learns Freud, is transformed, in Lacan's own work, into a deliberately literary style of teaching. While—as a subject of praise or controversy—the originality of Lacan's eminently literary, eminently "poetic" style has become a stylistic *cause célèbre* often commented upon, what has not been understood is the extent to which this style—this poetic theory or theoretical poetry—is *pedagogically* poetic: poetic in such a way as to raise, through every answer that it gives, the literary question of its non-mastery of itself. In pushing its own thought beyond the limit of its self-possession, beyond the limitations of its own capacity for mastery; in passing on understanding which does not fully understand what it understands; in *teaching*, thus, with *blindness*—with and through the very blindness of its literary knowledge, of insights not entirely transparent to themselves—Lacan's unprecedented theoretically *poetic pedagogy* always implicitly opens up onto the infinitely literary, infinitely *teaching* question: What is the "navel"[21] of my own theoretical dream of understanding? What is the specificity of my incomprehension? What is the riddle which I in effect here pose under the guise of knowledge?

> "But what was it that Zarathustra once said to you? That poets lie too much? But Zarathustra too is a poet. Do you believe that in saying this he spoke the truth? Why do you believe that?"
>
> The disciple answered, "I believe in Zarathustra." But Zarathustra shook his head and smiled.[22]
>
> Any return to Freud founding a teaching worthy of the name will occur only on that pathway where truth . . . becomes manifest in the revolutions of culture. That pathway is the only training we can claim to transmit to those who follow us. It is called—a style. (E 458)[23]

NOTES

1. Plato, *Meno.* 70a, 71a, 82a. Translated by G. M. A. Grube (Indianapolis: Hackell Publishing Company, 1980), pp. 3, 14 (translation modified).
2. *The Complete Psychological Works of Sigmund Freud*, translated from the German under the general editorship of James Strachey (London: The Hogarth Press and the Institute of Psychoanalysis), volume XIX, p. 273. Hereafter, this edition will be referred to as "Standard," followed by volume number (in roman numerals) and page number (in arabic numerals).
3. Jacques Lacan, *Ecrits* (Paris: Seuil, 1966), p. 233, my translation. Henceforth I will be using the abbreviations: "E" (followed by page number)—for this original French edition of the *Ecrits*, and "N" (followed by page number) for the corresponding Norton edition of the English translation *(Ecrits: A Selection*, translated by Alan Sheridan,

New York: Norton, 1977). When the reference to the French edition of the *Ecrits* (E) is not followed by a reference to the Norton English edition (N), the passage quoted (as in this case) is in my translation and has not been included in the "Selection" of the Norton edition.

4. Which for Lacan involves "the relationship of the individual to language": E 445.

5. Italics mine. As a rule, in the quoted passages, italics are mine unless otherwise indicated.

6. Anna Freud, *Psychoanalysis for Teachers and Parents*, translated by Barbara Low (Boston: Beacon Press, 1960), pp. 95–6.

7. Ibid., p. 105.

8. Catherine Millot, interview in *l'Ane, le magasine freudien*, No. 1, April–May 1981, p. 19.

9. Catherine Millot, *Freud Anti-Pedagogue* (Paris: Bibliothèque d'Ornicar? 1979).

10. Plato, *Meno*, 96 d, op. cit., p. 28 (translation modified).

11. Ibid., 82 e, p. 15.

12. "The abbreviation "TM"—"translation modified"—will signal my alterations of the official English translation of the work in question.

13. The abbreviation S-XI (followed by page number) refers to Jacques Lacan, *Le Séminaire, livre XI, Les Quatre concepts fondamentaux de la psychanalyse* (Paris: Seuil, 1973). The following abbreviation "N" (followed by page number) refers to the corresponding English edition: *The Four Fundamental Concepts of Psychoanalysis*, edited by Jacques-Alain Miller, translated by Alan Sheridan (New York: Norton, 1978).

   As for the rest of Lacan's Seminars which have appeared in book form, the following abbreviations will be used:

   S-I (followed by page number), for: J. Lacan, *Le Séminaire, livre I: Les Écrits techniques de Freud* (Paris: Seuil, 1975);

   S-II (followed by page number), for: J. Lacan, *Le Séminaire, livre II: le Moi dans la théorie de Freud et dans la technique de la psychanalyse* (Paris: Seuil, 1978);

   S-XX (followed by page number), for J. Lacan, *Le Séminaire, livre XX: Encore* (Paris: Seuil, 1975).

   All quoted passages from these Seminars are here in my translation.

14. Abbreviated for Lacan's texts published in *Scilicet: Tu peux savoir ce qu'en pense l'école freudienne de Paris* (Paris: Seuil). The roman numeral stands for the issue number (followed by page number). Number I appeared in 1968.

15. As soon as analytic knowledge *is* exchanged, it ceases to be knowledge and becomes opinion, prejudice, presumption: "the sum of prejudices that every knowledge contains, and that each of us transports. . . . Knowledge is always, somewhere, only one's belief that one knows (S-II, 56).

16. Sophocles, *Oedipus the King, translated* by David Grene, in *Sophocles I,* (Chicago & London: The University of Chicago Press, 1954), pp. 25–6.

17. The therapeutic analysis of patients is "interminable" to the extent that repression can never be totally lifted, only displaced. Cf. Freud's letter to Fliess, dated April 16, 1900: "E's career as a patient has at last come to an end . . . His riddle is *almost* completely solved, his condition is excellent . . . At the moment a residue of his symptoms remains. I am beginning to understand that the apparently interminable nature of the treatment is something determined by law and is dependent on the transference." Hence, Freud speaks of "the asymptotic termination of treatment." (Standard, XXIII, 215) Freud's italics.

18. The occasional master's pose—however mystifying to the audience—invariably exhibits itself as a parodic symptom of the analysand.
19. Plato, *Apology*, 22 a–c, in *Dialogues of Plato*, Jowett translation, edited by J. D. Kaplan (New York: Washington Square Press, Pocket Books, 1973), p. 12.
20. Ibid.
21. "There is," writes Freud, "at least one spot in every dream at which it is unplumbable—a navel, as it were, that is its point of contact with the unknown" (Standard, IV, 111).
22. Nietzsche, *Thus Spoke Zarathustra*, translated by Walter Kaufmann (TM), in *The Portable Nietzsche* (New York: the Viking Press, 1971), p. 239, "On Poets."
23. The news of Lacan's death (on September 9, 1981) reached me as I was writing the section here entitled "The Interminable Task." The sadness caused by the cessation of a life as rich in insight and as generous in instruction, was thus accompanied by an ironic twist which itself felt like a typical Lacanian turn, one of the ironies of his teaching: teaching terminable and interminable ... Few deaths, indeed, have been as deeply inscribed as a lesson in a teaching, as Lacan's, who always taught the implications of the Master's death. "Were I to go away," he said, some time ago, "tell yourselves that it is in order to at last be truly Other."

I have deliberately chosen not to change, and to pursue, the grammatical present tense which I was using to describe Lacan's teaching: since his life has ceased to be, his teaching is, indeed, all the more present, all the more alive, all the more interminably "what it has never ceased to be: an act that is yet to come."

2

Learning the Subject of Desire

DEREK BRITON

The fundamental presupposition of my approach to Lacan is the utter incongruity of a "synchronous" reading of his texts and seminars: the only way to comprehend Lacan is to approach his work as a work in progress, as a succession of attempts to seize the same persistent traumatic kernel. The shifts in Lacan's work become manifest the moment one concentrates on his great negative theses: "There is no Other of the Other," "The desire of the analyst is not a pure desire." . . . Upon encountering such a thesis, one must always ask the simple question: who *is* this idiot who is claiming that *there is* an Other of the Other, that the desire of the analyst *is* a pure desire, and so on? There is, of course, only one answer: *Lacan himself a couple of years ago.* The only way to approach Lacan, therefore, is to read "Lacan *contre* Lacan."

—Slavoj Žižek, *The Metastases of Enjoyment*

DISCERNING DESIRE

Desire, according to Jean Laplanche and Jean-Bertrand Pontalis, is one of the most slippery terms in the psychoanalytic lexicon. The notion of desire at play in the Freudian doctrine, for example, they judge "too fundamental to be circumscribed"; and although in the Lacanian corpus, desire is treated more specifically—"desire appears in the rift which separates need and demand"— the two deem it, in the last instance, equally uncircumscribable: reducible neither to need, since it is "a relation to phantasy," nor to demand, since "it seeks to impose itself without taking the language or the unconscious of the other into account."[1] Where, then, does one even begin learning desire, let alone discerning its relation to knowledge in Lacan's thought?—the task I have agreed to undertake in this chapter. Well, one way, as one of my more pragmatically minded colleagues is fond of putting it, is "to dig where you stand."[2] I have chosen, therefore, in the absence of any obvious starting point, to draw upon a recent experience of my own to explore desire's relation to knowledge in Lacan's thought.

KNOWLEDGE AND TRANSFERENCE

If Shoshana Felman is to be taken at her word (and I think she is); if learning proceeds "not through linear progression but through breakthroughs, leaps, discontinuities, regressions, and deferred action"; if "the analytic learning process puts in question . . . the progressivist view of learning as a simple one-way road from ignorance to knowledge"; if knowledge "is not a substance but a structural dynamic . . . is not contained by any individual but . . . is essentially, irreducibly dialogic," then learning desire and discerning its relation to knowledge will entail an act of transference, an act of dialectical engagement with Lacan's *sujet supposé savoir*, with a "subject presumed to know."[3] This has certainly proven to be the case in my own struggle(s) to come to terms with Lacan's thought—to learn desire.[4]

It was after presenting a paper to a critical pedagogy conference—on the implications of psychoanalytic theory for pedagogic practice, a paper that draws extensively upon Felman's "Teaching Terminable and Interminable"[5]—that one such struggle was to begin. Although the overall response to my paper was positive, questions were raised about the viability of a learning strategy premised on psychoanalytic principles. It was impossible, in the limited time available, to identify the concerns that prompted these questions, I assumed them to be of an ethical nature, concerns about the propriety of a pedagogy premised on psychoanalytic principles. (Only much later would I realize that this judgment was more a reflection of my own concerns than those of my interlocutors.) The ensuing exchange did convince me of one thing, however: I needed to investigate the implications of psychoanalytic theory for pedagogic practice more closely.

Several weeks were to pass before an opportunity to reflect on that exchange would present itself. (I had, in the meantime, made some minor corrections to the paper in question and submitted it for publication.) The process of introspection I was finally to embark upon offered little insight into the concerns of my interlocutors however.[6] But it did reveal, somewhat to my surprise, that what I remembered most vividly about the polemics following my presentation was not the questions of my interlocutors, but the sense of guilt their probing had invoked in me.[7] Why our exchange should have elicited guilt I could now only wonder. What could possibly be its source? Perhaps a suppressed kernel of knowledge whose presence would subvert the argument I advanced in the paper? Maybe a lacuna in my understanding of Lacan, a mar I had glossed over, repressed, rather than addressed? I knew I would have to work through my thoughts and feelings associated with the event before an answer to these questions would be forthcoming. This working through would entail an act of transference on my part, a willingness to place an other in the place of subject presumed to know, an other I had (re)turned to a number of times before.

THE TROUBLE WITH TRANSFERENCE

Of Lacan's many commentators, one in particular, Slavoj Žižek, "the Giant of Ljubljana," has proven especially alluring to me.[8] It is to Žižek that I inevitably (re)turn whenever I find myself struggling to make sense of Lacan's thought, to learn desire—which is more often than I care to admit. In preparation for this particular return, I began rereading the paper I had delivered to the critical pedagogy conference. In so doing, my attention was drawn to a citation I had culled from Žižek:

> The Lacanian notion of the imaginary self . . . exists only on the basis of the misrecognition of its own conditions; it is the effect of this misrecognition. So Lacan's emphasis is not on the supposed incapacity of the self to reflect, to grasp its own conditions—on its being the plaything of inaccessible unconscious forces; his point is that the subject can pay for such reflection with the loss of his [or her] ontological consistency.[9]

The point I remembered wanting to make, the point I had called upon Žižek to support, was simply this: that the imaginary self is an *effect* of misrecognition, a point succinctly made in the first two lines. That I had chosen to include the remaining lines now made little sense: far from supporting my argument that teachers should embrace reflection as a pedagogic strategy, they actually undermined it!

I remembered being puzzled by these lines when first I read them, being mystified by their indictment of concerted introspection: "the subject can pay for such reflection with the loss of his [or her] ontological consistency." Could this possibly mean that assuming the position of subject presumed to know for an other, assisting an other to interpret his or her "resistance," her or his symptom, to the point of dissolution might result in psychosis? Perhaps some of the guilt invoked by my presentation stemmed from a failure to pursue this anomaly when first it presented itself to me. What troubled me more, however, was why, if the knowledge transference discloses is, in fact, the very knowledge the subject *must* repress in order to maintain his or her ontological consistency, Felman would advocate dissolving that resistance, that is, providing the subject, through an act of interpretation, with knowledge of his or her underlying support—with the truth of her or his symptom?

A closer inspection of Felman's text convinced me that this is, in fact, what she advocates: "by structurally occupying the position of the analysand's unconscious, . . . the analyst . . . makes the patient learn what would otherwise remain forever inaccessible to [her or] him" (83). This knowledge is relayed to the analysand through his or her own signifiers, which "the analyst *returns* to the patient from his [or her] different vantage point, from his [or her] non-reflexive, asymmetrical position as an Other. . . . Coming from the Other, knowledge is, by definition, that which comes as a surprise" (82). Although the subject is ignorant of "that knowledge which is inaccessible to itself because it cannot tolerate knowing that it knows" (82), such knowledge can be accessed through the mediation of the Other: unlike the subject, then, who is constitutively split and lacking, the Other is whole, lacking nothing. The analyst can, on this account, by occupying the position of the Other, make available to the analysand, through an act of interpretation, the underlying support of his or her symptom, that very knowledge which would otherwise remain inaccessible to him or her—the truth. But why, if the price of truth is psychosis, would Lacan advocate such a course of action?

That Felman has simply gotten Lacan wrong is, of course, one possibility. She certainly would not be the first, given the tangled web that constitutes Lacan's thought. But Felman's is no passing foray into Lacan's oeuvre. Unlike others, whose brief sojourns yield only what they set out to find, Felman presents a careful and well-supported analysis of Lacan's thought. Convinced of the veracity of Felman's text, I decided there must be something I was missing, something I was overlooking. It was only through a return to Žižek, through attributing him with the very knowledge that I lacked, that I would finally resolve this dilemma. This return, however, was to draw me into the prickly debate on the nature of knowledge/truth and its relation to desire in Lacan's thought. It is to this debate that I now turn.

THE DESIRE FOR TRUTH

As early as the 1950s, social scientists began turning away from ahistorical, "scientific" modes of inquiry toward contextualist approaches that accommodate historical and cultural forms of difference.[10] Such modes of inquiry tend, however, to be premised on conceptions of knowledge that differ significantly from those of their scientific counterparts: they abandon all hope of, all desire for, Truth. Proponents of these new modes of inquiry, dismayed by the totalizing consequences of past attempts to circumscribe Truth, idealist and materialist alike, declare all aspirations to Truth misguided—paternalistic, at best; despotic, at worst. But the remedy such thinkers prescribe for the West's *malaise episte-mologique* has proven too bitter a pill for many to swallow. Few are willing, even to escape the thralls of "scientism," to abandon themselves to the play of the sig-nifier, to trade the promise of certainty for the ambiguity and indeterminacy of language.[11] Those who reject linguistic conceptions of truth/knowledge, how-ever, are faced with the task of finding a mode of inquiry that accommodates dif-ference while retaining the desire for, the possibility of, Truth—a formidable challenge. That such a mode of inquiry exists—the product not so much of a de-sire for Truth but of another desire: a desire to understand desire—is something I was about to learn. It was to take the mediation of yet another desire, how-ever—my desire to resolve the conundrum of transference—to alert me to this fact. Desire, I was beginning to realize, works in mysterious ways.

Is it not desire, after all, that compels so many to reject *post*prefixed solu-tions to the current epistemological crisis—the desire to retain Truth's reas-suring aura and History's comforting promise? Is it not this very desire that fuels so many reproaches of contemporary thought, that exudes from even the most cursory of such condemnations? Consider Salman Rushdie's sniping caricature of the French, for example:

> The French, these days, would have us believe that this world, which they call "the text," is quite unconnected to the "real" world, which they call "the world." But if I believe (and I do) that the imagined world is, must be, con-nected to the observable one, then I should be able, should I not, to locate it; to say how you get there from here. And it is not easy, you see, to be pre-cise . . .[12]

Such testimonies to Truth, however—their popular appeal notwithstand-ing—demand substantiation if they are to be taken seriously. And it is on this count that Rushdie and so many other defenders of Truth come up short.

Upon what, for instance, does Rushdie base his claim that "the imagined world is, *must be,* connected to the observable one"? What is the inarticulable *je ne sais quoi* that supports his belief in an incontrovertible "connection" be-tween imaginary and real? It is somewhat ironic, then, but not unfitting, that at the very point where Rushdie finds himself at a loss for words, up against the very limits of language, at the point where words fail, where "it is not easy, you see, to be precise . . . ," that Truth's defense is taken up by one so quintes-sentially French: Jacques Lacan.[13] Clearly *not all*—to coin a distinctly Lacan-ian turn of phrase—"the French, these days, would have us believe that this world . . . is quite unconnected to the 'real' world."

PSYCHOANALYSIS AND TRUTH

Rushdie, of course, is far from alone in identifying Frenchness with textualism—for many the epitome of poststructuralist thought.[14] But followers of Lacan, such as Žižek, are quick to point out that to label Lacan a textualist simply because he is French is not only to ignore "the radical break that separates him from the field of 'post-structuralism'" but also to overlook how "even the propositions common to the two fields obtain a totally different dimension in each."[15] Lacan's claim that "there is no metalanguage," for instance, or "his thesis that truth is structured like a fiction" has, Žižek contends, "nothing at all to do with a post-structuralist reduction of the truth-dimension to a textual 'truth-effect.'" Why? Because Lacan is singular in his insistence on one thing: "psychoanalysis as a truth-experience." It is, however, only in light of textualist critiques of Lacan—critiques that chastise him for positing a material support for Truth, for ascribing to an ingenuous realism, an indefensible metaphysics of presence—that the irony of labeling him a poststructuralist becomes fully apparent.[16]

Although such textual critiques acknowledge the enigmatic nature of Lacan's materialism—"this odd materiality of the letter . . . is neither idealism nor materialism, although the emphasis is placed, after it has been distorted, on the second of these two terms"[17]—they tend to reject Lacan peremptorily as simply another perpetrator of metaphysical sophistry. But to dismiss Lacan as a sophist of either a metaphysical or a textualist persuasion is to move a little too quickly.[18] Such dismissals tend to result from failed attempts to situate Lacan's enigmatic materiality within the Western philosophical tradition, within its twin branches of idealism and materialism. But it is in displaying such deference to conventional parameters of thought that Lacan's critics foreclose on much that is unique to, and distinctive of, his thinking.

LACAN'S "CRITIQUE OF PURE DESIRE"

That Lacan's thinking, along with that of other twentieth-century French intellectual greats, was significantly influenced by Alexandre Kojève's Sorbonne lectures on Hegel's *Phenomenology* is now a commonplace.[19] For Kojève, knowledge/truth and meaning are one and the same, as are meaning and desire: the meaning of life, of human struggle, for example, *is* its truth, and that truth corresponds to, is a function of, human desire:

> Desire directed towards a natural object is human only to the extent that it
> is "mediated" by the Desire of another directed toward the same object: it is

human to desire what others desire, because they desire it. Thus, an object perfectly useless from the biological point of view (such as a medal, or the enemy's flag) can be desired because it is the object of other desires. Such a Desire can only be a Human desire, and human reality, as distinguished from animal reality, is created only by action that satisfies such Desires: human history is the history of desired Desires.[20]

There can be little doubt that Kojève's Hegelian conception of history—the meaning of history resides not in the concrete events that comprise the stuff of history, its objective content, but in that fundamental absence that escapes each successive attempt at mastery: human desire[21]—inspired Lacan to begin identifying the meaning of *any* chain of events, that is its truth, with that which escapes each of the successive attempts at mastery that constitute that chain: its object of desire. I, for one—and seemingly Felman, for another— had certainly understood this identification of meaning with knowledge/truth and the correlation of meaning with desire to be a central axiom of Lacan's thought. And, in turning to Žižek, I was to find confirmation of this fact— but with a vertiginous twist!

In attributing Žižek with the knowledge I lacked, I had committed myself to a much closer reading of his work. That reading was to reveal something I had previously overlooked—or had chosen to ignore: Žižek is a Lacanian of a particular sort, one of a school of Slovenian Lacanians whose reading of Lacan has been much influenced by the work of Jacques-Alain Miller and a small coterie of his followers.[22] This enclave of analysts did not undertake the task for which they are best known—the codification of Lacan's thought—until late in Lacan's life, due, primarily, to Lacan's dislike of formal systems, which led him to frown upon those who attempted to systematize his thought. Led by Miller, Lacan's heir apparent, this avant-garde began the systematic documentation of Lacan's thought, "pointing out the distinction between the different stages of his thinking, and placing an accent on the theoretical importance of the last stage, in which a central role is granted to the notion of the *Real* as that which resists symbolization."[23] Due to the efforts of this intimate circle and those of others since inspired by its work—most notably Žižek and other members of the Slovenian Lacanian school—it is now possible to consider Lacan's corpus in light of a single, overarching aim:

Is not his entire work an endeavor to answer the question of how *desire* is possible? Does he not offer a kind of "critique of pure desire," of the pure faculty of desiring? Are not all his fundamental concepts so many keys to the enigma of desire? Desire is constituted by "symbolic castration," the original loss of the *Thing*: the void of this loss is filled out by *objet petit a*, the fantasy-object; this loss occurs on account of our being "embedded" in the symbolic universe which derails the "natural" circuit of our needs: etc., etc.[24]

What soon became apparent to those who participated in the codification of Lacan's thought, however, is that his "critique of pure desire" not only proceeds in three distinct stages but also undergoes radical revision in the movement from one stage to the next.

THE TERNARY NATURE OF LACAN'S THOUGHT

This was certainly a revelation to me. Could this—my failure to appreciate the ternary structure of Lacan's thought—be the source of my bewilderment and guilt? It was only through yet another return to Žižek, through attributing him, once more, with the knowledge that I lacked, that I would learn the answer to this question. That return, however, was very quickly to make one thing clear: in pursuing a single, "synchronous" reading of Lacan, I had unwittingly foreclosed on a crucial possibility: "the only way to comprehend Lacan is to approach his work as a work in progress, as a succession of attempts to seize the same persistent traumatic kernel."[25] Perhaps the answers I was seeking resided in the interstices of Lacan's thought, in the transitions between one stage of his thinking and the next, in "the shifts" that "become manifest the moment one concentrates on his great negative theses"?

Žižek characterizes the three stages of Lacan's thought as follows.[26] In the first, Lacan's focus is on how the word entails the death of the thing, how once something is snared in the symbolic web, it is more present in its concept than the thing itself: "Hegel puts it with extreme rigour—the notion is what makes the thing be there, while, all the while, it isn't."[27] Once ensnared in the symbolic network, the thing falls prey to the word, so that even when we focus on the thing itself rather than its concept, we find it inscribed with a lack. Consequently, Lacan's teachings during this stage stress how, to have knowledge of a thing, "we must have recourse to the word which implies an absence of the thing." Lacan finds in the *Fort* and *Da* game of Freud's grandson a perfect example of this process of ensnarement:

> I talked about the *Fort* and *Da* with you. It is an example of the way in which the child enters naturally into this game. He starts to play with the object, or more exact, with the simple fact of its presence and its absence. So it is a transformed object, an object with a symbolic function, a devitalised object, already a sign. When the object is there he chases it away,

when it isn't there he calls it. Through these first games, the object passes, as if naturally, on to the plane of language. The symbol comes into being and becomes more important than the object.[28]

Žižek maintains that the advent of Lacan's second stage of thought is signaled by a shift in focus from the word "to language as a synchronic structure, a senseless autonomous mechanism which produces meaning as its effect." This shift reflects Lacan's theoretical transition from phenomenology to structuralism, from the pursuit of psychoanalysis as a field of meaning to one of differentiality—the signifier, as such. It is during this stage that Lacan (1) develops an interest in the relation of the Imaginary to the Symbolic—"the opposition between the imaginary level of the experience of meaning and the meaningless signifier/signifying mechanism producing it"; (2) identifies the Imaginary with Freud's notion of the pleasure principle—positing it as a realm in search of homeostatic balance; and (3) equates the Symbolic with Freud's death drive—positing it as a site of "blind automatism [that] is always troubling this homeostasis." Once ensnared in the web of the signifier, the subject is exposed to a mortifying effect: "he [or she] becomes part of a strange automatic order disturbing his [or her] natural homeostatic balance."

The shift from the second to the third stage of Lacan's thinking is marked by a growing preoccupation with the Real as impossible. During this third and final stage of his thinking, Lacan's focus shifts from the Imaginary/Symbolic relation—from discourse/language as a synchronic structure—to that of the Symbolic/Real, to the thing itself, *das Ding*. The origins of this shift, according to Žižek, can be traced to Lacan's teachings in the late 1950s, to his seminar on the ethics of psychoanalysis in particular—*The Seminar of Jacques Lacan. Book VII: The Ethic of Psychoanalysis*. Therein, the Symbolic is no longer identified with the death drive—that is, posited as the realm beyond the pleasure principle—but with the pleasure principle itself: "the unconscious 'structured like a language,' its 'primary process' of metonymic-metaphoric displacement is governed by the pleasure principle." It is the Real, not the Symbolic, that now constitutes the beyond of beyond the pleasure principle for Lacan.

Consequently, it is the Symbolic, rather than the Imaginary, that Lacan now posits as pursuing homeostasis, an equilibrium incessantly perturbed by "*das Ding*, the Thing . . . at its very centre, some strange, traumatic element which cannot be symbolized, integrated into the symbolic order." In another characteristic reversal, the death drive, earlier conceived as the Symbolic's threat to the illusory homeostasis of the Imaginary, now assumes the form of a threat to the very existence of the symbolic order itself, implying the "possibility of its radical effacement, of 'symbolic death'—not the death of the so-called 'real object' in its symbol, but the obliteration of the signifying network itself."

In carefully considering the different elements at play in each of these three periods of Lacan's thought, one thing became clear: the final stage of Lacan's thinking serves as the focus of Žižek's work, and the second as that of Felman's "Teaching Terminable and Interminable." In failing to recognize and distinguish between the different stages of Lacan's thought, I had overlooked something of more than theoretical significance: how, in the transitions from one stage to the next, Lacan reconstitutes the very aim of the psychoanalytic process, its central concepts, and its point of termination. Gaining insight into this transitional dimension of Lacan's thought was to involve yet another return to Žižek.

RETHINKING PSYCHOANALYTIC PRACTICE

What that return to Žižek revealed is that during the first stage of his thinking, Lacan's "emphasis is on the word as medium of the intersubjective recognition of desire." The subject's symptom is treated as a yet-to-be-symbolized imaginary element of his or her personal history. Through analysis, such symptoms are interpreted and given a place in the subject's symbolic network, giving meaning, retroactively, to what at first manifested itself as a meaningless trace. Analysis, during this period, comes to a close "when the subject is able to narrate to the Other [her or] his own history in its continuity; [her or] his desire is integrated, recognized in 'full speech (*parole pleine*).'"

With the advent of the second stage, however, Lacan's emphasis shifts to the sense of irredeemable loss—symbolic castration—that accompanies the subject's entry into language, into the differential order of the signifier: the Symbolic. The Symbolic is identified with the death drive, with the mortifying effect of the signifier's blind automatism on a subject, who, in the register of the Imaginary, conceives of himself or herself as a unified whole. During this stage, analysis culminates "when the subject is ready to accept [her or] his fundamental loss, to consent to symbolic castration as a price to be paid for access to his [or her] desire."

The third and final stage of Lacan's thought, however, is marked by a rejection of the Symbolic as an intersubjective guarantor of meaning, in favor of the big Other as flawed, constituted around a nonsensical, unsymbolizable "little piece of the Real": *das Ding*. To mask this nonsensical absence at the very heart of the Symbolic, the subject fabricates a fantasy to breach the unbearable emptiness of the void he or she must otherwise face. The final moment of analysis during this stage is "defined as 'going through the fantasy' . . . not its symbolic interpretation but the experience of the fact that the fantasy-object, by its fascinating presence, is merely filling out a lack, a void in the Other." The analysand's task, then, is to recognize that there is nothing behind the fantasy, that its sole function is to mask the void at the very heart of the big Other.

In conflating Felman's reading of Lacan with that of Žižek, I had inadvertently juxtaposed commentary on the second stage of Lacan's thought—wherein "the Imaginary register is presented as a series of variants that must be referred to a stable symbolic matrix"[29]—with that on the third, wherein "the Real is the rock upon which every attempt at symbolization stumbles, the hard core which remains the same in all possible worlds (symbolic universes)"[30] Not realizing that Lacan's thought proceeds in three distinct stages and that Lacan subjects it to radical revision in the transition from one stage to the next, I had failed to give due consideration to this significant shift in focus. It was to Žižek that I turned, once more, to gain a fuller appreciation of this turn in Lacan's thinking.

SYMPTOM AS CIPHERED MESSAGE

There is, Žižek notes, in the final years of Lacan's teaching, a tendency toward universalization. There is, for example, a "universalization of the symptom" to the point that "we can even say that 'symptom' is Lacan's final answer to the eternal philosophical question 'Why is there something instead of nothing?'—this 'something' which 'is' instead of nothing is indeed the symptom."[31] Symptom is not, however, the only concept Lacan elevates to the level of generalizability during this period. The generalizability of symptom is, in fact, predicated on the universalization of another concept: *foreclosure*. Whereas in the 1950s, Lacan restricts the use of foreclosure to the domain of psychosis, employing it to designate "the exclusion of a certain key-signifier (*point de capiton*, Name-of-the-Father) from the symbolic order," in the final years of his teaching, he employs it to designate an exclusion "proper to the order of the signifier as such; whenever we have a symbolic structure it is structured around a certain void, it implies the foreclosure of a certain key-signifier." It is this generalization of foreclosure that makes possible the notion of symptom-as-real that Lacan begins to favor in the last years of his teaching, a notion seemingly at odds, however, with such earlier claims as "the unconscious is structured like a language" and the symptom is "a symbolic formation *par excellence*, a cyphered, coded message which can be dissolved through interpretation because it is already a signifier." It is this earlier notion of symptom that informs Felman's text and that leads her to advocate its dissolution through an act of interpretation—the very course of action Žižek cautions against, based on the revised notion of symptom Lacan introduces in the final stage of his thought. I was beginning to understand, finally, why "to explain this apparent contradiction, we must take into account the different stages of Lacan's development."

At the onset of the 1950s, for example, Lacan posits the symptom as a coded communiqué addressed to the big Other, an encrypted message whose true meaning is to be conferred upon it at a later date: "in the symptom, the subject gets back, in the form of a cyphered, unrecognized message, the truth about his [or her] desire, the truth that he [or she] he was not able to confront, that he [or she] betrayed."[32] On this reading, the symptom is a product of failed communication, an articulation of the repressed word in ciphered form: more than just interpretable, the symptom is actually formulated with interpretation in mind. In fact, there can be no symptom without transference, without the presupposition of some subject that knows its meaning in advance: "Precisely as an enigma, the symptom, so to speak, announces its dissolution through interpretation: the aim of psychoanalysis is to re-establish the broken network of communication by allowing the patient to verbalize the meaning of [her or] his symptom: through this verbalization, the symptom is automatically dissolved."[33] The formation of the symptom *presupposes*, then, an all-knowing symbolic order, an omniscient big Other that already knows its meaning—its truth. The meaning or truth of the symptom, therefore, is clearly a function of *intersubjective communication*, as is readily apparent in Lacan's schema of the four discourses—of the master, the university, the hysteric, and the analyst.

LACAN'S FOUR DISCOURSES

It was not until the 1960s drew to a close that Lacan, somewhat uncharacteristically, consolidated his thinking on intersubjective communication into a theory of sorts—that of the four discourses. Lacan goes to great lengths to explain the resultant schema, which "indicates how differently structured discourses may produce certain psychological effects which in turn produce certain sociological affects—ruling [the discourse of the master], educating [the discourse of the university], opposing [the discourse of the hysteric], and revolutionizing [the discourse of the analyst]"; and how "four primary effects are produced by the particular location of the terms/factors and the generated discursive practices at the inter- and intra-subjective levels."[34] The four effects are those of *agent, truth, other,* and *production*; the terms/factors those of master signifier (S$_1$), knowledge (S$_2$), the split or divided subject ($\cancel{S}$), and that which must be excluded, the surplus of signification, *le plus-de-jouir, objet petit a*, the symptom, (a). The invariable, quaternary structure of the four effects identifies the parameters of the four discourses—of master, university, hysteric, and analyst.

The Structural Coordinates of Lacan's Four Discourses

agent	other
truth	production

Lacan posits the following relations among the schema's four effects: the two leftmost effects—those of *agent/truth*—depict the position occupied by the source of communication, the sender of a message. The two rightmost—those of *other/production*—denote the position of the destination of communication, the receiver of a message. In both instances, the element above the bar, whether that of *agent* or *other*, represents that which is conscious and dominant in the subject; the element below, whether that of *truth* or *production*, that which is repressed and subordinated. In the process of intersubjective communication, the position of *agent* is occupied by the term (S$_1$, S$_2$, a, or $\cancel{S}$) most dominant in the subject initiating communication, by the factor that overdetermines the message; the position of *truth* by that which supports, albeit in a covert manner, the *agent* initiating communication; the position of *other* by that which is activated and most dominant in the subject receiving the message;[35] the position of *production* by that which is covertly elicited in the subject receiving the message.

Lacan's Four Discourses of Master, University, Hysteric, and Analyst

(1) Discourse of the Master

$$\frac{S_1 \;\rightarrow\; S_2}{\cancel{S} \;\leftarrow\; a}$$

(2) Discourse of the University

$$\frac{S_2 \;\rightarrow\; a}{S_1 \;\leftarrow\; \cancel{S}}$$

(1) Discourse of the Hysteric

$$\frac{\cancel{S} \;\rightarrow\; S_1}{a \;\leftarrow\; S_2}$$

(2) Discourse of the Analyst

$$\frac{a \;\rightarrow\; \cancel{S}}{S_2 \;\leftarrow\; S_1}$$

If we look to the discourse of the master, for example, we see that from the location of *agent*, the master signifier (S_1) seeks to impose its rule (S_2) on any listener that takes up the position of *other*, interpellating that listener as a subject, who, to identify with its rule, *must* reject all other forms of knowledge; this surplus knowledge (a) is repressed to the position of *production*. Since this byproduct of interpellation (a) cannot be explained within the parameters of the subject's conscious knowledge (S_2)—its repression is the condition for the possibility of (S_2)—the subject can only experience this surplus as an absence or lack. This lack, manifested in terms of a desire for completeness (a), motivates the subject to pursue fulfillment through the only means available: the dogma of the master signifier (S_2). The repressed divided subject, therefore, moves to support the promulgator of the message—the *agent* (S_1)—and in so doing reproduces the discourse of the master. The truth of this discourse, then, is the divided subject ($\mathcal{S}$), whereas its production is the *objet petit a*, the *pas-tout* or not-all, *le plus-de-jouir* or surplus knowledge/enjoyment, the remainder, the repressed, the object-cause of desire, the symptom.

Of Lacan's four discourses, Žižek notes:

> The first is the *discourse of the master*: a certain signifier (S_1), represents the subject ($\mathcal{S}$) for another signifier or, more precisely, for all other signifiers (S_2). The problem is, of course, that this operation of signifying representation never comes off without producing some disturbing surplus, some leftover or "excrement," designated by a small *a*. The other discourses are simply three different attempts to "come to terms" with this remnant (the famous *objet petit a*), to "cope" with it.[36]

In the discourse of the university, for example, a preconstructed, neutral body of knowledge (S_2) functions as the *agent* of communication, and the symptom (a) as *other*; the outcome, or *production*, of this discourse is a repressed divided subject ($\mathcal{S}$), and its *truth* is the existing master signifier (S_1), which serves to support the agent's semblance of neutrality. In the discourse of the hysteric, however, a dominant divided subject ($\mathcal{S}$) functions as the *agent* of communication, and a new master signifier (S_1) is posited as *other*; the desired *production* of this discourse is plenitude, in the form of a new body of knowledge (S_2) that will satisfy the subject's desire for stability, coherence, and meaning: "the discourse of the hysteric is at work when the discourse in use does not express, cannot embody, the underlying despair of the divided subject; at best, its symptoms are manifested"; consequently, the *truth* of this discourse is the symptom, the *objet petit a*, "which provides the support for the dominant divided subject as well as its essential *pas-tout* character."[37] In the fourth and final discourse, the symptom (a) functions as the *agent* of communication and the dominant divided subject ($\mathcal{S}$—the analyst) as *other*, the *production* of this discourse is a new master signifier (S_1), and the *truth* of this discourse is a new body of knowledge (S_2) that supports *le plus-de-jouir*: a body of knowledge "that is qualitatively different from the mathematical knowledge produced in the discourse of the master and university, the very knowledge which the hysteric rejects."[38] Žižek cautions, however, that "what we must not forget is that the matrix of the four discourses is a matrix of the four possible positions in the intersubjective network of communication"; that is, "within the field of *communication* qua *meaning*."[39] Consequently, in Lacan's theory of the four discourses "meaning itself [truth/knowledge] is always intersubjective, constituted through the circle of communication."[40]

SYMPTOM AS REAL

What Lacan's relentless pursuit of desire would subsequently reveal, however, is that the symptom does not simply dissolve upon being interpreted. Consequently, after noting how "even after the completed interpretation, the subject is not prepared to renounce his [or her] symptom," Lacan began considering the possibility that the symptom's meaning, its truth, was not *only* a function of the intersubjective network of communication—the play of the signifier—but also an expression of enjoyment, *jouissance*.[41] More than a ciphered message, the symptom also serves as the vehicle, as the means, to organize the surplus knowledge/enjoyment resulting from the subject's interpellation, its entry into the Symbolic. Lacan identified the uncipherable knowledge/truth of this new dimension of the symptom—that which resisted explanation in terms of the intersubjective truth of the big Other—with *fantasy*, formulating a series of oppositions to distinguish its truth from that of the symptom proper:

> Symptom is a signifying formation which, so to speak, "overtakes itself" towards its interpretation—that is, which can be analyzed; fantasy is an inert construction which cannot be analyzed, which resists interpretation. Symptom implies and addresses some non-barred, consistent big Other which will retroactively confer on it its meaning; fantasy implies a crossed out, blocked, barred, non-whole, inconsistent Other—that is to say, it is filling out a void in the Other.

In introducing the notion of fantasy, Lacan added a second stage to the psychoanalytic process: the first stage, as always, demanded the interpretation of the analysand's symptom—and the subsequent isolation of the fantasy-formation serving to organize the analysand's enjoyment and block further interpretation; the final, and crucial step, however, now involved "going through the fantasy, . . . obtaining distance from it, . . . experiencing how the fantasy-formation just masks, fills out a certain void, lack, empty place in the Other."

Lacan's continued pursuit of desire, however, revealed this two-stage process to be equally ineffective in eradicating the symptom. In many cases, the symptom persisted long after the analysand penetrated his or her fantasy. This prompted Lacan to reconceptualize the symptom as *sinthome*, the neologism he coined to designate "a certain signifying formation penetrated with enjoyment . . . a signifier as a bearer of *jouis-sense*, enjoyment-in-sense." This reconceptualization of symptom as *sinthome* reflects Lacan's turn from a linguistic conception of knowledge/truth—wherein truth is a function of the subject, of the intersubjective network of communication, of meaning—to a materialist conception of knowledge/truth—wherein truth is a function of the object, of the object in the subject, of the subject's material support:

> Symptom, conceived as *sinthome*, is literally our only substance, the only positive support of our being, the only point that gives consistency to the subject. In other words, symptom is the way we—the subjects—"avoid madness," the way we "choose something (the symptom-formation) instead of nothing (radical psychotic autism, the destruction of the symbolic universe)" through the binding of our enjoyment to a certain signifying, symbolic formation which assures a minimum of consistency to our being-in-the-world.

It is in the final stage of his thought, then, that Lacan identifies the symptom, or more properly, *sinthome*, as *substance*, as that which is not subject, as that which is *Real*. But as with the concepts symptom and foreclosure, Lacan's notion of the Real also undergoes significant revision in the transitions from one stage of his thinking to the next.

REVISIONING THE REAL

In the 1950s, for example, Lacan, according to Žižek, envisages the relationship among the Real, Imaginary, and Symbolic as that between "the *Real*—the brute, pre-symbolic reality which always returns to its place—then the *symbolic* order which structures our perception of reality, and finally the *Imaginary*, the level of illusory entities whose consistency is the effect of a kind of mirror-play—that is, they have no real existence but are a mere structural effect."[42] In the late 1960s and early 1970s, however, the Real begins to display characteristics remarkably similar to those ascribed to the Imaginary during the 1950s. For instance, in Lacan's very first seminar, trauma "is defined as an imaginary entity which had not yet been fully symbolized, given a place in the symbolic universe of the subject"; in the 1970s, however, trauma is defined as "a hard core resisting symbolization." The point not to be overlooked in this shift is that it becomes irrelevant—literally, immaterial—whether the traumatic event "'really occurred' in so-called reality; the point is simply that it produces a series of structural effects." It is as something that *must* be presupposed, after the fact, to explain certain anomalies in the symbolic order, that the Real assumes its materialist—albeit paradoxical—status.[43]

The paradox of the Lacanian Real, then, of Lacan's enigmatic materiality of the letter—"by 'letter' I designate that material support that concrete discourse borrows from language"[44]—is that while it does not exist in the sense of being present in reality, its properties are such that its *effects* are readily apparent there: "it exercises a certain structural causality, it can produce a series of effects in the symbolic reality of subjects."[45] The Real is "an element which, although nowhere actually present and as such inaccessible to our experience, nonetheless has to be retroactively constructed, presupposed, if all other elements are to retain their consistency."[46] Herein resides the explanation of such Lacanian concepts as *sujet supposé savoir*: "it does not exist, but it produces a decisive shift in the development of the psychoanalytic cure"; and the *objet petit a*—"a pure void which functions as the object-cause of desire."[47]

The singularity of Lacan's materialism, as Joan Copjec adroitly notes, derives from his distinction between two kinds of existence, between existence in the sense of "'The' woman does not exist (*la femme n' existe pas*)"—in which case existence is "implied by the verb *exister*,"—and existence in the sense of "There is some of One (*Il y a d' l'un*)," in which case existence is implied "by the phrase *il y a*":

> The existence implied by the first is subject to a predicative judgment as well as to a judgment of existence; that is, it is an existence whose character or quality can be described. The existence implied by the second is subject *only* to a judgment of existence; we can say only that it does or does not exist, without being able to say what it is, to describe it in any way.[48]

As to the charge of idealism—Lacan's supposed linguistic conception of knowledge/truth, his privileging of the signifier—Copjec retorts:

In fact, the opposite is true; it is the rejection of the linguistic model, properly conceived, that leads to idealism. For the argument behind the adoption of this model—something cannot be claimed to exist unless it can first be stated, articulated in language—is no mere tautology; it is a materialist argument parallel to the rule of science which states that no object can be legitimately posited unless one can also specify the technical means of locating it. The existence of a thing materially depends on its being articulated in language, for only in this case can it be said to have an objective—that is to say, a verifiable—existence, one that can be debated by others.[49]

DESIRE AND TRUTH/KNOWLEDGE

It is not, then, that Lacan does not advance a linguistic conception of knowledge/truth, an intersubjective, communicative theory of knowledge that correlates meaning with desire, but that he, in the transition from the second to the third and final stage of his thinking, abandons this communicative model of meaning for a materialist conception of truth, a theory of knowledge that equates truth not with the play of the signifier but with the disquieting presence of the Real. It is through this shift, according to Žižek, that "the emphasis of the notion of *transference* is radically displaced"[50]—as a comparison of the Lacan of *Seminar XI* and the Lacan of *Logic of Fantasy* readily reveals.

It is in *Seminar XI* that Lacan undertakes to stand Descartes on his head. While Descartes, in formulating his *Cogito*, equates thinking with being—*cogito ergo sum*; I think, therefore, I am—Lacan notes how the subject must, in fact, choose between thought and being—"I think where I am not, therefore I am where I do not think."[51] Lacan insists, however, that there is really only one choice the subject can make: thought. For it is only through thinking that the subject can have being; psychosis is the only alternative. But as Žižek notes, when the subject chooses thought, "he [or she] gets it, but truncated of the part where thought intersects with being—this lost part of thought, this 'un-thought' inherent to thought itself, is the Unconscious."[52] In attributing existence to the "I" that remains after all that can be doubted is removed, Descartes, according to Lacan, made a fundamental error. Far from being the "thinking substance" Descartes imagines it to be, the "I" is nothing more than the empty form of thought, thought stripped of all empirical content. Lacan reveals this "I" to be not "a substance, a 'thing which thinks,' but a pure point of substanceless subjectivity, a point which is nothing but a kind of vanishing gap baptized by Lacan 'subject of the signifier' (in opposition to 'subject of the signified'), the subject lacking any support in positive, determinate being."

Some two years later, however, in his seminar *Logic of Fantasy*, Lacan "accomplished one of the reversals of his previous position so characteristic of his procedure and offered the opposite reading of Cartesian doubt." Although still forced to choose between thought and being, Lacan now deems the subject's only possible choice to be that of being; consequently, the Unconscious becomes the thought lost through the choice of being, as opposed to thinking:

> Lacan's new paraphrase of *cogito ergo sum* is therefore: *I* (the subject) *am in so far as it* (*Es*, the Unconscious) *thinks*. The Unconscious is literally the "thing which thinks" and [is] as such inaccessible to the subject: in so far as I am, I am never where "it speaks." In other words, I am only in so far as something is left unthought: as soon as I encroach too deeply into this domain of the forbidden/impossible thought, my very being disintegrates.

Žižek notes how this reversal introduces the paradoxical notion of a subject constituted through misrecognition, the ontological precondition for which is the *repression* of a certain knowledge, a knowledge that must remain forever unknown to the subject: the *unconscious*. The choice of being, however, is actually the choice of *fantasy*, since it is fantasy that gives consistency to, and provides the parameters for, *reality*—the fantasy-frame incessantly besieged by scraps of knowledge jettisoned from the unconscious to disrupt its homeostasis:

Fantasy, in its most basic dimension, implies *the choice of thought at the expense of being*: in fantasy, I find myself reduced to the evanescent point of a thought contemplating the course of events during my absence, my non-being—in contrast to *symptom*, which implies *the choice of being*, since . . . what emerges in a symptom is precisely the thought which was lost, "repressed," when we chose being.[53]

Consequently, while the Lacan of *Seminar XI* "defines transference as a supposed knowledge relying upon being (that is, upon the '*objet petit a*' *qua* remainder-semblance of being lost in the forced choice of meaning)," the Lacan of *Logic of Fantasy* defines transference "as a breakthrough into the domain of knowledge (thought) lost in the forced choice of being." Initially, then, "we had knowledge that relied on the remainder-semblance of being"; finally, however, "we have being (of the subject towards which we maintain a relationship of transference) on to which some impossible/real knowledge is hooked." The full significance of this shift is most readily apparent when considered in light of the fundamental revisions the Lacan of the 1970s makes to the thought of the Lacan of the 1950s; that is, in light of the latter Lacan's reconceptualization of the relation between knowledge/truth of desire as a function of the subject and knowledge/truth of desire as a function of the object; more precisely, between knowledge/truth of desire as a function of the *inter*subjec*tive network of communication*, the big Other; and knowledge/truth of desire as a function of the Thing, *das Ding*, the impossible Real.

THE OBJECTIFICATION OF TRUTH

In the 1950s, for example, "the object was *devalorized* and the aim of the psychoanalytic process was consequently defined as '(re)-subjectivization': translation of the 'reified' content into the terms of the intersubjective dialectic." It is during this period, the heyday of psychoanalysis, that we find Kojève's influence still weighing heavily on Lacan's thought. For Kojève, the meaning of desire resides not in the *materiality* of the desired object but in the *immateriality* of desire itself—and he is singular on this point: "desire directed towards a natural object is human only to the extent that it is 'mediated' by the Desire of another directed toward the same object."[54] Consequently, the meaning of desire—knowledge/truth of the desired object—is posited as a function of the meaning the subject attributes to the object, rather than the subject-independent attributes of the object itself. Such an antimaterialist conception of knowledge/truth clearly informs Lacan's thought during this period: "in the 1950s, the object is reduced to a medium, a pawn, in the intersubjective dialectic of recognition (an object becomes object in the strict psychoanalytic sense in so far as the subject discerns in it the other's desire: I desire it not for its own sake but because it is desired by the other)."

In the 1970s, however, "the object that comes to the fore is the *objet petit a*, the object which renders possible the transferential structuring of the relation between subjects (I suppose a knowledge in another subject in so far as 'there is in him something more than himself,' *a*)." In fact, from the 1960s on, Lacan introduces new terms to his lexicon, seemingly to distance himself from his earlier work. Lacan, for instance, not only refers much less often to the signifier, preferring the term "letter," but also "avoids speaking of 'intersubjectivity,' preferring the term 'discourse,'" which is "in clear opposition to the 1950s, when he repeated again and again that the domain of psychoanalysis is that of intersubjectivity"—that which distinguishes the latter from the former, of course, is "the addition of the object as fourth element to the triad of the (two) subjects and the big Other as medium of their relationship."

This shift in emphasis from the subject to the object of psychoanalysis—more precisely, to the object *in* the subject—in the last years of Lacan's teaching certainly helped to explain the conundrum of transference: whereas the symptom (as ciphered message) must be interpreted early in the analysis (dissipated to reveal the fantasy-formation, the barrier to further interpretation), the symptom that remains after the analysand goes through her or his fantasy (the final, material support of the subject's ontological consistency, the *sinthome*) must be allowed to persist, since its eradication entails psychosis. But if the symptom must persist after the analysis ends, what signals the end of the psychoanalytic process? It was in pursuing an answer to this question that I would stumble across that to another: that of the source of my guilt, the very absence that had prompted my return to Žižek and initiated the process of inquiry recapitulated herein.

THE SUBJECT OF A QUESTION

It was only after prescribing a definitive account of knowledge/truth as a function of meaning, of the intersubjective network of communication, of the Symbolic, (the schema of the four discourses) that Lacan—due to the failings of this approach—turned his attention to explicating knowledge/truth as a function of *le sinthome*, of the Real, of "the One of *jouis-sense*, of the signifier insofar as it is not yet enchained but rather freely floating, permeated with enjoyment ... enjoyment that prevents it from being articulated into a chain."[55] However, since Lacan continued to define the signifier as "that which represents the subject for another signifier"[56] but no longer posited the meaning—knowledge/truth—of the signifier as a function of the Symbolic, of the discourse of the master, university, hysteric, or analyst, the question of just what exactly the status of this preinterpellated, presubjectivized subject is needed to be addressed.

According to Žižek, "the Lacanian answer would be, roughly speaking, that before subjectivation as identification, before ideological interpellation, before assuming a certain subject-position, the subject is the subject of a question."[57] This subject is not to be confused, however, with the subject of the Western humanist tradition, that is, the *poser* of a question; this subject is the *product* of a question: "it is an answer of the Real to the question asked by the big Other, the Symbolic order"; in fact, "the subject is the void of the impossibility of answering the question of the Other." It is not, however, the nature of the Other's question—its content—that excludes the possibility of response, but its very form: "the question [as such] lays open, exposes, denudes its addressee, it invades his [or her] sphere of intimacy ... it aims at a point at which the answer is not possible, where the word is lacking, where the subject is exposed in his [or her] impotence." But what exactly is it in the subject that the question targets, what is it that constitutes the subject's prelinguistic, most intimate core? According to Freud, it is the subject's *Kern unseres Wesens*; to Lacan, *das Ding*:

> The real object of the question is what Plato, in the *Symposium*, called—
> through the mouth of Alcibades—*agalma*, the hidden treasure, the essen-
> tial object in me which cannot be objectivated, dominated.... The
> Lacanian formula for this object is of course *objet petit a*, this point of Real
> in the very heart of the subject which cannot be symbolized, which is pro-
> duced as a residue, a remnant, a leftover of every signifying operation, a
> hard core embodying horrifying *jouissance*, enjoyment, and as such an ob-
> ject which simultaneously attracts and repels us—which *divides* our desire
> and thus provokes shame.

It is, however, through functioning in this obscene manner, in aiming at the
object in the subject that is more than the subject, that the Symbolic's unanswerable question serves to constitute the subject: "there is no subject without
guilt, the subject exist[s] only in so far as [she or] he is ashamed because of the
object in [herself or] himself, in its interior." The Symbolic's question elicits a
sense of shame and guilt in the subject that serves to divide, to hystericize the
subject: "the subject as such is hysterical . . . constituted through [her or] his
own division, splitting, as to the object in him [or her]." At once fascinating
and repulsive, the object in the subject, that aspect of the Real at the subject's
very core, is "that of a 'death drive,' a traumatic imbalance, a rooting out. Man
as such is 'nature sick unto death,' derailed, run off the rails through fascina-
tion with a lethal Thing."[58]

IDENTIFICATION WITH THE THING

The processes of interpellation and subjectivization, according to Žižek, are
nothing more than strategies the subject employs to avoid confronting this
traumatic element at its very core: the subject's attempts to *de*hystericize itself
through identification. What is obscene about the question, about its very
form, is that it aims beyond that which the subject identifies with to the traumatic element at its core, triggering the very sentiments of shame and guilt
the subject seeks to avoid through identification. This certainly helped to explain the feeling of guilt I had experienced during the exchange that followed
my presentation. In identifying with Felman's conception of a pedagogy
premised on psychoanalytic principles, I had found an answer to the Other's
unanswerable question of how pedagogy should best proceed; when that conception of pedagogy was challenged, however, I found myself confronted,
once more, with that which I had sought to avoid through identification: the
unanswerable question.

The guilt I had experienced during the exchange following my presentation was a product of my *re*hystericization, a consequence of my interlocutors' questions, questions that, by taking seriously, I had allowed to destabilize my identity with Felman and reacquaint me with the unsettling presence of the Real at my very core. In so doing, I had unwittingly stumbled into the very position the analysand finds himself or herself in as the psychoanalysis draws to a close: coming to terms with the unsettling presence at his or her very core, with the intrinsically hystericized state of his or her being, is an indication that the analysand has reached the end of the psychoanalytic process. This state of resolve is achieved through an inversion—the reversal, of the Other's unanswerable question: "at the end of the psychoanalysis the question is, so to speak, returned to the Other, the impotence of the subject displaces itself into the impossibility proper to the Other: the subject experiences the Other as blocked, failed, marked with a central impossibility—in brief, as 'antagonistic.'"[59] In redirecting the Other's question, the subject seeks not to eradicate her or his symptom, to dehystericize himself or herself through identification with some aspect of the Symbolic, but to embrace the *sinthome*, to identify with the little piece of the Real that constitutes her or his very being.

It is this identification with the symptom that Lacan designates *passage à l'acte*. As opposed to "acting out"—the subject's attempt, no matter how seemingly demented, to communicate with the Symbolic, to discover the meaning, the truth, of his or her symptom in the intersubjective network of communication, in the omniscient big Other—Lacan's "passage to act" denotes the subject's withdrawal from the Symbolic, the dissolution of the social bond, the subject's transition into "subjective destitution," wherein she or "he has no name . . . no signifier to represent [her or] him, which is why [she or] he retains [her or] his consistency only through identification with [her or] his symptom."[60] It is, then, in choosing to identify with the symptom, rather than eradicate it, that the subject is finally dehystericized, that the psychoanalysis comes to a close. For, in identifying with the *sinthome*, the subject reconstitutes the very parameters of knowledge/truth, revealing the total incommensurability of truth as meaning—as a function of the Symbolic—with truth as that which *must* be presupposed to explain the very existence of the Symbolic, as a function of the Real. It is for this reason that Lacan's thought is best understood "as a work in progress, as a succession of attempts to seize the same persistent traumatic kernel,"[61] to grasp the truth of the Real, of the object in the subject, in its very indeterminacy:

> In psychoanalysis . . . truth belongs to the order of contingency; we vegetate in our everyday life, deep into the universal Lie that structures it, when, all of a sudden, some totally contingent encounter—a casual remark by a friend, an

incident we witness—evokes the memory of an old repressed trauma and shatters our self-delusion. Psychoanalysis is here radically anti-Platonic: the Universal is the domain of Falsity *par excellence*, whereas truth emerges as a particular contingent encounter which renders visible its "repressed." . . .

Lacan's final lesson is not relativity and plurality of truths but the hard, traumatic fact that in every concrete constellation *truth is bound to emerge* in some contingent detail. In other words, although truth is context-dependent—although there is no truth in general, but always the truth *of* some situation—there is none the less in every plural field a particular point which articulates its truth and as such *cannot* be relativized; in this precise sense, truth is always One.[62]

IN CONCLUSION

It is always difficult to draw an inquiry of this nature to a close, for there really is no close. My own struggle to learn desire, to come to terms with Lacan's thought, continues, and hopefully will continue, for years to come. The controversial nature of Lacan's work means there will always be much to come to terms with. As for the work of Žižek, it continues to allure, frustrate, and inspire me. While it may well seem so, the struggle to learn desire I reiterate herein was not contrived for the purposes of this text; it really did proceed from a desire to resolve certain difficulties arising from my own attempts to appropriate psychoanalytic principles for pedagogic practice. Had I set out deliberately to investigate desire's relation to knowledge in Lacan's thought, I am not sure where, exactly, an inquiry of that nature would have taken me. One thing my struggles with Lacan have taught me is that I never really know what it is I'm trying to resolve until I resolve it. I remain convinced that, despite its controversial and enigmatic nature, psychoanalysis—and Lacan's thought in particular—holds great promise for education. I hope this chapter, which really only begins to address desire's relation to knowledge in Lacan's thought, will provide some encouragement to those considering taking up Lacan's work—learning desire.

NOTES

1. Jean Laplanche and Jean-Bertrand Pontalis, *The Language of Psychoanalysis* (London: Hogarth, 1973), 482–83.
2. The colleague in question is Bruce Spencer, of Athabasca University, Alberta.
3. Shoshana Felman, *Jacques Lacan and the Adventure of Insight: Psychoanalysis in Contemporary Culture* (Cambridge: Harvard University Press, 1987), 31–33. All future references to this work will be made in the text.

4. The irony is that, in order to re-present this struggle cogently and coherently, I must attribute it with a sense of "linear progression" and continuity that were markedly absent from my original struggle with desire. That I am now able to impose a sense of order on that struggle is the result of a great many "breakthroughs, leaps, discontinuities, regressions" and much "deferred action." I fear that of all the contributors to this volume, I have posed the greatest problem for Sharon Todd, the editor. The self-analysis I recount in this chapter has extended for well over a year, and has entailed much head scratching, chin rubbing, hand wringing, and rewriting—not to mention missed deadlines! I am still not sure that it is over; however, for the purposes at hand, I have attempted to bring a sense of closure to the process.

5. The paper, a reworked version of an earlier presentation to an interdisciplinary curriculum theory conference has since been published: Derek Briton, "The Decentred Subject: Pedagogical Implications," *JCT: An Interdisciplinary Journal of Curriculum Studies* 11, no. 4 (1996), 57–73.

6. These concerns were to remain secret to me, as, perhaps, they were to the questioners themselves, something that "is best exemplified by a well-known Hegelian dictum according to which the secrets of the ancient Egyptians were also secrets to the Egyptians." Slavoj Žižek, *The Sublime Object of Ideology* (London: Verso, 1989), 178.

7. Only later would I learn that such a feeling of guilt is one to which those who aren't in the know are prone: "an indeterminate Kafkaesque feeling of 'abstract' guilt, a feeling that, in the eyes of Power, I am a priori terribly guilty of something, although it is not possible for me to know what precisely I am guilty of, and for what reason—since I don't know what I am guilty of—I am even more guilty; or, more pointedly, it is in this very ignorance of mine that my true guilt consists." Slavoj Žižek, *The Metastases of Enjoyment* (London: Verso, 1995), 60.

8. I am attracted to Žižek's reading of Lacan for a number of reasons, not the least of which is his ability to reframe certain problematic aspects of Lacan's thought through reference to the work of Hegel and vice versa.

9. Žižek, *Sublime*, 68.

10. See, for example, Peter Winch, *The Idea of a Social Science and its Relation to Philosophy* (London: Routledge & Kegan Paul, 1958).

11. Habermas describes scientism as "the conviction that we can no longer understand science as *one* form of knowledge, but rather must identify knowledge with science." Jürgen Habermas, *Knowledge and Human Interests*, trans. Jeremy J. Shapiro (London: Heinemann, 1972), 4.

12. Salman Rushdie, *Imaginary Homelands: Essays and Criticism, 1981–1991* (London: Granta, in association with Viking, 1991), 118.

13. As Catharine Clément notes, Lacan "is French to the very tip of his tongue, down to his erudite and antiquated way of citing a text in Latin, Greek, or any other language—and without translation." Cited in Elizabeth Grosz, *Jacques Lacan: A Feminist Introduction* (London: Routledge, 1990), 193.

14. That Rushdie, normally a defender of difference, is willing to employ, in the defense of Truth, a strategy he so often decries—the vilification of the Other through a process of crass homogenization—testifies to the intensity of desire that fuels so many condemnations of post-prefixed discourses.

15. Žižek, *Sublime*, 153–54.

16. See, for instance, part 2 of Jean-Luc Nancy and Phillipe Lacoue-Labarthe, *The Title of the Letter: A Reading of Lacan*, trans. François Raffoul and David Pettigrew (New

York: SUNY, 1992), for a Derrida-inspired, textualist critique of Lacan's "meta-physics."

17. Ibid., 29.

18. Of such overly zealous dismissals Žižek notes: "The perception of Lacan as an 'anti-essentialist' or 'deconstructionist' falls prey to the same illusion as that of perceiving Plato as just one among the sophists. Plato accepts from the sophists their logic of discursive argumentation, but uses it to affirm his commitment to Truth; . . . along the same lines, Lacan accepts the 'deconstructionist' motif of radical contingency, but turns this motif against itself, using it to assert his commitment to Truth as contingent. For that very reason, deconstructionists and neopragmatists, in dealing with Lacan, are always bothered by what they perceive as some remainder of 'essentialism' (in the guise of 'phallogocentrism,' etc.)—as if Lacan were uncannily close to them, but somehow not 'one of them.' Slavoj Žižek, *Tarrying With the Negative: Kant, Hegel, and the Critique of Ideology* (Durham, N.C.: Duke University Press, 1993), 4. See also Slavoj Žižek, *For They Know Not What They Do: Enjoyment as a Political Factor* (London: Verso, 1991), 196–97, for a succinct appraisal of Lacan's understanding of the contingent nature of Truth.

19. According to Julian Pefanis, Kojève's weekly lectures on Hegel's *Phenomenology*, presented at the Sorbonne throughout the 1930s, had a significant impact on French thought, drawing future intellectual greats such as "Sartre, Merleau-Ponty, Lacan, Bataille, Queneau, and a host of existentialists, Catholics, Communists, and surrealists who eagerly awaited the event of Hegel's epiphany." Pefanis, *Heterology and the Post-modern: Bataille, Baudrillard, and Lyotard* (Durham, N.C.: Duke University Press, 1991), 11.

20. Alexandre Kojève, *Introduction to the Reading of Hegel: Lectures on the Phenomenology of Spirit*, ed. A. Bloom (New York: Basic Books, 1969), 6.

21. Kojève's *historicist* conception of knowledge—the correlation of meaning with that which is absent from, rather than present in, history—differs markedly from historical materialist conceptions of knowledge, from the *historicism* that correlates the meaning of historical events with their particular historical circumstances. Whereas historicism, in declaring knowledge historically relative, abandons Truth for truth(s) and History for history(s), Kojève's historicist conception of knowledge retains both the promise of Truth and History. See Žižek, *For They Know Not*, 101, for a discussion of the important distinction Lacan, too, makes between historicism and historicity.

22. See Ernesto Laclau's preface to Žižek's *Sublime*, wherein Laclau states of the Slovenian Lacanians and the focus of Miller's work, respectively: "The Slovenian Lacanian school . . . possesses highly original features . . . its insistent reference to the ideological-political field . . . ; [its] use of Lacanian categories in the analysis of classical philosophical texts . . . , above all, Hegel. . . . Its special combination of Hegelianism and Lacanian theory currently represents one of the most innovative and promising theoretical projects on the European intellectual scene" (xi–xii); and "[a group of analysts] (Michel Silvestre, Alain Grosrichard, etc., led by Jacques-Alain Miller) has attempted to formalize Lacanian theory, pointing out the distinction between the different stages of his teaching" (x).

23. Ibid., x.

24. Žižek, *Tarrying*, 3.

25. Žižek, *Metastases*, 173.

26. Unless specified otherwise, the citations included in the following two sections are from Žižek, *Sublime*, 131–33.

27. Jacques Lacan, *The Seminar of Jacques Lacan: Book I, Freud's Papers on Technique, 1953–1954*, ed. Jacques-Alain Miller, trans. John Forrester (New York: Norton, 1991), 243.

28. Ibid., 178.

29. Laclau, preface to *Sublime*, x.

30. Žižek, *Sublime*, 169.

31. Unless specified otherwise, the citations included in this section of text are from Žižek, *Sublime*, 71–73.

32. Žižek, *Enjoy Your Symptom: Jacques Lacan In Hollywood and Out* (New York: Routledge, 1992), 54.

33. Žižek, *Sublime*, 73.

34. Dragan Milovanovic, "Lacan's Four Discourses, Chaos, and Cultural Criticism in Law," *Studies in Psychoanalytic Theory* 2, no. 1 (1993): 16. Milovanovic is a member of the Slovenian Lacanian school.

35. As Milovanovic notes, "An understanding of the message presupposes that the factor occupying this location is responsive; this very responsiveness provides the primary mechanism by which the receiver is constituted, or *interpellated*, by the dominant factor . . . the other entering one of the particular discourses, must become receptive to the message being sent." Ibid., 7.

36. Žižek, *Looking Awry: An Introduction to Jacques Lacan Through Popular Culture* (Cambridge: MIT Press, 1992), 130.

37. Milovanovic, "Four Discourses," 14.

38. Ibid., 17–18.

39. Žižek, *Looking*, 131.

40. Ibid., 181, n. 11.

41. Unless specified otherwise, the citations included in this section of text are from Žižek, *Sublime*, 74–75.

42. Žižek, *Sublime*, 162.

43. Examples of such Real events that *must* be presupposed to explain the effectivity of the symbolic order are the primal parricide, as presented by Freud, and the struggle of Lordship and bondage, as presented by Hegel.

44. Jacques Lacan, *Écrits: A Selection*, trans. Alan Sheridan (New York: Norton, 1977), 147. I borrow the term "materiality of the letter" from Nancy and Lacoue-Labarthe, *Title*, 29.

45. Žižek, *Sublime*, 163.

46. Žižek, *Tarrying*, 33.

47. Žižek, *Sublime*, 163.

48. Joan Copjec, *Read My Desire: Lacan Against the Historicists* (Cambridge: MIT Press, 1994), 3.

49. Ibid., 7–8.

50. Žižek, *For They Know Not*, 147.

51. Lacan, *Écrits*, 166.

52. Unless specified otherwise, the citations included in this section of text are from Žižek, *For They Know Not*, 146–48.

53. Žižek, *Tarrying*, 64.

54. See note 21.

55. Žižek, *Looking*, 132.

56. Lacan, *Écrits*, 316.

57. Unless specified otherwise, the citations included in this section of text are from Žižek, *Sublime*, 178–181.

58. Ibid., 181.

59. Ibid.

60. Žižek, *Looking*, 139–140.

61. Žižek, *Metastases*, 173.

62. Žižek, *For They Know Not*, 196.

Part 2

Desire and Recognition

3

Fantasy's Confines

Popular Culture and the Education
of the Female Primary-School Teacher

JUDITH P. ROBERTSON

Having been passionate about the movies, I have been able to observe the
power of cinema to produce the unexpected—feelings and affects for which an
account cannot easily be made. In retrospect, there is no doubt in my mind that
those great teacher films of the late 1960s (*To Sir with Love*, *Up the Down
Staircase*, *Rachel, Rachel*, and *The Prime of Miss Jean Brodie*) influenced my decision to become a teacher. I formed wishful attachments to screen teachers
like Jean Brodie, investing in them utopian hopes about devotion, defiance,
and heroic solutions to learning and its discontents. I recognize my stubborn
old tendencies in the hurried optimism of the beginning teachers I teach. Not
only my own fantasies of teaching, but also those of my students encourage me
to examine what idealistic expressions mask: the hesitancy, for example, to
reckon with the vulnerabilities, ambivalences, and uncertainties of classroom
life. In fact, it is possible as a beginning teacher to form a philosophy of education without ever seriously considering the limitations of mastery that education opens up.

Researchers within teacher education are only just beginning to pay attention to ways in which fantasy life affects the process of learning to teach. Beginning teachers actively deploy the material of everyday life—including
images of teaching from film and other forms of popular culture—to help
shape their thinking and learning. The means by which reader engagement
with popular culture affects categories of meaning-making in schooling in
complex and unexpected ways has been discussed by Sol Cohen, Jane Gallop,

Henry Giroux and Roger Simon, Judith Robertson, and Sandra Weber and Claudia Mitchell,[1] to name but a few.

Yet within this literature, few studies examine how desire figures in specific instances of screen identification or how fantasy engagement with screen heroes and screen stories affects what gets said or left unsaid about the work of teaching.[2] For example, investigators are just beginning to grapple with the question of what beginning teachers actually draw upon to form their ideas and practices as "raced" and gendered social subjects.[3] How do heroic identifications influence the way beginning teachers define their understandings and aspirations in the classroom, and what can be said about the limits and anxieties that trouble these effects? What objects of appeal underlie how teaching gets imagined within some teaching communities, and how can particular habits of imagination be linked to specific historical and social circumstances that help shape the restrictions and expectations of primary teaching? By examining how individuals take hold of certain ideals through forms of language, educators can learn how beginning teachers come to think in different ways about teaching and how particular fantasies of teaching in white primary-school women teachers, namely the erotic notions of mastery and salvation, ignore issues of "race," gender, and other kinds of conflict in education.

FIGURING DESIRE IN PEDAGOGY: A MEDITATION

What can be said about desire in pedagogy? The idea is difficult . . . messy . . . so difficult, in fact, that even thinking about having to write about this topic (disorderly, boundless thing) inspires panic. With desire I associate a sense of urgency. Desire makes me want things. Inside. It is big rather than small. It deposits me into its pocket, forcing me along like necessity. In this regard desire is a serious, insistent thing. It feels like gravity, only it doesn't pull me down. Instead, it pushes me on. Desire is something interminable. It is ceaselessly, constantly there.

Is desire the same as a wish? No—it is larger and more insistent. When I listen to desire I hear two hungry syllables (there . . . there . . .) and two long vowels that sound their names persistently. In utterance desire sounds attenuated and prolonged. I hear "ire" in desire. . . excitement and ardor. I hear "fire" in desire . . . animation.

Wishes will never do for desire. It is after all impossible to imagine a streetcar named "wish." All seriousness and urgency gets dissipated in the attempt to substitute one word or thing for the other. Wishes can not stand in for desires, because wishes are domesticated things—desires that have been schooled in patience and forbearance. Wishes are desires gone calm.

Pedagogy is for two people . . . or three . . . sometimes more. In pedagogy, there's an exchange, something circulates, something mobilizes—hands, bodies, minds, and the

actions/words that go between. Pedagogy is a practice, an event. Something happens,
having to do with power and energy between people and desires that live inside. It can
be witnessed. It is experienced. It can be felt as something delicious or, in bad times,
something that hurts. When the time of pedagogy is over, the learner and teacher can
feel deep loss. Desire has lost its partner and doesn't want to dance alone. Desire in ped-
agogy leaves traces of joy and sorrow on people and events and the world. What is the
desire that pedagogy desires? I will tell a true story that happened about learning to
teach, in which desire figures . . . I am the teacher/researcher in the story.

WISHING UPON A FILM IN TEACHING

I watch a movie with twelve women. Based on real events, the movie, *Stand and Deliver*,[4] is about a male, Hispanic math teacher (Jaime Escalante) who teaches disadvantaged high-school kids to do advanced calculus. In so doing, the teacher helps secure for barrio students the status of advanced placement in college. Based on newspaper and other accounts of Escalante,[5] the small-budget, community-based movie is shot on location. The story turns on a moral crisis. It explores the racism evinced by the larger educational community (the Educational Testing Service at Princeton) in the face of unprecedented test-score success by impoverished Chicana and Chicano students. The energetic teacher hero is characterized by the innovative distance he is willing to go to inspire *ganas* (desire to learn) in his students. The protagonist earns vindication for his efforts. It is difficult not to be touched by his powerful teaching credo: "You are the true dreamers . . . and dreams accomplish wonderful things."

I wanted to comprehend more precisely how the emotional responses of the women could be most fully articulated. Accordingly, I asked the women to view the movie while keeping this question in mind: "Focus on one or more moments of intense feeling for you in this movie. Describe the image, character, scene, or event that evoked this feeling. Try to relate your feeling to either an event you remember or a desire or pleasure aroused in you by watching this film."

We watched the movie together. Afterward, I was surprised to observe that in writing and speech the women returned to a single, fleeting scene from the film, in which students demonstrate explicit love for their cherished teacher. In terms of the development of the film plot, it is neither predictable nor inevitable that this scene (more than any of the others) should captivate teacher viewers. One of about two hundred scenes in a one-hundred-and-ten-minute film, it lasts for only about ninety seconds. Viewers experience it only once. There are ostensibly more gripping moments on which to focus, such as the teacher's trials and reflections on his own imperfections in teaching, his tendency to disqualify his own significant abilities and successes, student agitation and gang tensions, and the problematic relationship between racism and group standardized testing. Although these moments stimulated some postviewing debate, when asked to tell about the moment of their most deeply felt association with the screen, five out of twelve viewers referred to a scene depicting a theatrical posting of love of students for their teacher. What is the significance of this pattern of response?

One explanation is that the narrative quality of representation or conventions of verisimilitude inscribed in the scene itself determine the intense engagement. The story, for example, charts the teacher's genuine surprise when adoring students publicly display through speeches and a gift their gratitude for what he has helped them to learn. Editing techniques and camera movement (for example, close-ups and reverse shots), as well as a pulsing sound track work like a grammar that functions syntactically to assist in telegraphing the intended affective messages of the scene (i.e., struggle, hope, and transcendence). Moreover, Edward James Olmos gives a tour-de-force performance as teacher in the drama. It appears, then, that the sequence animates a deeply felt viewing experience in beginning teachers because the story, sounds, acting, and images provide a vicarious space through which to observe and learn about some realities of classroom life.

However, the problem with this argument is that what the scene makes ardently visible is not so much a lived reality as a desired, imagined reality of classroom life: the promise of student-teacher devotion and the miraculous transcendence of the trials and mistakes of teaching and learning. Thus, the scene captivates the women precisely because of the dynamics of the fantasy it inscribes. It replays the wish that solutions to the tensions of teaching and learning can depend on magical displays of student devotion. The point of curiosity, then, is how and why the women's identifications focus on this particular fantasy within the film.

INTERPRETING TEACHER IDENTIFICATIONS IN VIEWING

The analysis of viewer responses to *Stand and Deliver* involved interpreting the significance of categories of repetition (thematic and tonal) that organized viewers' collective responses (oral and written) to the entire movie. I placed highest interpretative value on those repetitions demonstrated either by a group of readers in response to a single scene, or by a single reader repeatedly in relation to a single scene, object, or effect. The frequency of group attention to the "posting of love" scene, coupled with the repetitious speech acts generated by single viewers about it, qualified the scene as pivotal in terms of its affective usefulness in preservice learning.

Freud first mapped out the reality of the repetition compulsion in human behavior. In questioning the significance of repetition, he stated that the point of departure for speculation should not be consciousness because consciousness may not be the most universal trait of mental processes.[6] Freud reconceived the notion of consciousness as something that arbitrates between inner and outer realities. Consciousness, he wrote, is a function of the system that lies on the borderline between outside and inside worlds: "it must be turned towards the external world and must envelop the other psychical systems."[7] The repetition, he said, is like the effect of two facing mirrors endlessly reflecting each other.[8] Like an instinct, the repetition functions dynamically to conserve and restore an earlier state of plenitude in human beings.[9] In interpreting the repetition effect, verbal elements became increasingly central to Freud's understanding of psychic behavior.[10]

I revised broad thematic categories as the analysis progressed. In tracing the manifestation of subjective realities, some researchers contend that investigators should use transcribed words as a source of evidence to allow "a current and felt experience to be reckoned."[11] In trying to understand the ways in which individuals endeavor perpetually to keep inner and outer realities separate yet interrelated, researchers need to find "a way of interpreting the silences, breaks, and inconsistencies" in workers' accounts of experience, in a way that recognizes "the subjective encodings of its impact."[12] Working with the women's texts in this way was like working with discursive fragments to gain access to a continuing historical process that draws on interior life. Accordingly, in order to conceptualize the psychic dynamics of learning, I listened not only to the manifest content of the women's thoughts and feelings, but also to enigmatic qualities such as contradiction, silence, and groping to make meaning through tentative speech, repetitions, laughter, and even jokes.[13] In my efforts to comprehend the voice and meaning of desire in the women's screen attachments, I observed the principle that the manner in which words are expressed (i.e., with hesitation, urgency, contradiction, disregard for standard conventions) can teach about the lived character of thought itself.

THE FANTASY OF THE LOVE LETTER IN TEACHING

The statements reproduced in the following text were written and spoken by the women one day after viewing *Stand and Deliver*. Some viewers expressed pleasure that a teacher's labor can receive praiseworthy valuations—if not from society at large, then at least, and not insignificantly, from students. Others recounted fascinating daydreams about their imagined futures in teaching. The daydreams spoke of "receiving a text" years before or later.

One of the scenes which I found moving was the one in which Escalante's students brush the principal aside impatiently in order to honor their teacher with a plaque . . . I don't remember the . . . words at this moment . . . but I recall the students crowding around Escalante . . . in a manner that suggested their gratitude, their love, even, for him, and a special relationship. . . . The movie makes me think of how dedicated teachers don't expect appreciation for their efforts because that isn't their goal at all. They will work countless hours without reward and never give it a thought, so that when their efforts are noticed and appreciation shown, they are surprised. (Meg, journal)

One scene which evoked intense feelings was the scene in which the children of Jaime Escalante reward him for all of his hard work and dedication with a plaque. I felt very touched at that moment. The students were ecstatic with their own accomplishments and greatful [sic] that their teacher inspired them and believed in them. It was a beautiful moment in the film. (Jaye, journal)

Kids loving their teacher as opposed to just being respected in another job—the intrinsic rewards of being a teacher (pointed out by his wife in his moment of despair). (Vinny, journal)

[In a soft dreamy voice, like she's telling a story] One year there's this child in my class who dreams . . . *[laughter from others]* of being a writer. And I foster this hope in them and encourage them and inspire them and then *[finishing off quickly]* one day they write a book and dedicate it to me! *[Still sits looking proud as though she has actually had this wonderful thing happen.]* (Still, utterance)

[Dreamy voice] I'm in my classroom. And everything's set up and it just seems like . . . just . . . ummm. . . . I see myself teaching and working with them and it just seems such a . . . umm. . . . How do I say it? . . . I don't really see myself . . . ummm . . . . Oh, come back to me, okay? (Devon, utterance)

I prefer to think about years later, getting letters from kids I'd taught, saying how things would be different if . . . (Meg, utterance)

There were many moments of triumph. Oddly, one that stands out is where Pancho is waiting on his test results. He goes to the mail box, takes the paper out, and expresses such triumph when he reads the results. I figure this stands out for me because, corny as it sounds, it was a very similar feeling for me when I finally got into the Faculty of Education. As I watched the scene, it brought back that feeling of, "I did it!" The movie evoked feelings of desire. Desire that I can one day give children the chance to find a moment of self-triumph. (Annie, journal)

Given Freud's notion that speech performs as a vehicle through which unconscious effects are established, the repetitious figures directly observable in the women's language are immediately striking. Clearly, the arrival of a gratifying message by post is a recurrent theme. For example, Still's fantasy pertains to a text that will someday arrive as a gift sent by a student whom she encouraged to become a writer. The book's dedication inscribes its debt to her. Meg and Jaye both fantasize (from the movie) about students crowding around and brushing aside a powerful person (the principal) in order to pay "greatful" tribute (a plaque) to the teacher. Meg (like Still) says she enjoys dreaming about receiving a letter years later. And Annie invokes pleasurable identifications that remember letters received. In each case, the letter informed the woman that her dream had come true—her seemingly impossible dream to enter teacher education and become a teacher.

What does it mean that after witnessing Escalante's scene of triumph, four women fantasize about receiving tributes by mail? How do the women's viewing responses profit them in terms of helping them make themselves (through discursive play in daydreams) into subjects of teaching? Frigga Haug remarks that although Freud had little to say in his work about the significance of daydreams, he did hypothesize that their imagined scenes function as psychic fulfillments of unconscious wishes and satisfy either erotic desires or aspirations to power and ambition.[14] According to Haug, Freud saw the division as a gendered one, that is, that men dream of ambition, whereas women satisfy erotic desires. He referred to the shame and protectiveness that is likely to attend daydreaming. Indeed, these emotions played throughout the seminar in the tones of tentativeness and groping that marked the speech of the women who consented to reveal their daydreams and in the collective laughter produced to cover initial embarrassment. Freud conceived that the essence of the imaginary happiness experienced in daydreams is "the independence of desire from the approval of reality."[15]

Common lexical elements link the women's enunciations (including their daydreams) in response to the film. First, the speakers imagine receiving by post a tribute (i.e., it is posted—a book, a letter, a plaque). To receive a notice by post is to render it (through fantasy) unspeakable, unsayable. If the message could be spoken, it would be said. But because it cannot be said, it must arrive (be communicated) via another semiotic corridor that will post its meaning.

Second, the women's posted texts symbolize simultaneous revelation and concealment. What the postings reveal are honor, triumph, acknowledgment, and debt owed. What they conceal is the actual content of the message. For instance, Devon's fantasy message arrives by post, but its seal cannot be opened. Hence, its message is simply absent to her consciousness, as well as ours. Note, too, how Meg falters on the specific wording of the missive: "I don't remember the . . . words at this moment." Elsewhere she trails off, leaving the actual message unuttered: "getting letters from kids saying things would be different if. . . ." The postings also conceal the actual identity and temporality of the sender. For example, a text arrives by post "one day . . . years later . . . from this child . . . kids I'd taught . . . them." Meg projects one additional concealment onto the fantasy scene: the recipient of the letter must enact concealment of her anticipation. The addressee hides her expectation of tribute because (according to the tautological logic that governs the fantasy) dedicated teachers "don't expect appreciation for their efforts . . . they will work countless hours without reward . . . so that when their efforts are noticed . . . they are surprised" (Meg, journal).

The readers' fantasies show them taking hold of certain forms of language to impose order on their world. Fantasy may be treated as a source of evidence in its own right. "One does not have to possess or own the truth, in order to effectively bear witness to it; that speech as such is unwittingly testimonial."[16] The rhetorical figure of Meg's fantasy is (among other things) hagiographical: teacher as saint, martyr, paragon of detached love. Connected to this figure of desire is a story, also recounted by Meg. In her journal, she recalls how once in her work in a nursery she succored a little boy who was misunderstood by others. The child blossomed under her care. The boy was "hyperactive . . . considered hard to deal with." He was "switched to my group . . . I had little problem in dealing with him." Meg writes of the transformation that came over the boy: he started looking every day for her beige car to arrive at school. The child's mother sent a note to the principal expressing "in such glowing terms (my work) that I was totally taken aback." Suddenly, Meg cuts short the story: "I would be too embarrassed to repeat her exact wording. Ugh, this is starting to look like a lot of back-patting. Such a note was totally unexpected" (Meg, journal).

Meg's reverie (i.e., her memory and recounting of the little lost boy found) functions for her in socially specific ways in terms of her learning. She recasts the event as a romantic allegory in which the teacher's role is both heroic and subservient. But if, as Meg writes, the teacher's desire for acknowledgment must be concealed, of what psychological use to Meg is this fantasy? Why does desire configure itself as demurring sainthood in this beginning teacher's imagination of teaching? Why does she need to produce these symbolic figures (possibly standard tropes among primary teachers),[17] and why, in turn, to disavow (through producing the figures) her hunger for payment and reward in teaching?

Meg's verbal disclaimer functions on one level as a concealment. The con-

cealment virtually reproduces what the fantasy letter strategically performs—
which is another concealment. The repeated concealments function psychologically in similar ways. The women variously dream of posted texts, which
offer tributes sent by imaginary children in vaguely defined imaginary times.
But to whom do the imaginary children and tributes really belong? Who constitutes the point of address? The enunciations replay desires addressed by the
addressees to themselves. They function as the locus of a transfer. In Freudian
terms, the women engage in a complex mirror game through the sequence.
The senders post tributes to themselves, thus concealing and revealing what
cannot be spoken: a desire for recognition and to be the container of that
(knowledge) which their (imaginary) students must attribute to them in order
to be (themselves—imaginary teachers and children) complete. What is psychologically present is a text that arrives by post, endowing the landscape of
primary teaching with a legitimacy and value that must otherwise remain hidden, denied, and ignored. Through fantasy, the longing the women feel to be
recognized as knowing and worthy subjects in teaching gets restored to language. It is posted.

The epistolary fantasies would appear to allow the women expression of the
powerful drive of Eros in teaching. The letters clearly render wishes of love.
Moreover, they are narcissistic and idealized projections, in the way that Julia
Kristeva, drawing upon Freud, describes as follows:

> What is universal in the love situation is, on the one hand, . . . the narcissis-
> tic investment which is a necessity for the living being to last, to stay alive,
> to preserve itself. And on the other hand, the idealisation. The possibility
> for this living being to project [the] self through an ideal instance and to
> identify with it. And this can be found in different kinds of friendship,
> sympathy, love, homosexual, erotic—differently orchestrated. The emphasis
> may be put in this situation more on violence, or more on narcissism, or
> more on idealization, or more on the erotic, and so on. But the two compo-
> nents: narcissism and idealisation will last, will endure.[18]

The generalities that Kristeva associates with loving relationships organize
the women's fantasies of teaching. Once upon a time tokens (will) arrive as
though sent by lovers. That will be a "greatful" day (as rhetorically encapsu-
lated by Jaye's semantic confusion). The tokens are narcissistic investments
(signed, sealed, and delivered by the self to the self) in anticipation of the triumphant day when creative agency will at last be allowed dominion through
teaching (a romantic idealization of the pedagogical encounter). The addressee of the posted missive is an ideal imaginary I, and the addresser is an

ideal, imaginary other. Their triumphant fusion through subjective fantasy (and the feelings connected with this moment—ecstasy, beauty, sublimity) constitute the women's desire to "be a teacher and make (that) difference."

Fantasy that organizes teaching as a dream of love blocks some significant tensions from consciousness. A woman who commits herself to teaching with selfless devotion to the love object (working countless hours without reward and never giving it a thought) is not only subdued but also dispossessed of a vocabulary for articulating what is rightfully hers: dignity, compensation, and recognition for her efforts. Such a figure repudiates the legitimate expectation that she can be open and deserving of the erotic potential of pedagogical relationality. Moreover, the idealized projection of dominion over the (loved) other in teaching introduces a hierarchy of valuation. The fantasy testifies to a hidden self-aggrandizement that may at the same time function as a disavowal[19] of the desire for separateness and omniscience. In this respect, the rendering of love through the letter disavows the reality of aggressive strivings in the wish. The act of disclaiming power and aggressivity through a dream of love brings the projection back into the boundaries of the social, the ideological, and the institutional. Not only do the women in this study appear in fantasy to accept the gendered subject position offered primary teachers, but this very process may be a contextualization of the contemporary specificities of those wish fulfillments Freud pointed to.[20]

Epistolary fantasies in women learning to teach often function in contradictory ways as a means of subjectivization within the logic of schooling. When primary-school women practice fantasies in response to *Stand and Deliver* (through posted texts, saintly composure, and search-and-find expeditions for lost children), they project themselves powerfully into anticipatory futures, albeit in socially obedient ways. Only saints can conduct business by virtue of disembodied detachment and stainless modesty. Only saints do not have to contend with what it actually feels like to spend one's days forfeiting that to which they are entitled. If the martyr within Meg's vision could be restored to speech, what would she say? Whose tyranny justifies her intermission, and whose desire produces her obedience?

DESIRE AND THE UNSAID IN FANTASIES OF DEVOTION

In her elaboration of how cinema functions as a "technology of subjectivity" in society, Teresa de Lauretis contends that movies offer spectators places in which to replay fantasies that are both in the text and in the viewer. Patterns of identification have less to do with the formal qualities of the text (the narrative or conventions of verisimilitude) than with the dynamics of the fantasy inscribed.[21] Similarly, for Freud, all experience is metaphoric because it echoes the intense experiences of infancy and early childhood, and everything that finds its way into thought represents instincts that cannot be expressed other than by ideas.[22] In de Lauretis's discussion of viewing response, she suggests, like Freud, that the contents and structure of early fantasies are inseparable in their effects in spectatorship. Intense experiences in viewing enable the replaying of positions of desire in which viewers find their places in a film's fantasy, and an "original" fantasy (founded as it is on early, unresolved conflicts) exercises its capacity through the ongoing structuration of subjectivity, a process irrevocably wedded to representational practices. The "original" satisfactions that viewers' fantasies replay may never be known, embedded as they are in experiences of the deep past. Even so, fantasy enables and activates powerful structures of feeling in film viewing, even as narrative conventions shape the materials of the story.

Epistolary fantasies in women learning to teach are indications of pedagogical desire, with the fantasy of the posting of love itself the *mise-en-scène* (or the direction in which desire is staged). Four elements organize the structure: the teacher, the student, the posting and receiving of pleasure from the gift of love, and the promise of transcendence over the chaos of learning and teaching. If the fantasy serves as a psychologically useful structure through which the beginning teacher demonstrates her legitimate wish to be recognized as a worthy and knowing subject of teaching, what now can be said about the conflictive or unacknowledged aspects of the desire?

Viewer responses to *Stand and Deliver* provoke important theoretical debate about what the desire for loving acknowledgment in education portends, how common or deeply rooted the impulse is, what forms it takes in pedagogy, and the possible, unremarked relations that may exist among figures of desire, and structures of confinement, or opportunity in education. In terms of the relations between images and cultural codes of teaching, learning to teach, and constraints within education, I offer the following speculations.

A persistent and infelicitous finding within educational research has been that learning during the preservice year reproduces conservative values, beliefs and attitudes (including class, "race," and gender relations) that students bring with them into teacher education.[23] Problematically, however, "[W]e do not have very strong empirical evidence confirming the fact that teachers actually incorporate elements into their perspectives in ways consistent with the theoretical arguments. . . . Clearly, more direct study of the formal and hidden curriculum of teacher education courses and of the ways in which the messages of these courses are received and interpreted by students is needed."[24] My research suggests that important relations exist among the semiotic provocations of popular culture texts, devotion fantasies, and the production of self-regulating structures of desire in beginning female teachers. Arguably, such interactions help to sustain psychocultural desires that circumscribe even as they provide imaginary resolutions to the conflicts, tensions, and inequities of schooling.

Psychoanalysis teaches that fantasies of devotion contain structures of idealization and narcissism that screen hostility and hide it from consciousness. Idealization is "the mental process by means of which the object's qualities and value are elevated to the point of perfection. [A film viewer's] identification with the idealized object contributes to the formation and elaboration of the individual subject's so-called ideal agencies (ideal ego, ego-ideal)."[25] Jean Laplanche and Jean-Bertrand Pontalis make the point that when viewers imaginatively associate with scenes of transcendence, perfection, or flawlessness, this act of identification supports the formation of an ideal ego that hides its own aggressiveness. What is blocked from learning is the full recognition of the other, who serves (in fantasy) the seemingly straightforward function of self-affirmation.[26]

In the devotion fantasies of women learning to teach, an unrecognized conflict may derive from the fact that the "other" (the fantasized student who performs the work of adoring) is negated, except as a condition of self-affirmation on the part of the teacher. In theory, it is the teacher herself who is aggrandized and nourished in the posting of the letter and who fulfills the useful function as love object. The dreamer psychically symbolizes herself as knower and consecrated bearer of the gift of knowledge. In psychoanalytic terms, the figure is an ego-ideal.

Psychoanalysis teaches that idealization and narcissism are unconscious processes, both stubborn and hidden. In therapeutic situations, the analyst strives to make the analysand aware of the unbearable, conflictive aspects of unconscious processes. In what ways—if any, then—may the story of the love letter be educative and transformative for beginning teachers? If the idealization at work in the fantasy formation displays the beginning teacher's imaginary relation with her ego-ideal as teacher, then it is a deceptive relation that functions in several ways. For educative purposes, teachers should think about how the dreamer is simultaneously served and deceived by the enigmatic fantasy of the love letter.

Arguably, the devotion fantasy serves as an important "enabling metaphor" for the making of white primary-school women teachers. As a rhetorical device, "devotion" performs the manifest function of assisting the women to reason a way out of subject-object tensions, while ignoring the latent relations of power and privilege inscribed.[27] Semiotically and strategically, the marker acts as a figure of division by reifying a "natural," unchanging, unchangeable social division. Psychologically, it sanctions a rhetorical role that empowers the women with goodness, exalted status, and hallowed feelings of love. It could be said to characterize them with high value at the same time that it distances them from a subordinate class of unmarked others. Self-evidently valid and natural, the devotion fantasy omits or conceals important information. It says nothing, for example, about the low prestige of teaching little children. It refuses comment on the wearing routine of material preparation and cleanup in early-childhood programs. It omits, precisely by the manifestation of absence itself, reflections on the ideological conditions that motivate linkages between devotion and racialized, heterosexualized "norms" in schooling.

Yet, despite what the fantasy leaves unsaid, the viewers of *Stand and Deliver* do recognize and take offense at the hierarchical system that places them (as teachers of young children) on the subaltern rung of the educational ladder. For example, Annie fumes about being told that "early primary teachers are nothing more than overrated baby-sitters." "This angers me," she says, "not because I would ever question the awesome responsibility of a teacher, but because many individuals in society do . . . teachers, particularly at the primary level, (do not) get the respect they deserve." Anja, too, expresses frustration about aspects of the work she has chosen: "God! We're very vulnerable out there . . . you really have to know how to play this big political game of power. Power of people. Power of influence. Power of wealth. And you know? We are servants. You know? I am there to serve. Where does it go? Surviving. Surviving and maintaining a sense of dignity."

Here, the women expose aspects of gendered subjectivity not disclosed in the central fantasy of the love letter. Their worries about "awesome responsibility," "service," "no respect," "survival," and "dignity" shed light on the defensive and life-sustaining qualities of the love fantasy. The women's experience of children's demands and their knowledge of how belittled work with children can be may evoke the real fear that they, as teachers, will fail. The dream of love is one way of forgetting the persecutory potential of the work of being together and making knowledge. It is one way of entering the pedagogical arena without worrying about the low intellectual valuation and social prestige that primary teaching accords.

The dream of love may also help the women reason their way out of another unpleasant possibility: that the imaginary child who constitutes the women's subjectivity as teacher may in reality not post love but may rather post hate, rejection, boredom, refusal, or ignorance. The fantasy defensively and productively hides its fear that pedagogy can—and, indeed, does—get derailed. It thus enacts psychic recognition and misrecognition that allow the beginning teacher to persist with her passion to teach.

At the same time, when white female teachers worry about the burdens of service and "awesome responsibility" in teaching, they imagine themselves not so much as agents of possibility, but rather as victims or objects of disenfranchisement. I believe that, especially within the viewing context of *Stand and Deliver* (a film that, explicitly raises questions concerning teacher agency, white privilege, and racism), it is necessary to consider whether the women's failure to speculate about the "other" enslaved does not, in fact, constitute silence (and by implication consent) about white women's own unacknowledged imbrication within spheres of racialized and sexualized privilege. Fantasies of teaching as devotion and as a burden of service can be said to function as enabling metaphors that ignore or distort the latent relations of white, heterosexualized power and privilege inscribed in student-teacher and teacher-community relations.

These speculations raise questions about unmarked whiteness in those who see themselves as (subaltern) subjects in education's story and point to the need for further inquiry into whether and how dreams of love may clear the way for unmindful participation in structures of racialization, sexualization, and engenderment in schooling, where "the one who knows" is the white teacher and the "other" (blacks, girls and women, or children as ignorant) is understood as impoverished in his or her marked ignorance. Fantasies of love may provide legitimacy for feelings of omnipotence over and against those who need "raising up" or "salvation." Tactically, the structure could help to consolidate a "proper civility" in white female subjects who teach, who are enabled (in part by dreams of devotion) to keep the terms of their lease within projects of imperialism, colonization, and patriarchy and yet not be deadened by it.

It is important for teacher education that "enabling" disavowals are part of disabling idealizations of children and their gratitude. The fantasy of the love letter provides insight into how the desire for mastery and domination becomes woven into the fabric of selfhood as teacher and how investments in love in fact obstruct the work of education. The process is buttressed by semiotic provocations (i.e., cultural images and stories) that possess beginning teachers in purposeful ways to create versions of selfhood that are recognizable and acclaimed within a particular interpretive community, a community of teachers. In this way, psychic and social selfhood is always negotiating its blind intentionality through and with itself.[28]

FANTASY'S CONFINES IN IMAGES
AND PRACTICES OF EDUCATION

It remains to show what a teacher movie has to do with the production of a fantasy formation about receiving love letters from students. What are the relations among the film text, the viewing experience, and learning to teach? And what are the limits of the fantasies teachers (and filmmakers) make when they imagine teaching?

The love letter (in both the film and the reading formation) functions as an imaginary sign, just as the posting of the letter signifies an imaginary act. In both film and real life a phantasmatic structure is at play that connects the addressee and addressed over time through the symptom of the letter. Teacher education needs to address the implications of unconscious fantasy within the conditions of white women learning to teach primary school. This is especially so today, because the fantasy hitches onto existing cultural formations that are very much a part of the women's living present.

The story of teaching as a dream of love exists simultaneously in many social places. For example, it exists in the film *Stand and Deliver*, through the narrative structures and representations of devotion that help to characterize the teacher hero. It also exists widely in the intertextual field that circulates popular images of teaching, images that petition would-be teachers long before they pass over the threshold of faculties of education. Scenes of students paying tribute to teachers activate some of the most stirring moments of teacher movie viewing, present in such films as *Maedchen in Uniform*, *The Corn Is Green*, *The Miracle Worker*, *To Sir with Love*, *The Prime of Miss Jean Brodie*, *Dead Poets Society*, and *The Browning Version*. In fact, in many teacher movies the narrative crisis hangs on an ironic reversal of the gift of love, in which the students' payment of tribute precipitates a moment of great existential crisis for the teacher (as in both *Maedchen in Uniform* and *The Prime of Miss Jean Brodie*).[29] In other teacher films, screen students never get to post their love to teachers at all, because a nasty administrator gets to the passionate teacher first (as in *Conrack* and *Sylvia*) and dismisses him or her. This reversal is simply another narrative organization for staging the representation (of lack thereof) of desire for the (missing) gift of love in teaching.

But the dream of love in teaching exists as something more than simply a transhistorical, transnational, popular culture phenomenon. The structure may be thought of as symptomatic of a particular set of circumstances involving white women's struggles with the affects and uses of power and desire in the post-Enlightenment age. The fantasy can be understood in part by placing it within the historical context of teacher formation in Europe and North America that began one hundred and fifty years ago and drew initial inspiration from religious (Christian) perspectives.

Historians of education make clear that from the very inception of institutionalized teacher education, godly perspectives were incorporated through which to ground visions of purity, progress, and selflessness in teaching. Thus, Keith Melder characterizes early teacher-education seminaries as conservative sites that functioned as a vehicle for dealing with cultural changes by alleviating male anxieties about the growing freedom of women.[30] Early teacher-training facilities functioned as places in which to inculcate in women "a willingness to dedicate herself to a life of service to others."[31] Mary Lyon, the founder of the first normal school, was emphatic that the women who taught there were to be considered the secular counterpart to preachers.[32] Similarly, Jennifer Nias observes that Kay Shuttleworth, founder of the first teacher-training college in England, envisioned a band of "intelligent Christian(s) . . . entering on the instruction of the poor with a religious devotion to their work."[33] Almost every female teacher in Nias's study responded to the request to explain what it was "to feel like a teacher" by saying that it was to serve others by "being in control."[34] Diane Manning's examination of the oral testimonies of women who taught between 1920 and 1960 also found that women were attracted to teaching because of the prospects teaching offered to influence and serve.[35]

Attributing meaning to patterns of viewer response in educational research requires addressing the issue of what psychocultural use is served for viewers in passionate and repetitive moments of screen engagement. It involves acknowledging that investments in particular images allow people to construct something for themselves out of the material at hand, something having to do with need, demand, habit, hope, pleasure, and even profit. Sharon Cook illustrates how children have been useful to twentieth-century, educated, white heterosexual Canadian women as representable objects ("little," "innocent," in need of "segregation and protection") for propagating a vision of a sanctified and moral public and private order. The author illustrates how children get figured into educational reports, images, and "discoveries" in such a way that society imagines itself moving forward through the young. At the same time, Cook paints a vivid picture of tension through her descriptions of Bands of Hope and Little White Ribboners, moving across the Canadian landscape according to a "logic" motivated equally by the ethical concerns of child health and nurture and the guarantee of imperialism's project.[36]

Women's desire for agency and social justice in the public realm has been an important factor in attracting them into elementary classrooms, and the tradition of females who see themselves as "crusaders" and "missionaries" is a long-standing one in early childhood education. Although contemporary fantasies of devotion in women learning to teach seem to be conditioned by factors that are timeless and universal, in fact they are very much shaped by contingencies of the present. Salvation impulses in education perform socially specific functions that are not always easy to see. For example, when Valerie Walkerdine writes about the paradigm of child-centered learning (which possesses currency in many teacher-education programs today), she shows how the rhetoric and practices of child-centeredness function toward the production of teacher and child identities in late twentieth-century classrooms.[37] Child-centered discourses position the woman teacher as benevolent overseer of a landscape of elemental and natural goodness. Children are configured as governed by universal laws of development that guard their steady progress as individuals toward rational autonomy and freedom, and the teacher functions as empathetic facilitator of their evolution. Childhood is presented within the scene as a romantic, unique, innocent, and teleological force.

What is forgotten in the fiction is that centering children in this way does not in any natural way best develop their potential as learners. Children not only consistently circumvent teachers' intentions in child-centered activities, but the very notion that children can "discover" the truth through "individualized activities" is a denial on many levels. It denies that any discursive system (including those that posture as "individualized") produces its own particular truths, no matter how these truths are veiled or fictionalized. It denies that the "rational" learner who is ostensibly a product of child-centered practices is not in mastery of either knowledge or the self. Finally, it withholds from learners the legitimate right to expect that teachers will intervene in learning in ways that may feel discomfiting, that may not be easily understood, that may be insistently directive, and that are not always experienced as ego affirming.

Because it is difficult to engage such perilous knowledge head on, it is necessary to understand more about those moments in which discourse itself becomes productive in specific ways. Neither moralism nor denial does much to comfort this work, and both of them ignore the role of the unconscious in discourse and forget how undermining its effects can be in language. Dreams of love do not resolve the difficulties of teaching, nor, ultimately, do they increase its pleasures. In some ways, devotion fantasies help put into place a subjective reality that is bound to experience dismay. Teacher educators can develop ways to assist beginning teachers in disrupting fantasy's confines. Popular culture can be used within pedagogy to explore what fantasy hopes for and ignores when it imagines teaching. Screenplay pedagogy can work to disrupt those moments of feeling trapped in a history produced but not unchangeable. Part of the lesson involves imagining how to teach in the absence of miracles. A popular song sums it up aptly: "Too much love will kill you, if you don't read all the signs." Writers such as Frantz Fanon put it differently when they describe the process by which the reason of the powerful objectifies victims as unreason, knowing the position of victim as already circumscribed by otherness. Similarly, cultural theorists Toni Morrison and James Snead bid workers to understand how claims to freedom in literature and film occur in the presence of the unfree.[38]

Dreams of love in teaching are compensatory figurations, ways of "bringing culture to the people," privileged ways of "cultivating uncultivated bodies and minds." Some women learning to teach avail themselves of this pervasive structure of feeling in education. They use the idealization strategically; that is, they unconsciously rove among many possible scenes of classroom life and retrospectively settle upon this one as their favorite. The structure offers them a powerful place to replay a desire for recognition that possesses them. But in turn, "the object becomes the very structure of representation through which it fails to be thought, the impasses of conceptual thinking itself."[39] The fantasy straps into place the discourses that mark the place of the subject in primary-teacher education, and it deserves to be disquieted. Shared by both spectator and filmmaker, one and the same scenario sustains respective and mutual desires. It is the posting of love in acknowledgment that the women problematically long for.

NOTES

I am indebted to faculty members at the University of Toronto and the Ontario Institute for Studies in Education who guided this work in its earlier formulation as a dissertation: Roger Simon, Deanne Bogdan, and Dennis Thiessen. For their continued encouragement and demands, I wish to thank Deborah Britzman, Geoff Milburn, Sharon Todd, and the anonymous reviewers of this paper who challenged my thinking about education and psychoanalysis in instructive ways. I wish to acknowledge the Social Science and Humanities Research Council of Canada for the generous funding that enabled me to finish the research.

1. See Sol Cohen, "Postmodernism, the New Cultural History, Film: Resisting Images in Education," in *Paedagogica Historica* (in press); Jane Gallop, ed., *Pedagogy: The Question of Impersonation* (Bloomington: Indiana University Press, 1995); Henry Giroux and Roger Simon, "Popular Culture as a Pedagogy of Pleasure and Meaning," in H. Giroux, Roger Simon, and contributors, *Popular Culture, Schooling and Everyday Life* (Toronto: Ontario Institute for Studies in Education Press, 1989), 1–30; Lynn Joyrich, "*Give Me a Girl at an Impressionable Age and She Is Mine For Life*: Jean Brodie as Pedagogical Primer," in *Pedagogy*, ed. Gallop, 46–63; Judith Robertson, "Screenplay Pedagogy and the Interpretation of Unexamined Knowledge in Primary Teaching," *TABOO: The Journal of Culture and Education* (in press); Sandra Weber and Claudia Mitchell, *That's Funny, You Don't Look Like a Teacher: Interrogating Images of Identity in Popular Culture* (Philadelphia: Falmer Press, 1995).

2. However, the question of how the predispositions of beginning teachers affect their

knowing and thinking as teachers is well established in teacher education research. In *Schoolteacher: A Sociological Study* (Chicago: University of Chicago Press, 1975), Dan Lortie established that neither teacher education nor later experiences in the workplace function significantly to alter beginning teachers' initial beliefs about teaching. Some researchers since Lortie have seen school life, with all its hierarchies, obligations, rituals, and rules, as an important variable in determining how beginning teachers learn the complexities of their work. See, for example, Mark Ginsburg and Renée Clift, "The Hidden Curriculum of Preservice Teacher Education," in *Handbook of Research on Teacher Education*, ed. W. R. Houston (New York: Macmillan, 1990), 450–68; Jesse Goodman, "The Political Tactics of Teaching Strategies of Reflective Active Preservice Teachers," *Elementary School Journal* 89 (1988), 23–40; Tom Popkewitz, ed., *Critical Studies in Teacher Education: Its Folklore, Theory, and Practice* (Philadelphia: Falmer Press, 1987); John Smyth, ed., *Educating Teachers: Changing the Nature of Pedagogical Knowledge* (New York: Falmer Press, 1987); Ken Zeichner and Daniel Liston, *Teacher Education and the Social Conditions of Schooling* (New York: Routledge, 1991). Such findings challenge the view that teacher socialization is a passive process—or even an entirely reasonable one. They demonstrate that particular habits in teaching take root precisely because of the tendency of beginning teachers to consolidate previous strategies and fictions of learning. See also Deborah Britzman, *Practice Makes Practice: A Critical Study of Learning to Teach* (New York: State University of New York Press, 1991); Jennifer Nias, *Primary Teachers Talking: A Study of Teaching as Work* (New York: Routledge, 1989); Carolyn Steedman, *Childhood, Culture and Class in Britain: Margaret McMillan, 1860–1931* (New Brunswick, N.J.: Rutgers University Press, 1990); and Valerie Walkerdine, *The Mastery of Reason: Cognitive Development and the Production of Rationality* (London and New York: Routledge, 1988).

3. For discussions of the social geography of whiteness, racialized gender, and genderized race in education, including how race is assumed, learned, and naturalized through schooling, see Cameron McCarthy, *Race and Curriculum: Social Inequality and the Theories of Politics of Difference in Contemporary Research on Schooling* (Philadelphia: Falmer Press, 1990), and Cameron McCarthy and Warren Crichlow, eds., *Race, Identity, and Representation in Education* (New York: Routledge: 1993).

4. Ramon Menendez, director, *Stand and Deliver* (1987). Based on *Walking on Water* (screenplay) by Ramon Menendez and Tom Musca. Screenplay available from Script City, 8033 Sunset Blvd. Suite 1500, Hollywood, CA 90046. Tel. 213–871–0707. Videotape available from Warner Communications Company, 4000 Warner Blvd., Burbank, CA 91522.

5. See Jay Mathews, *Escalante, the Best Teacher in America* (New York: Henry Holt and Company, 1988). Original inspiration for the movie came from the *Los Angeles Times* on December 7, 1982, "Fourteen Students Retake Test After Scores are Disputed—Principal Charges Minority Bias." The article proved slightly wrong. Eighteen students at Garfield had taken the advanced examination and twelve students accused of copying retook the test (Mathews, *Escalante*, 1–6).

6. Patrick Mahony, *Freud as a Writer* (New York: International Universities Press, 1982), 56.

7. Sigmund Freud, *Beyond the Pleasure Principle*, vol. 18 of *The Standard Edition of the Complete Psychological Works of Sigmund Freud* (hereafter referred to as *SE*), trans. and ed. James Strachey (1920; reprint, London: The Hogarth Press, 1955), 24.

8. Mahony, *Freud as a Writer*, 57.

9. Freud, *Beyond the Pleasure Principle*, 36.

10. To arrive at the categories of repetition in the women's language, I numbered and then coded each written and verbal response to the movies, based on about seven hundred pages of transcripts from writing, interviews, and seminar discussions. I indicated in parentheses the pseudonym of the speaker and whether the words were uttered or written. Repetitions, "errors," and non-verbal expressions such as "ah . . . um" were included and later interpreted for evidence of ideas or affects. I added punctuation to utterances and indicated pauses or hesitation with ellipses. When words were accompanied by gesture or forcefulness, I relayed this information in italics and parentheses. The women's written language was not otherwise "polished" in any way. This meant reproducing "errors" (i.e., neologisms or malapropisms) without the use of "sic" or editorial revision. If the written text was a very long one, I used ellipses to lift out key passages in the sequence.

11. Carolyn Steedman, *The Tidy House: Little Girls Writing* (London: Virago, 1982), 26.

12. Luisa Passerini, "Work Ideology and Consensus Under Italian Fascism," *History Workshop: A Journal of Socialist Historians* 8 (1979), 82–109.

13. The challenge of making sense of the gendered relations at play in the women's discourse was assisted by discussions in M. Devault, "Talking and Listening from Women's Standpoint: Feminist Strategies for Interviewing and Analysis," *Social Problems* 37, 96–116; and P. Thompson, L. Passerini, I. Bertaux-Wiame, and A. Portelli, "Between Social Scientists: Responses to Louise A. Tilly," *International Journal of Oral History* 6, 19–39.

14. Frigga Haug, *Beyond Female Masochism: Memory, Work, and Politics*, trans. R. Livingston (London: Verso, 1992), 56–59.

15. Sigmund Freud, *Five Lectures on Psycho-analysis*, in *SE*, vol. 11, 9–55.

16. Shoshana Felman and Dori Laub, *Testimony: Crises of Witnessing in Literature, Psychoanalysis, and History* (New York: Routledge, 1992), 15.

17. See Nias, *Primary Teachers.*

18. Julia Kristeva, "Histoires d'Amour / Julia Kristeva in Conversation with Rosalind Coward," in *Desire*, ed. Lisa Appignanesi (London: Institute of Contemporary Arts, 1984), 24.

19. According to Freud, disavowal functions as a mode of defense for dealing with external reality in which individuals refuse to recognize the reality of a traumatic perception; see *An Outline of Psycho-analysis*, in *SE*, vol. 23, 144–269. My argument is that Meg disavows the reality of her desire for power, an unconscious strategy that allows her to hold on to two incompatible positions at the same time (i.e., women want/do not want power).

20. My thanks to one of the anonymous reviewers of this paper for suggesting this interpretation.

21. Teresa de Lauretis, *The Practice of Love: Lesbian Sexuality and Perverse Desire* (Bloomington: Indiana University Press, 1994), 128.

22. See Freud, *My Contact with Josef Popper-Lynkeus*, in *SE*, vol. 22, 221; and Freud, *Unconscious Emotions*, in *SE*, vol. 14, 177.

23. For critical examinations of the socially reproductive effects of teacher education, see, for example, Deborah Britzman, "Cultural Myths in the Making of a Teacher: Biography and Social Structure in Teacher Education," *Harvard Educational Review* 56 (1986), 442–72; Britzman, *Practice*; Sharon Feiman-Nemser and M. Buchmann, "When Is Student Teaching Teacher Education?" *Teaching and Teacher Education* 3 (1987), 255–73; G. Riseborough, "Pupils, Recipe Knowledge, Curriculum, and the Cultural Production of

Class, Ethnicity, and Patriarchy: A Critique of One Teacher's Practices," *British Journal of Sociology of Education* 9 (1988), 39–54; Kenneth Zeichner and Jennifer Gore, "Teacher Socialization," in *Handbook of Research*, ed. W. Robert Houston, 329–48.

24. Ibid., 338.

25. According to J. Laplanche and J.–B. Pontalis, some post-Freudian authors make a distinction between the terms "ideal ego" and "ego-ideal"; see *The Language of Psycho-Analysis* (New York: W. W. Norton, 1973), 201. According to Freud, the ego-ideal constitutes a model to which the indivudal tries to conform and is the principle upon which the formation of human groups is accomplished (Freud, *SE*, vol. 18, 116). The ideal ego refers to an ideal of narcissistic omnipotence modeled upon infantile narcissism (Freud, *SE*, vol. 14, 94). For the purposes of my argument here, with its emphasis on Meg's heroic identification and its implication for her entry into a group (white, female primary teachers), the ego-ideal is my main focus (although both meanings pertain).

26. Here, identification also plays out in fantasy the process of incorporation, where the object (the student) is taken into the subject (the teacher), thereby "devouring" it, "killing" it in order to preserve the loss of love. I wish to thank Sharon Todd for suggesting this interpretation.

27. See Carole Taylor, "Positioning Subjects and Objects: Agency, Narration, Relationality," *Hypatia* 8 (1993), 55–81.

28. I am indebted to Roger Simon for this association, which he offered me in June 1995.

29. These films may be thought of as examples of the genre of the "lesbian fairy tale," discussed by Ruby Rich in "*Maedchen in Uniform*: From Repressive Tolerance to Erotic Liberation," *Jumpcut* 24–25, 44–50 and by Andrea Weiss, *Vampires and Violets: Lesbians in the Cinema* (London: Jonathan Cape, 1992).

30. See Keith Melder, "Masks of Oppression: The Female Seminary Movement in the United States," *New York History* 55 (1974), 261–78.

31. Ibid., 268.

32. Ibid., 278.

33. Nias, *Primary Teachers*, 17.

34. Ibid., 189.

35. See Diane Manning, *Hill Country Teacher: Oral Histories from the One-Room School and Beyond* (Boston: G. K. Hall and Company, 1990).

36. See Sharon Anne Cook, *"Through Sublime and Shadow": The Women's Christian Temperance Union, Evangelicism, and Reform in Ontario, 1874–1930* (Kingston: Queen's University Press, 1995).

37. See Valerie Walkerdine, *The Mastery of Reason* and *Counting Girls Out* (London: Virago, 1989).

38. See especially Toni Morrison, *Playing in the Dark: Whiteness and the Literary Imagination* (Cambridge: Harvard University Press, 1992) and James Snead, *White Screeens/Black Images: Hollywood from the Dark Side* (New York: Routledge, 1994). Both authors demonstrate convincingly that images and stories in literature and film are produced and read in codified ways that potentially reproduce (through figures of division) racialized categories of valuation and ways of thinking.

39. Jacqueline Rose, "Where Does the Misery Come From? Psychoanalysis, Feminism, and the Event," in *Feminism and Psychoanalysis*, ed. R. Feldstein and J. Roof (Ithaca: Cornell University Press, 1989), 25–39.

4

Say Me to Me

Desire and Education

REBECCA A. MARTUSEWICZ

What is love's knowledge, and what writing does it dictate in the heart?
—Martha C. Nussbaum, *Love's Knowledge*

... I'm afraid of disappointing you. With the desire to fulfill your expectations comes a specific anxiety, the one whose mimetic nature is only confirmed by overly explicit denials: the anxiety of facing the other.
—René Girard, "The Founding Murder in the Philosophy of Nietzsche"

It is always something bad to injure one's own power of thought, since thought is the condition of all that is good.
—Simone Weil, *Lectures on Philosophy*

I know that little girl's passion for questions. The pleasure of the questions. Warm sun on her back. Looking at grass. "Why do I see green? Does my mother see the same green, or is her green blue, like my sky? Does this sky touch me?" Something moves her. There's a limit here; she knows she can't know the answers, and yet ... something else. I feel her desire to share these questions, for someone else to feel the intensity, the wonder of it all. And perhaps to be touched by another's wonder too, a desire for connection to the world and to the other, through this passion to know.

She runs into the kitchen. She runs in there with her questions. "Mom! Could your green be my blue? What is the sky?" She gives them to her. She wants her to love them, too, to love her questions. At four she knows that love is in those questions, a particular kind of love. It's impossible that her mother should not know this, too. But the woman does not turn; she remains at the sink.

I'm not sure this scene ever really happened or whether I have created it out of some vague and lingering confusion, where the joy of thinking about the world and its mysteries mingles with a sense of disappointment. It is a disappointment connected at once to this wonder about the world—a sense of caring and love for the unknown—and to a strong desire to be loved myself, loved for my questions. For me. Two kinds of love and desire intertwine, one a strong love of the world, a desire to know it, to think and to understand; the other a desire *to be loved*, affirmed *because* I want to know this world. Throughout my life, I have felt the collision of these two forms in a variety of contexts: my mother's kitchen, an academic conference, and now as I write.

I have felt the rush of creation that comes in the wake of asking a particular question. And I have felt the disappointment of not getting it right, or more accurately, of not getting back what I wanted, the burgeoning violence that this latter desire invites. A violent disappointment seeps in, pulls me down, stops the questions and the joy. I use the word *violent* here because the strength of the disappointment can kill the creative process (which I will argue for as the educational process) and become harmful both to me and to others. It shuts down thought, which can only harm our ability to find new and better ways of living together.

I begin from the premise that the forces shaping forms of desire "are the cultural codes and representations which derive from the historical and collective relations between men and women."[1] Desire, in all its forms, said or unsaid, is culturally learned and maintained, and certain forms are at the crux of the perpetuation of social and psychic violence, as well as violence to the earth and to other sentient and nonsentient beings. Yet, there is also a kind of desire that motivates our struggles against domination and toward a shared truth. I do not mean desire as a transcendental force but rather individually experienced desire generated out of and through our relation to each other, to the earth and its creatures, that motivates and is generated within the struggle to care for each other. Desire for a better world, for justice, and for truth generates questions and pushes us to challenge forms of social injustice by offering new ways of thinking and being.

This essay explores this contradictory relation, the points at which the desire for affirmation or recognition overtakes the desire for truth, stopping the questions and ultimately the joy that makes education possible. What is this desire for love, and why does it too often turn so heavy? What are the particular contexts and political relations within which such disappointment and the accompanying possibility of self-negation get generated? What are the effects of these negative effects of desire for education and the possibility of new thoughts for the world?

These are clearly ethical and aesthetic questions. I approach these questions here autobiographically, reflecting both on my own particular life and on the broader culture I live in and exploring ways of living justly in this culture.

Mostly, I'm interested in these problems in terms of their relation to pedagogy. I am a teacher. And I am a student (at least in the broad and informal sense). A particular definition of pedagogy informs both my teaching and my learning but more generally, as much as I can make it do so, my living. Although pedagogy is often thought of in primarily technical terms (the set of skills and behaviors needed for teaching), I would like to broaden that definition and to think about pedagogy in terms of the generative relation between teacher and learner. I believe strongly that pedagogy is defined as any relationship between two or more people, or between someone and another communicating form, through which often unpredictable expressions—words, dances, songs, thoughts, creative effects and possibilities of all—kinds get generated. So I use the term pedagogy broadly, but I truly see it, experience it and believe in it as a relation which occurs on very common, microlevels of all kinds.

Moreover, I want to argue for a definition of *education* that also goes beyond the technical, this time toward the ethical. For me, *education* is what happens when we engage such multiple possibilities (created pedagogically) in the search for better, more just ways of living in our communities and with our fellow creatures. The search, which we could call the search for truth, cannot happen if the possibilities are not allowed to flourish. Put succinctly, if too simply: a more just relation with the world cannot be brought into being unless we create ways to allow, engage, and act upon these possibilities collectively. It is this very commitment that pushes me to teach, to ask questions, and to encourage my students to ask their own questions that will open pathways for thinking.

My concern in this paper is with a particular and, I think, too common danger that lies in the path of this endeavor. Specifically, I want to explore how the violent effects of certain forms of desire turn us away from the conditions necessary for education.

QUESTIONS

Let me begin with some thoughts about questions. What is it to ask a question? To ask is always a repetition, a repetition of the "why" or the "how," for example, as the play between what we know and don't know, between the thought and the unthought, and always between the said and the unsaid. As such, a question is an invitation to the play of multiplicity that operates between the given and the virtual. I mean that when we ask why, when we repeat that linguistic function, we are opening a *space* in which there are an indefinite number of possible answers for us to choose. I'm convinced that this space, a space of pure difference, is where the possibility and the thrill of teaching come from. This space and its indefinite creation is precisely what allows and ensures different possibilities to spring forth. For as we attempt to answer why and to choose the best solution, yet another set of whys come, and the space of possibility, never separate from, and yet irreducible, to our attempts to say something, is opened once again. Gilles Deleuze puts it this way:

> Just as solutions do not suppress problems, but on the contrary discover in
> them the subsisting conditions without which they would have no sense,
> nor do they saturate the question, which persists in all the answers. There is
> therefore an aspect in which problems remain without a solution, and
> therefore without an answer. It is in this sense that problem and question
> . . . have their own being.[2]

This space of question and solution is the boundary between the world and our attempts to comment on it. It is at once a limit and an empty space, forming the condition for both what has been said and what is to come. And though I have said that it was the questions that made me run to the kitchen, it is actually this limit space that generates for me the senses of awe and joy. This relational space is what generates the wonder at all those possibilities for understanding myself and others in this world, for loving this world. These senses fuel my life. This is why I so joyfully ran. And this is why I teach.

To teach (perhaps especially to teach teachers) is to share with others the exhilaration and the difficulties of opening oneself (and others) onto this limit space, of stepping out to a precipice, and confronting the unthought. To be there in that process of repetition and difference is what education means; it's what it means to love the world. That was what I discovered in the grass—that I could ask a question and recognize the essential limitations of finding an answer while still experiencing the desire to know. This joyous recognition of the fullness and limitation of this space was what I was so excited to share with my mother.

So then, what is the problem? (Yet another question!) Where does the disappointment come from, and more important, what can it do? What is its violence?

To ask a question is always to want something. In the scene I shared at the beginning of the paper, I ran to my mother with my questions because I had been touched by something. A recognition of the limit space had brushed me. I ran because I wanted to share a sudden understanding that as humans we have a capacity for perceiving and searching for truth that is limited by the very function that allows us to think—our power to name the sky blue or the grass green. I ran for the sheer joy of that truth.

And I ran for myself. This is important, for there is an intensity of aspiration in the asking of those questions, aspiration for the world and aspiration for myself.

SAY ME TO ME

I cannot separate myself, me, from the aspiration to ask or from the exhilaration of facing the unthought. Part of the desire that pushes me to ask about this world, that pushes me to that precipice, is a desire to understand myself in this world. That is, there is the desire (and the anxiety) to face the other that both is and is not "me."

This is the desire for the unthought, for an unsaid and unknown other to "say me to me."[3] But the unthought does not give me *me*. It gives me nothing, which is to say, everything: the questions come flooding. And so I run to known others—my students, my teachers, my lover, and my mother. I give them my questions, and I search for myself in their responses. And this is where the problem lies, for the other cannot give me to me, except to the extent that this "other" is me and does not yet exist. I may search for myself "out there," but the me whom I seek is always already other than the me they may reflect back. To get caught in a desire for the "me" is a prelude to violence, because to give those questions in the illusion of a return of myself is to forget or deny the other. The desire for the "me" is inescapable, but the me is, strictly speaking, unattainable, except to the extent that it is given in "the other of the me" itself or in the questions that are generated in the thought about the world. Jacques Derrida puts it this way: "When he writes himself to himself, he writes himself to the other who is infinitely far away. . . He has no relation to himself that is not forced to defer itself by passing through the other."[4]

In our teaching, our writing, our loving, we search for others who will affirm our lives, share our aspirations, our questions, who will care that we are alive and help to connect the "me" to the world. And yet, this "me" is inevitably tied to those questions I keep mentioning, to the limit space and the desire to transcend the limitations of our ability to find answers. Again, the questions tie "me" to the other. The questions are "me" and other, tied to this earth, to the ones I love, and to my limited time here. And yet they also mark what I do not know, what is not yet thought, the indefinite movement of difference in identity and in knowledge; tied to a "me" who does not exist, the questions are always different and deferred as soon as they appear. The danger lies in the experience of this difference as a failure, either to fulfill or to be fulfilled. Such a weighty disappointment can shut down thinking and the play of questions, leading to a kind of terrorism of the soul.

You can see the problem. We search for identity, for connection to the world, and for love, and at the same time, we seek transcendence from this imperfect "humanity," this essential emptiness of being. That is a critical existential problem: to desire to be more than human, although we are "all too human." That is, we learn that while we want to know, our knowing is limited by the tools that we have at our disposal, the relation between our ability to name and to perceive, for example.

I learned this in the grass, and I'm learning it again as I read philosophy. The first thing we know about ourselves is that we are not perfect. As Simone Weil told her students, "The only mark of God in us is that we know we are not God." And yet we are not satisfied with this imperfection; we believe it should not be so, that we should, and perhaps could, transcend the limit space. "We feel we should not be imperfect and limited; if it were perfectly right and proper to be so, then we would not think ourselves imperfect."[5] And so, like Alice's bright object on the shelf above—sometimes like a doll and sometimes like a toolbox—and the empty shelf she always seems to find as soon as she tries to look,[6] the "me" is never where I thought it to be.

Our relation to imperfection is the source of both joy and violence. Around this experience of ourselves circulates desire for the truth. It pushes us to problematize ourselves, to ask questions about who we are in the world. Since the imperfection or limitations never go away (although we may push past some limits, others are always on the horizon), neither do the questions. They continue to circulate, as I argued earlier, indefinitely.

And this is often quite difficult because the ego is also present in this process. Another desire may manifest itself in the desire to be perfect, to seek the recognition of others. Here, desire helped along by the ego may turn toward negative forms of power and the illusion of oneself as having reached or neared the status of God. We don't have to go far for examples. History has given the world its share of despots in politics and in philosophy, too. But such desire for power, recognition, or affirmation is not to be found only in those extreme cases. The ego operates in all of us. The desire for power over others and the violence it entails are a cultural and psychological monster fed by the belief that we ought not be imperfect.

René Girard's well-known work *Violence and the Sacred* helps to illuminate the ways in which violence may follow upon this experience of imperfection. According to Girard, the desire to be affirmed by the other involves the desire for that which we perceive the other to want and is thus essentially mimetic. Desire in this case is focused on the object of desire of the other, an object perceived as holding within it Being and thus the power to deliver the "me." The subject believes that the object of the other's desire holds the key to *her* being, therefore affirmation from the model—the parent, the teacher—has the effect of deliverance from uncertainty and arrival at Being. Such an experience of fullness is, of course, illusory and easily deflated. Fullness is quickly exchanged for nothingness and disappointment. And as Girard teaches us, such shifting positions too often lead to jealousy, rivalry, and the escalation of violence, as disciple and model struggle over who is to be first with the object.

This is the economy of the ego, the plane of exchange, where the reward of affirmation is the currency sought: "Love me. Say it. Say my name." The movement from affirmation to rejection and back to affirmation creates tremendous energy. This is the energy that so fascinated Hegel. An essentially violent energy, he believed it to be the basis for transcendence. Perhaps Hegel was writing too close to his own ego; he missed what plays on the body and on our hearts as we stand on the precipice. He was too fascinated with mind to pay attention to those affects.

But referring to Hegel this way is only an expression of my own will to power. A story of my own would serve better here. The story that I want to tell is really a series of stories strung together by three statements. It is both about education and about ego as each comes to circulate and tease in the pedagogical relation. Tracing this series of events in my own life, moments marked particularly by the bodily experience of the desire for affirmation and its dangerous effects, I will explore the difference between the will to truth (structured by the free play of questions) and the will to power (structured by mimetic desire).

ON EGO AND EDUCATION: THREE STATEMENTS

Three statements comprise my story: (1) "You have not risked," (2) "You have arrived," and (3) "Those were very different papers." These statements form a sort of developmental series, though not in the sense of any predetermined ontological or teleological series. Rather, this is a series made meaningful by the relation that each statement has to the other two. These statements were made and heard separately, in three different years, at an annual conference of curriculum scholars, known colloquially as the Bergamo Conference.

In 1989 I presented a paper that was part of my dissertation. It was a sound paper and was fairly well received, but I was unexcited. I said so to a friend, a person with whom I have shared many questions and who had really been a primary teacher and model for me for many years. He responded: "You have not risked. You have presented what you know." What could that mean? I had no idea, but the statement shook me. I felt very uncomfortable. Something was stirring me up. I felt mobilized.

The next year, I presented again. This paper was indeed a risk. I had written about the joy of teaching. Although the details of the analysis are not important, the effects of the experience are. The words in that paper and their effects had come from my heart, from the knowledge in my body of the joy created as one works hard to say something, to teach something to someone else. I remember feeling very peaceful as I presented it, even while my heart was racing. I had danced up to the precipice. And this time, without any question from me, I heard from my mentor, "You have arrived." I had indeed "arrived"; I thought I was in heaven as my friends and colleagues praised my work. I certainly was basking in the glow of recognition and affirmation. But as I was to discover, this was a most dangerous arrival!

The pragmatic effects of that statement, expressed within a particular context and in a particular set of circumstances as part of a series, sent me into the economy of my ego. This was the reward it was waiting for, to finally be heard, to have my peers, my colleagues, my teacher say my name: "Rebecca, you have arrived." Operating in the textual relation of this comment and the circumstances of my life—all the old longings, the disappointments, and the desires—was a powerful "order word."[7] Gilles Deleuze and Felix Guattari use this concept to describe incorporeal transformations of bodies that are affected in statements. As Deleuze and Guattari argue, "to order, question, promise or affirm is not to inform someone about a command, doubt, engagement or assertion but *to effectuate these specific, immanent and necessarily implicit acts*" [emphasis added].[8]

To say "You have arrived" was not to inform me of that event but to effectuate it, to effectuate a specific, incorporeal, transformative arrival. I don't mean that this transformation was necessarily to a new and better place. And I don't mean that it occurred as a result of any intention of the speaker. It was an arrival incited by the statement, colliding with and fueling a specific kind of desire, a desire for the pleasure of affirmation and the power of recognition. This was a pleasure quite different from that taken in the questions and the writing of that paper. This was a pleasure taken in the *power* that I felt in the event of recognition, both transported by and not reducible to the words of my teacher. The "being recognized" by my peers and my teacher happened in the transformative power of the order word, as an event. I had instantly taken a new position in the academic game; I moved upstream; it felt good to hear my name.

But I was scared, too. Defensive. I remember asking myself, "What if I never write such a paper again?" It was my ego speaking. This statement, made violent by mimetic desire, was taking my heart.

The desire for recognition, the energy of the ego, is fueled by the sense of nothingness that the limit-space brings. Denying the moment of absolute fullness, the ego rushes in to fill the void. A kind of happiness ensues, a happiness created from a sense of power and control over the void: "I'm something! Look at me!" Girard's thesis seems all too clear here.

Truth was and is a powerful object of desire for me, and I must admit that in the presence of this teacher, I believed I had access to truth. I felt sure that I had finally found a person who would not disappoint me, but rather who would share with me this love of the limit space and grant me the kind of understanding that I had been searching for, someone who would "say me to me."

His words "You have arrived" meant to me that I had arrived where I believed *he* was, that I had grasped what I believed *he* wanted (a certain knowledge of the limit-space and/or the ability to express it), and that I had therefore achieved some sort of fullness. His words gave me the "me" my ego had been seeking. Or at least an illusion of me.

Powerful academic woman? But what a dangerous identity to covet! Powerful academic woman propelled up the mountain by a massive ego energy, by the belief that I was no longer empty. It was a temporary gusto, of course. I felt the fear of losing my position, or perhaps it was the fear of the certain danger of that position. As Michel Serres has so aptly demonstrated, it is when one is in the maximum position that one is most vulnerable to the violence of others.[9] A sense of competition and rivalry settled upon me; and as always, it too quickly became evident that something was amiss: me.

The year following my "success" is important. I wrote yet another paper. It was a struggle. I've struggled before; I'm struggling now. Indeed, the work to bring something to life—to create something—is usually difficult, an odd mixture of frustration and exhilaration. But this was different. I felt no joy in it. When I think of that summer, I understand the expression "her heart wasn't in it," but I pressed on, motivated by the previous year's success. When I finally presented, I felt none of the exhilaration of the year before, though there was anxiety. I said so, again to my teacher. "Those were very different papers," he responded. A fairly innocuous statement on its own, but I sank a million miles. That old disappointment was seeping in again: I'm nothing! Pain flooded my body. Chained to this very weighty desire, my heart was like a ton of bricks.

At home I wept. And for months afterward I was in the bluest, blackest intellectual/psychological place, unable to think, going through the motions with my students. The sense of fullness was replaced by defeat. In the passage from fullness to nothingness, the whole mimetic process escalated—the disappointment, the anger, the jealousy, the sad passion.

René Girard has written of this vertigo, describing the process of instability and alternation that accompanies mimetic desire. In the mimetic structure, the need to be first with the object of desire leads to rivalry and competition between the model and the disciple. Oscillation between victory and defeat escalates the violence in social relations—and the need for a sacrifice.[10] Girard's analysis of tragedy in Greek mythology shows that this sacrifice is necessary to avoid total destruction in a community and usually involves the selection of a scapegoat. In order to protect the community from the escalation of conflict, scapegoats are sent away in exile or are offered up in sacrifice, in a symbolic, but necessary, purging of violence from the community.

In my case, the rivalry that I felt most sharply was not with my mentor (at least not explicitly) but with myself. The violence was not turned upon an outside other but rather inward, upon myself. Rather than engage external conflict, I chose myself first as rival (Will I ever write such a paper again?) and later as scapegoat. Simone Weil warns against such self-injury. To turn violence upon one's self is ultimately, she tells us, an ethical problem, since it is injurious to thought, and thought is the only passage that we have toward a different world.[11]

It's difficult to write about that time. I was afflicted, sick and sad from the wrong passion. I had been headed for this place for a year, maybe two. This was what the "arrival" had really been about. My pain was, to use a phrase coined by Deleuze and Guattari, "naked, vegetative egoism."[12] Teaching was impossible because I could not turn my attention outward toward the other.

I had taken a trip through a writing and thinking process that was quite simply an example of what happens when our attention is not focused on a problem that we sincerely feel. This was not writing as thinking; this was an academic exercise. It failed because it was primarily motivated by the desire for recognition, by self-love and not by love of the truth, not by a concern for the world. The sacrifice that I had imposed was a serious ethical problem precisely because I could not engage thought outward to the world and to the other. The questions stopped; I was not able to open myself to the limit space. And I suffered for myself. An ugly suffering.

So there I was the following spring, feeling defeated and considering not going to Bergamo. As the May 15 deadline for proposals approached, I found myself in a kind of paralysis. Throat-constricting, stomach-knotting panic. What was I going to propose? I began to struggle. I had no question! No project, no problem. Time was closing in. This was impossible! Visions of failure swamped me. This was my conference, my summer writing time. "But I have no problem!"

But, of course I did. How is it possible to be so disturbed and not to have a question? How funny! The problem was I had no problem. Questions flew to the screen of my computer. Laughter began to buoy me. What shuts down problem making? Where is this fear, what are its affects? What is this ambition about? What kind of desire is this? Why am I so obsessed with presenting at this conference?

Finally, I had to go way down into a very bad, painful place, to be lost before I could begin to discover the joy again. I had to be confronted with my vulnerability, my imperfection, my ego. I nearly drowned in the violence of my own self-absorption, a self-disgust born of the very text of my life, born of the will to power. The self-negation had shut down my ability to think, until I was so frustrated that I could not bear it. I had to wait until that moment for something else to kiss me.

That something else is born of the same text of my life, but it is not about power. I don't really have a name for it. It doesn't really exist as a thing or a body. Perhaps this is what Michel Serres calls the "educated third." Perhaps we could name it "love." Or "the good." Or "truth." Our words will not capture what it is, and yet it is only because we struggle to name it that it keeps returning. It is what makes it possible to struggle for justice in the world. I had to wait for the love of the truth to become stronger than my ego. When love came, I found the courage to peer over the edge again, to face the limit-space. To write, and to think, and to ask my questions. These are the necessary conditions for education, for teaching and for learning.

Those of us in academia know all too well what comes to interfere with the will to truth. We are all too familiar with the will to power and its ugly effects. The institutions that we work in thrive on competition and rivalry. Violence is a part of our daily lives there, producing and reproducing the psychological, social, and even ritual relations that I have been describing. I am not suggesting that we could easily escape their effects.

Neither am I suggesting that we should rid ourselves of the desire for love or affirmation or even that such a desire necessarily leads to violence. Rather, I am pointing to contradictions that seem to plague us: our need to transcend our imperfection while we will never close the gap between the world and our attempts to represent it or between what we "know" and what we do not. Perhaps that is what needs to be affirmed, this "me" that will never be full and is always fuller than we can yet imagine. Instead, we trap ourselves in the belief that we could somehow avoid the problem of imperfection, gain power over it through the fullness of self, of "me." And in so doing, we stop the necessary ethical struggle, the attention to other. And this includes the other "me" that is in fact yet to come. In short, we stop educating ourselves and others.

THE QUESTION OF GENDER

When I first wrote and presented this paper, I steered clear of the question of gender that circulates in this story. I'm not sure why, except that I was somehow not ready to confront it. I do think it is an important piece of the dynamic that needs to be addressed if we are to understand what goes on for women and men as we struggle within these academic settings as teachers and as students. I do not pretend to be able to do that in the necessary depth here, but I do want to say something about it and perhaps point to what needs to be done.

Clearly the desire for truth is shot through with relations of power and identity that include gender. The ability to ask questions in particular contexts and the ability to have them heard are not the same for men and women because of the ways in which we come to be defined and thus think of ourselves as "knowers," or question makers. Did I run to my mother with my questions hoping that she, a woman, would be the one to confirm them? Was my disappointment about some perception that she could not or would not engage me this way? Did she not engage me because of her own self-negation as a knower? Or out of some fear that I might be hurt if I began to understand myself as able to ask questions of the world?

All these questions swirl through this text, and I must admit that I cannot clearly answer any of them with any certainty. But I suspect that the dynamics they suggest are somehow relevant and that the self-violence that I periodically engage in is caught in the politics of gender, desire, and identity. What happens if we entertain René Girard's theory and invite gender politics to play a part in mimetic desire? Why was my model a man? What dynamics got played out with him that would not have been there if he were a woman?

Girls, and boys for that matter, are born into, and grow up, in a culture in which social relations are hierarchized by gender. Identities are made in participation with a powerful system of meaning that presents men and boys as stronger, smarter, and more apt to achieve independent, autonomous lives, simply by virtue of their gender. In a culture structured by male dominance and, moreover, as Adrienne Rich has taught us, by compulsory heterosexuality, the question of how gender plays in the dynamic of mimetic desire becomes important. To what extent and in what ways is "fullness of being" and the role of model represented as masculine and played out for women by men? I'm certain that in my own life, my father was such a figure, and though I have had women who were mentors, none had the impact on me that male figures have had. Much of the history of feminist research has been focused on the ways that forms of "fullness" get coded in masculine terms and used as the standard for humanity.

Certainly the problem of "imperfection" must be experienced differently, perhaps more violently for women than for men. Women have, after all, been defined historically in Western discourses—medical, philosophical, and popular—as imperfect men. With men's experiences viewed as the standard, these discourses and their accompanying identity formations produce a kind of double jeopardy of imperfection for women. The desire for affirmation and the potential for self-negation in this context seems particularly dangerous.

Looking at my own case, I am not surprised that I did not take the opportunity of success to engage in a rivalry with my mentor. I could not, since I did not see myself as even close to his equal. Instead, I engaged the competition with myself and experienced intense self-defeat as I turned the violence inward. It seems to me that this tendency is not uncommon for women, especially given the systematic processes of inferiorization that we experience daily. Moreover, women and girls do not generally grow up learning how to fight; instead we learn to be self-sacrificing, passive, and nurturing creatures.[13] Many women grow up learning that the varying degrees of violence that they receive daily—psychological, symbolic, and physical—are what they deserve as women. Self-abnegation is just part of the fallout of this cultural dynamic. Listening carefully to Weil, I'm interested in the ways that self-violence shuts down our ability to engage as thoughtful and thought-provoking participants in the struggles against injustice and toward a better world. What damage must it do to our efforts to engage ethically, politically, and pedagogically in the world?

Obviously, women as well as men continue to be thrilled by the desire for truth and to engage the questions that come. And, in spite of our socialization, women are clearly not immune to the desire for power that lurks in the shadows of this work and the resulting relations we create with others. But, though I continue to be critically interested in the specificity of women's lives, these contradictory desires generate problems that also exceed the boundaries of gender.

ON PEDAGOGY AND EDUCATION

Is there really an ego? Perhaps it is a conventional way of saying something about this desire for power and all the effects produced as we use language, as we try to say something about ourselves in this world. I'm not sure I understand desire yet. I do know what disappointment is, however. I have felt it in my gut. And I do know the joy that questions can bring. I have felt it down my spine and in my chest, a mixture of pride and surprise. Every teacher I know is familiar with this feeling. It's what makes teaching worth all the struggle and exhaustion. But schools and classrooms are not always places where questions and the desire for truth are nurtured and flourish.

Too many classrooms are places where the teacher is believed to be in the place of fullness or certainty, holding the answers, while the students struggle to prove themselves capable of attaining such heights. Or perhaps worse, students often simply stop caring, sinking into indifference about themselves or the world. Either way, the violence to self in these classrooms is too well known. The desire for recognition in this game is framed by hierarchical relations of power structured by the social relations of the school itself; it is caught in forms of domination that often lead to jealousy and other dangerous, even violent, effects. And as I have tried to demonstrate in this paper, too often our desire for power overcomes the will to truth, impeding the generative effects of pedagogy.

Even in so-called liberatory classrooms, "truth" is often seen to be had by some (the teachers) and not by others (the students), and liberation is seen as possible only when the students "get it," that is, the teacher or the school's version of the "truth."[14] Indoctrination and socialization are not education. Yet, too much of what we call "education" unfortunately falls into these categories, forcing students and teachers into modes of behavior and thought that often serve the interests of domination and existing power relations rather than promoting creative solutions to injustice.

I do not deny that a clear sense of purpose is necessary to teaching. Teachers, like writers, artists, or dancers, are in the business of communicating something to someone. Rather, I want to argue that the teaching-learning relation produces much more than what can be measured in the planned outcomes of our teaching efforts. Although teaching is always an intentional act, pedagogical relations have the power to create effects that escape intention, and these effects are what open the door to different visions and to new thoughts about the world. Both traditional and critical pedagogical approaches too often miss, deny, or ignore as errors or aberrations the fundamentally unpredictable, generative effects of pedagogy and hence the political, ethical, and aesthetic possibilities inherent in the teaching-learning relationship.

To care for the truth is to wait for the questions and perhaps to give them, but not as a matter of exchange. The care of the truth has nothing to exchange since it is a matter of accepting a moment of emptiness opened by a question, a space that forms the limits on our thought or a limit that gives form to our thought. This space, too often difficult to accept, is the condition for thinking itself. And also for teaching.

"Teachers with their students must learn to love the questions."[15] To learn to love the questions is really a matter of learning to learn, or better, learning to feel at ease in the uncertainty, even anxiety, brought on by the spaces opened up when one allows the questions to flutter into the open. But more than that, I believe learning to love the questions is a matter of beginning to feel at ease with a certain responsibility opened by the care of the truth. It is a responsibility governed by the necessity to choose, to make a decision, to struggle with the problem of value. And this is where the problem of ethics in education issues forth.

Standing at the edge of the unthought, even the unasked, and always the unsaid, is the moment of choosing. The choice is about what is "good," not as an *a priori* form waiting to be discovered but rather as something to be wrestled with and decided upon collectively. I mean that it is ultimately this question—what is the best way—that we are confronted with as members of any community. And it is this problem that students and teachers, too, must learn to love. No matter what we choose, the question of what is the best or right way will always come back, again and again in an infinite repetition. And though we can never finally answer, we must try. That's what it means to care.

To stand on this edge, *to endure it*, as Weil says, is an event, the ethical event of the question itself. I hear Heidegger, too: "The indefinability of Being does not eliminate the question of its meaning; it demands that we look that question in the face."[16]

If we stand, waiting on this edge, something happens: a question, an idea, a word that touches, stabs, caresses, burns—something to propel us toward an answer. If we turn away, we turn away from the care of the world and, ultimately, ironically, tragically, from care of ourselves. For me, to become educated is to attend to a kind of waiting. And this is precisely what it means for teachers and students to learn to love the questions.

To wait for the question is not to remain passive. Quite the contrary. It is to expend as much energy as possible in the attention to a problem. To push for the right word, even as none comes, or as too many flood our paper or our discussions with our students. It is to force our way up to the precipice, to that limit space—to wait for the question as that event that will again open us to some possible expressions, some ways to care.

That is the event that we must be worthy of—serene with. To choose and to choose again, even through all our errors, even through our most selfish or self-effacing moments. To wait for the question is to think; it is not a matter of knowing, or of certainty, or even of comfort, really. If we believe that a problem is simply a matter of overcoming uncertainty, we will be perpetually trapped in sadness and afflicted by the disappointing sense of failure. That is the ego's territory.

I know I need to say something more about education, perhaps specifically about teaching, but when I sit down to do it, I find that this "something more," eludes me. I take my dog to the park. We sit in the grass, with the sun on us. I think about Plato's sun, Deleuze's grass—two powerful metaphors for the truth. I think about the differences between these metaphors, their very different effects for thinking about thinking and about teaching. Plato's heights, Deleuze's surface; grass growing in whatever cracks open. That's a little like my sense of the constancy of questions; they spring up because of the cracks, the limit spaces in our words and our thinking.[17]

To teach is to bring our questions to others, to share as teacher and as students in this process of thinking about who we are on this earth. But that means, of course, facing the paradoxical space that circulates in our attempts to say or write or teach about this life and this earth, to face the constant and beautiful return of the question and our imperfection at answering. This means that teachers must learn to listen to and engage the questions posed by their students, even and perhaps especially when these questions are suprising or disconcerting, when they do not conform to preconceived expectations and goals. Yes, teachers *with* their students must learn to love the questions. That is the condition of education that we must be at peace with. It is indeed the condition for joy, for loving the world and ourselves as part of it. To be writing this now is a sort of pragmatics of such a love. We only have our analogies, our stories, our translations of the circumstances of our lives. And, as Michel Serres so passionately and tenderly writes: "Densely sown in the determinate, the possible accompanies us all through time. Without these temporal plateaus mixed with valleys, there would be no hope, no future; there would never be any change."[18]

I write this—and I teach—for the hope brought by the questions that spring from spaces between my writing and the grass, and for those with whom I'd like to share the wonder of green.

NOTES

1. John Brenkman, *Straight Male Modern: A Cultural Critique of Psychoanalysis* (New York: Routledge, 1993), 164.
2. Gilles Deleuze, *The Logic of Sense* (New York: Columbia University Press, 1990), 56.
3. I take this phrase and much of my thinking about the "me" from Jacques Derrida: "The ear of the other says me to me and constitutes the autos of my autobiography." Derrida, *The Ear of the Other: Otobiography, Transference, Translation*, ed. Christie McDonald and trans. Peggy Kamuf (Lincoln: University of Nebraska Press, 1985), 51.
4. Ibid., 88.
5. Simone Weil, *Lectures on Philosophy* (Cambridge: Cambridge University Press, 1979), 90.

6. I take this reference from Deleuze's analysis of Lewis Carroll's *Alice in Wonderland* in *The Logic of Sense*, 41.

7. Gilles Deleuze and Felix Guattari, *A Thousand Plateaus* (Minneapolis: University of Minnesota Press, 1987).

8. Ibid., 77.

9. Michel Serres, "Knowledge in the Classical Age: LaFontaine and Descartes," in *Hermes: Literature, Science, Philosophy*, ed. Josue V. Harari and David F. Bell (Baltimore: Johns Hopkins University Press, 1982), 15–28. See also Serres, *Detachment* (Athens: Ohio University Press 1989).

10. René Girard, *Violence and the Sacred* (Baltimore: Johns Hopkins University Press, 1977), 149–50.

11. Weil, *Lectures*, 196.

12. Deleuze and Guattari, *A Thousand Plateaus*, 35.

13. Recent research on adolescent girls bears this out. See, for example, Lyn Michael Brown and Carol Gilligan, *Meeting at the Crossroads: Women's Psychology and Girls' Development* (Cambridge: Harvard University Press, 1992); Mary Bray Pipher, *Reviving Ophelia: Saving the Selves of Adolescent Girls* (New York: Putnam, 1994); and Valerie Walkerdine, *Schoolgirl Fictions* (London: Verso, 1990).

14. Jennifer Gore has written extensively about the "regimes of truth" operating in some forms of critical and feminist pedagogies. See her, *The Struggle for Pedagogies: Critical and Feminist Pedagogies as Regimes of Truth* (New York: Routledge, 1993).

15. Maxine Greene, *Landscapes of Learning* (New York: Teachers College Press, 1976), 145.

16. Martin Heiddeger, *Being and Time* (San Francisco: Harper and Row, 1962), 23.

17. See Gilles Deleuze and Claire Parnet, *Dialogues*, trans. Hugh Tomlinson and Barbara Habberjam (New York: Columbia University Press, 1987).

18. Michel Serres, *Rome: The Book of Foundations* (Palo Alto: Stanford University Press, 1991), 47.

Part 3

Desire and Voice

5

Knowledge as Bait

Feminism, Voice, and the Pedagogical Unconscious

LAURIE FINKE

Education, as Paulo Freire has pointed out, is never a neutral process. Either it facilitates "the integration of the younger generation into the logic of the present system," thereby encouraging students to internalize its values, or it becomes a "practice of freedom" and a means of enabling them to participate in the transformation of that system (1968, 15; see also Davis 1990). For the last two decades, feminist teachers committed to creating a feminist education that would also be a "practice of freedom" for students, especially for women, have attempted to promote more egalitarian classrooms responsive not only to differences of gender but also to those of class, race, sexual preference, ethnicity, and age. Crucial to this goal of developing new pedagogies that are participatory, experiential, and nonhierarchical—a goal shared with those practicing "liberatory," "oppositional," or "radical" pedagogies—have been concepts like "empowerment," "student voice," "dialogue," and "critical thinking." Under these various labels, however, efforts by both feminist and radical teachers to promote nonauthoritarian classroom environments have often ended up mystifying the very forms of authority they sought to exorcise, authority that is both institutionally and psychically embedded in the social relations of education. This has happened because the social relations inherent in education cannot so easily be reduced to a simple dichotomy between conformity and resistance. Indeed, that dialectic continually founders on the rocks of such anxiety-producing paradoxes as the feminist teacher who attempts to subvert the institution of education while participating in its unequal system of rewards and punishments, or the feminist student who tries to bring down the patriarchal system while maintaining a GPA high enough to get into graduate school, or even the nonfeminist student negotiating a graduation requirement. The social relations of education can be comprehended only within a complex network of intersecting oppositions that include not only conformity and resistance but also identification and rebellion, love and power; they must account not only for the vertical relations between teacher and student but also for the horizontal relationships among students.

Because they cannot articulate a pedagogical politics that is not simply oppositional, many feminists who write about pedagogy sometimes write as if they believe that the classroom is a universal and ahistorical space. Such critics often misrepresent the classroom, which, far from being universal and generic, is a local and particular space embedded within a specific institutional culture that serves a range of disciplinary and institutional objectives. To be sure, both feminists and other radical educators have already begun to examine the political shortcomings of pedagogies that strip students and teachers alike of their specific political investments in the name of "rational" analysis and "critical thinking" (Ellsworth 1988; Tetreaut and Maher, 1993; Penley 1986; and Treichler 1986). Although I do not wish to ignore the significance of these critiques, I want to explore the psychic investments that come into play in feminist classrooms that may be mystified by an unexamined commitment to egalitarian ideas about learning. In particular, I shall examine the ways in which all pedagogy—including feminist pedagogy—is driven by a psychic interplay of desire and power among teachers and students. Although I recognize that this analysis is not unique to feminist teaching and that many of its particulars are shared by other radical teachers, my interest is specifically in what *feminist* teachers say about their teaching and with the ways in which psychoanalytic thinking might enable feminist teachers to come to terms with the roles of power and authority in their own teaching. I assume feminist pedagogy does not exist in a vacuum. It interacts with, influences, and is influenced by other approaches to teaching. This essay is one instance of an attempt to bring feminist teaching into dialogue with other radical pedagogical practices—in particular with the practices of psychoanalysis. This is what I mean by the "pedagogical unconscious" that appears in my title, a term Gregory Jay has used to describe student resistance and ignorance not as a passive state—as an absence of information—but as an "active dynamic of negation" that effective teaching must engage (1987, 789). Such a concept, tied to a feminist political analysis of the social relations of gender, should enable a more complex vision than feminist pedagogy has allowed of classroom dynamics, which are inevitably as conflicted as nurturing, as competitive as collaborative, and as contradictory as complementary.

Ordinarily, we consider teaching as a public practice that operates consciously and rationally; psychoanalysis, in contrast, is a privatized practice that engages the unconscious. For this reason, the two might seem antithetical (Penley 1986, 131; Millot 1979; Emerson 1983, 255–57). Feminist pedagogy seems a particularly hostile ground for psychoanalytic thinking because it shares with the liberatory pedagogy of Paulo Freire the belief that once oppression is rationally exposed through a critical analysis that springs from the dialogue between student and teacher, it can be effectively resisted. Feminist pedagogies have their origins in the consciousness-raising movement of the 1960s and therefore would subscribe to Freire's formulation of humans as "conscious beings, and consciousness as consciousness intent upon the world" (1968, 66; see also Treichler 1986, 68–69). Such a formulation would seem to have little political use for a concept of the unconscious, for that which is unknowable to consciousness.

But this appeal to consciousness-raising cannot tell us why the student who can intelligently critique patriarchal institutions in a brilliant seminar paper can still suffer from date rape, domestic violence, or even an eating disorder. And even the most politically correct feminist can suffer a crisis of sexual identity. Feminist teachers, however total their commitment to theoretical analysis, can neither banish entirely nor fully illuminate the psychic life of their students because the classroom itself is part of the cultural matrix within which its participants' psyches have been produced. Both teachers and students are, at least in part, constituted by the masculinist discourses and practices they oppose and seek to demystify. Feminist pedagogy, then, must avoid reproducing a simplistic inside/outside dichotomy that locates oppression, anxiety, and resistance either exclusively within the individual, the result of psychic forces of which the individual is not consciously aware, or exclusively outside of the individual in the cultural and historical forces that act on her. The one approach privileges neurosis—hysteria in particular—and the other victimization (Rose 1989). The former calls for a psychoanalytic pedagogy, the latter for a political one. The task of a feminist pedagogy seems to demand some integration of both approaches.

By writing an essay on psychoanalysis and pedagogy, I do not wish to suggest that feminist pedagogy can or ought to be explained only in psychoanalytic terms or to set psychoanalysis up as a "master" narrative for pedagogy. Nor do I wish, however, to engage in any apologia for bringing these two practices "in conversation" with each other. Although I am aware of the potentially productive feminist resistance to psychoanalysis—a resistance that is always political—there is already a large body of literature on this resistance, including several anthologies, conference proceedings, and polemics (Bernheimer and Kahane, 1985; Feldstein and Roof, 1989; Garner, Kahane, and Sprengnether, 1985). The process of thinking through the relationship between psychoanalysis and feminist pedagogy is undoubtedly an anxious one. Having no previous commitments to psychoanalytic feminism, I feel caught between the often keen insights of psychoanalytic feminist critics, on the one hand, and the distrust, the often open hostility, of other feminist scholars (my own divided self included), on the other. The political situation that such competing theoretical approaches creates within feminism potentially reduces all feminists either to naive and unsophisticated "empiricists" or dutiful daughters mimicking the master discourse. In the final analysis, it seems to me that feminism cannot be content either with an apolitical theory or with an untheorized politics. The question that then poses itself concerning the relations between psychoanalysis and feminist pedagogy is not only how psychoanalysis might reveal the unconscious of feminist pedagogy but, equally important, how a feminist pedagogy might repoliticize psychoanalysis.

For this reason, I want to begin my investigation of the dialogue between psychoanalysis and feminist pedagogy by exploring a literal scene of teaching—women's teaching in the shadow of patriarchy—that appears in a very political play, Shakespeare's *Henry V*. This scene, which describes a particular kind of pedagogy, is marginal to the main plot of the play, undoubtedly included to create "comic relief." It follows immediately on Henry's victory against the French at Harfleur. In it, Katherine, the French princess who will later be married to Henry to cement a dynastic merger between the English and French, learns some English from her lady-in-waiting. The "language lesson" is composed entirely in French.

> *Katherine:* Alice, tu es été en Angleterre, et tu parles bien le langage.
> *Alice:* Un peu, madame.
> *Katherine:* Je te prie m'enseigner; il faut que j'apprenne à parler. Comment appelez-vous la main en Anglais? (3.4 1–6)

The conscious, or rational, goal of this pedagogical exchange is to teach Katherine the language of her soon-to-be adopted country. This simple cognitive act posits a one-to-one correspondence between words and things in which signifiers can be exchanged between different languages while the signifieds remain unaffected by the exchange. *"La main"* can become "de hand," with no violence to the actual appendage.

The enunciation of this "language lesson," however, proves a more complex affair than the cognitive exchange of signifiers between teacher and student suggests. Ronald Schleifer defines enunciation as the "act of utterance, the performance of discourse," as opposed to the utterance or statement itself

(1987, 802). The exchange between Katherine and her lady-in-waiting is driven by conflicting articulations of power, desire, status, and resistance—not only those of the two characters in the scene but also of many others who are absent from it. "Teach it to me," Katherine says to her lady-in-waiting, "I *want* to learn it." But Katherine's desire reflects her acceptance of the realities of power and dynastic politics in the war between her father and her future husband. Katherine functions in the play as a token of exchange between the warring French and English monarchies, whose offspring presumably will unite the two realms and end their warfare (Henry VI, "in infant bands crowned King / of France and England"). As Alice proceeds to teach Katherine several words of English, we notice that the words she asks to have translated are all parts of her body: hands, fingers, nails, arm, elbow, neck, chin, and foot. As the scene progresses, what Katherine "learns" from her "language lesson" is far more than the English equivalents of French words. She also learns how the female body is constructed and deployed in the aristocratic and militaristic culture of "chivalry." She learns this not through the agency of the lady-in-waiting, the ostensible "teacher" in this transaction, but through the desires of those men who, although not actually present in the scene, establish the conditions of its enacting. In effect, the lesson has a subconscious; both Katherine and her lady-in-waiting have internalized the desires of others. Katherine is "schooled"—by another woman who is her social subordinate— to define herself as a body, an object of sexual exchange in the feudo-dynastic politics of late medieval—and Renaissance—England.

At the same time, Katherine resists both the conscious and the unconscious "lessons"—resists, that is, the desires both of those present and of those absent—by punning on French-English homonyms. In using the term "resistance," let me be clear that I am not speaking of conscious and effective political resistance that I might urge feminists to adopt as an agenda for change. What I mean is that Katherine plays the "student," adopting a position of resistance and ignorance that both Felman and Jay attribute to the pedagogical unconscious (Felman 1982; Jay 1987). Engaging this resistance, they argue, is crucial to any true pedagogical practice informed by psychoanalytic insight. Katherine mistakes the English "elbow" for the French *bilbow*, or sword, and the English "nail" for the French *mail*, mimicking (unconsciously?) the militaristic language that dominates the play but that is especially prominent in the preceding scene depicting Henry's siege of Harfleur (3.4. 29, 45). She also mistakes the English "foot" and "gown" for the French *foutre* and *con*, setting up an obscene pun that even late twentieth-century editions of Shakespeare refuse to gloss: "'Le foot' et 'le count'! O Seigneur Dieu! ils sont mots de son mauvais, corruptible, gros et impudique, et non pour les dames d'honneur d'user: je ne voudrais prononcer ces mots devant les seigneurs de France pour tout le monde. Foh! 'le foot' et 'le count'!" (3.4. 52–56). These obscene puns that she would refuse to speak in public, before *les seigneurs,* suggest her perhaps unconscious resistance to being reduced to a "good fuck" or a "cunt." This scene, then, subtly defines and limits Katherine's role within the play's politics, at the same time that it offers a mode of resistance—the slippage in and between languages—to its cultural and political imperialism. Although Katherine's "resistance" is contained by the play and the final courting scene covers over the slippages between the French and English languages, this scene provides a moment through which we might tease out a potential feminist politics of psychoanalysis.

In this scene, Katherine's unconscious desires, manifested in lapses of speech and in wordplay (see Freud 1960), are shaped by and in resistance to the political and social concerns of the Renaissance aristocracy within which individuals are gendered. In *Henry V,* the individual psyche and the social world are never seen in isolation from each other; the play discourages the separation of the individual and the social so central to the philosophy of liberal individualism. What complicates both feminist and psychoanalytic critiques of pedagogy is the liberal/Enlightenment concept of the individual embedded within the philosophies of education, psychoanalysis, and liberal feminism. All tend to conceive of the "individual" in opposition to the "social," so that consciousness, or the "psyche," is constructed as individual, whereas ideology, conceived of as false consciousness, operates in the realm of the social, particularly the political. The operations of the psyche and politics end up opposing one another rather than emerging in dialogic relation. The feminist critique of psychoanalysis asserts that psychoanalytic discourse explains ideology and history only in terms of universalized and static psychic formations (Smith 1989, 84–85). Implicit, if undeveloped, in the rereading of Freud by Lacan, however, is some recognition of the complex interrelationships between the individual and the social, the psychic and political. If, as Lacan has argued, the psyche is organized as a language, then, like a language, it must be a social process explained in terms of ideology, conceived not simply as false consciousness but in Althusserian terms as those lived practices, meanings, and values that effectively ensure the maintenance and reproduction of social power. In an effectively politicized feminist psychoanalysis, the individual woman's psyche must be construed as a social and ideological process, constituted by and within language and culture and not by some kind of privatized interiority. "Raising" her consciousness is not simply a matter of translating isolated private and prelinguistic experiences into discourse but of negotiating the ways in which she, like Katherine, is culturally and ideologically embedded in history. Both consciousness and the unconscious are processes, the ongoing productions of an internalized ideology in Western society of "individuality," which is itself an ideologically delimited and unstable sign.

Despite what it has to tell us about the relationships between the individual and her social environment, however, the "language lesson" in *Henry V* stands as a model against which a feminist pedagogy would want to define itself. Katherine merely parrots the list of words and sounds she has been "given"; her resistance to its conscious and unconscious agendas can be registered only through the subversion of mimicry. As I suggested earlier, it hardly constitutes an effective political resistance. Most feminist teachers, when they talk about teaching, speak of a desire to "empower" the learner to tell her own stories rather than ventriloquizing those of the dominant and masculinist culture. Even more specifically, they seek to give "voice" to those who have been silenced and alienated by traditional pedagogical practices that privilege hierarchy, authority, "rigor" (mortis), and exclusivity and that value abstract and rational knowledge over subjective and experiential knowledge.

The authors of *Women's Ways of Knowing* testify to the persistence of "voice" among the female students they interviewed as a powerful metaphor to describe learning experiences that contrasts with the metaphors of vision traditional pedagogies employ to describe cognition.

> What we had not anticipated was that "voice" was more than an academic shorthand for a person's point of view. Well after we were into our interviews with women, we became aware that it is a metaphor that can apply to many aspects of women's experience and development. In describing their lives women commonly talked about voice and silence: "speaking up," "speaking out," "being silenced," "not being heard," "really listening," "really talking," "words as weapons," "feeling deaf and dumb," "having no words," "saying what you mean," "listening to be heard," and so on in an endless variety of connotations all having to do with sense of mind, self-worth, and feelings of isolation from or connection to others. We found that women repeatedly used the metaphor of voice to depict their intellectual and ethical development; and that the development of a sense of voice, mind, and self were intricately intertwined. (Belenky et al. 1986, 18)

Yet despite the prominence of the metaphor "voice" within feminist pedagogy (see also Tetreaut and Maher 1993), it remains an elusive concept. We assume we know what we mean when we say we want our students to discover their own "voice," and the term itself becomes a kind of mantra we chant. But as an unexamined assumption, the metaphor of voice repeats Katherine's language lesson in *Henry V*, tying feminist pedagogy to an essentially female body. Yet even a moment's reflection on the voice as a physical attribute might serve to undermine the self-evident nature of the metaphor. When we hear our voices mechanically reproduced on a tape recorder, the experience is alienating. Frequently, we deny that they sound at all "like" our own voices; we might even deny altogether that they are ours, as my son did when at six years of age he heard his voice recorded for the first time. Furthermore, that "voice" that was once located in a body is now detached from it and infinitely reproducible, a simulacrum or copy without an original bodily presence to authorize it. Technologies such as the tape recording and the microphone that "supplement" the human voice may serve as examples of what Donna Haraway has called a "cyborg," that hybrid of machine and organism that calls into question the purity of the boundaries we have erected to hold chaos at bay, including the boundaries between self and other, human and machine, speaking and writing (1985). The interrogation of such boundaries may enable us to explore the peculiar forms of resistance feminist pedagogies have marginalized or missed altogether.

The metaphor of voice grounds feminist pedagogy in the (female) body and in an essentialist notion of a core "self," which produces language or "voice" manufactured out of "experiences." This "self" is assumed to precede social life so that the detrimental effects of a patriarchal society on the individual are correctable once adjustments have been made to release the "voice" that will speak for the "self." Yet all of these terms—"self," "voice," "experience"—have been placed under erasure by poststructuralist semiotics and by Lacanian psychoanalysis, which define these concepts in terms of their radical discursivity. The "self" that can have a voice is not independent and preexistent; it is fashioned out of the discursive and semiotic practices of patriarchy within and against which the gendered self fashions its "identity" (de Lauretis 1987). In this respect, the process feminist pedagogy seeks to describe is not the student's discovering a voice that is already there but her fashioning one from the discursive environment through and in which the feminist subject emerges. The difference may seem subtle, but it is crucial to a theoretical understanding of a feminist pedagogy of voice. Pedagogy attempts to intervene in the ongoing processes by which the subject is fashioned and to propel that fashioning in a particular direction. Feminist pedagogy as a "practice of freedom" attempts to fashion a female subject who is "empowered" to participate in the transformation of her world. But before we can consider what that might mean in pedagogic practice, we must consider what we mean by the "subject."

Poststructuralist analysis, particularly that dependent upon the works of

Lacan, replaces terms like "self" or "individual"—with their connotations of autonomy and unity—with the term "subject," which more fully captures the sense of subjection, of the self's fashioning by its insertion into an already articulated symbolic economy. What, I think, prevents this concept from becoming totalitarian (the subject is completely subjected to forces outside of her control) or quietistic (the subject can never do anything to alter or refashion herself) is that the subject is never fully complete; the subject is always in the process of being fashioned, always shifting and heterogeneous. As a result, this subject-in-process is always simultaneously a product and producer of the symbolic economy.

If poststructuralist semiotics is right in describing the formation of the subject as a discursive process, and if Lacanian psychoanalysis is correct in describing that subject as fundamentally heterogeneous, split, and not fully present or known to itself, then our very notion that what is significant about teaching is available for conscious, and rational analysis needs to be rethought. Pedagogy must also be characterized by some form of intervention in the "unconscious," by a dynamic interchange between the unconscious of both teacher and learner. It is crucial, though, to avoid the danger of reifying or mystifying the psychoanalytic "unconscious." After Lacan, the unconscious can no longer be seen as a "moral occult" (Brooks 1976, 202), nor is it a "reification of the human being" (Lacan 1982, 64). It is not a pre-existent entity any more than the "self" is. Like the conscious self, it is an effect of language, of enunciation. Lacan does away with the reified Freudian topography of ego, id, and superego and returns to Freud's earlier division between conscious and unconscious, attempting to describe a dynamic process by which the "self" comes into being—enters semiosis—through its interactions with the world: "Psychoanalysis can locate the unconscious, as Lacan does, not behind or below consciousness as an agent of impulses we do not recognize (but which is always susceptible to cognition), but rather inhabiting enunciation itself, a function, not a cause of discourse" (Schleifer 1987, 804). Since education is also a "function of discourse," such a view of the unconscious makes more plausible its appropriation as a critical term in a discussion of pedagogy.

What forms the unconscious—if we can talk about its having form at all— are the countless and innumerable pragmatic, semiotic, and linguistic "events" and cues we have encountered, internalized, and then forgotten but which form part of our production of language and meaning from infancy on. The process begins in infancy, in the infant's experience of her body in the premirror stage, which Lacan describes as laying down "letters," which are "the effects of touch, sound, the gaze, images, and so forth as they intermingle with sensory response" (Ragland-Sullivan 1986, 20). These "letters" operate as "local signifiers" that create and inform the unconscious. If the primary processes of the unconscious are laid down in infancy in these "letters," the process continues throughout the subject's lifetime and is crucial to understanding Lacan's notion of subjectivity as a culturally and linguistically mediated process. Lacan does not separate the conscious and the unconscious as rigorously as Freud does, although he recognizes them as distinct orders. Instead, in an effort to prevent the hypostasization of the unconscious, he introduces two new terms—the *moi* and the *je*—which mediate between the conscious and unconscious and prevent them from becoming reified concepts. "Subjects reconstitute themselves for each other . . . by exchanging ego (moi) through language (je) as symbols" (Ragland-Sullivan 1986, 43). The subject, then, is at once dual and contradictory; it is at the same time fixed and continually in play (calling upon both senses of that term). The unconscious simultaneously attributes "permanence, identity, and substantiality" to the subject and its objects and reveals the illusory nature of that unity in its "gaps, ambiguities, and scars" (Ragland-Sullivan 1986, 43).

The psychological growth and development of the individual is always thoroughly implicated in the social and, thus, in the ideological. "The process described as being 'assimilated' into culture . . . covers over a multiplicity of complex processes of reaction, resistance, subversion, acquiescence and acceptance" (Hodge and Kress 1988, 240). Outside of the family, the educational system is the primary "state apparatus" or "disciplinary mechanism" through which such assimilation takes place. In a chapter of *Social Semiotics* entitled "Entering Semiosis: Training Subjects for Culture," Robert Hodge and Gunther Kress attempt to describe a very small portion of this "assimilation"— both cognitive and psychological—that contributes to the formation of an unconscious in teaching of all kinds: in the informal exchanges between a mother and a toddler, in a nursery school "discussion," and in an elementary school "report." Teaching, then, I would argue, not only engages the unconscious but is implicated in the very formation of the unconscious itself. The unconscious constitutes what Shoshana Felman has called "a kind of *unmeant knowledge* which escapes intentionality and meaning, a knowledge which is spoken by the language of the subject (spoken, for instance, by his [sic] slips or by his [sic] dreams), but which the subject cannot recognize, assume as *his* [sic]" and thus appropriate (1982, 28). To agree with this statement is not to privilege the unconscious as some realm of freedom from authority. On the contrary, it is to engage with that authority precisely where it is the most effective because the least calculated.

This unmeant knowledge, spoken but recognized, suggests that knowledge, like the subject, is also fundamentally split and heterogeneous. Feminist pedagogies have recognized intuitively that traditional pedagogical strategies cannot "get at" this "unmeant knowledge," but they have been unable to theorize the consequences, to engage that unmeant knowledge and use it as a "practice of freedom" by interrogating the realm of their own authority. In practical terms, they have been unable to develop strategies to teach to such a conception of "unmeant" knowledge. Traditional pedagogy speaks of an exchange of information between conscious and rational egos. The teacher who has mastered a particular "field" of knowledge transmits that knowledge to students. This is the kind of teaching Freire describes with his metaphor of "banking," an educational practice in which deposits of knowledge are made in students by the teacher (1968). This transmission implies certain practices—the lecture, the Socratic dialogue, the exam, even the research paper—all of which function to manage the flow of information as a bank manages the flow of currency and all of which, despite our protests to the contrary, are still very much current teaching practice in most colleges and universities. Although teaching methods have doubtless advanced greatly over the days of the lecture and recitation, outside of the composition classroom (and most of our students spend much more time outside of it than in it) and in classrooms with anywhere from forty to one hundred students, we still primarily manage students by monitoring their exams and papers to make sure they have absorbed particular information, concepts, and skills. We do this not necessarily by choice, but because we play a role within an institution. In this institution, knowledge is conceived of as finite, so the method of transmission should be linear, temporal, continuous, and progressive (numbered sequences of courses, distribution requirements, and "capstone" courses are just a few of the practices that instantiate this concept of knowledge). Both students and teachers are universalized; the method is the same, whatever the historical moment, location, institution, discipline, or the gender, race, or class of the participants (see Graff 1987). But such practices quite often fail students (in both senses of the term) not simply because they are oppressive but because they deny what Felman calls the "irreducibility of knowledge." "Human knowledge," she writes, "is, by definition, that which is untotalizing, that which rules out any possibility of totalizing what it knows or of eradicating its own ignorance" (1982, 29). Such a conception of knowledge as always unmasterable requires a mode of teaching, a practice that, much like the analytic situation, proceeds not progressively through time but through resistance and "through breakthroughs, leaps, discontinuities, regressions, and deferred action" (1982, 27).

The practical consequence of this discontinuous view of learning is to return us to the question of voice from a new direction. We may ask ourselves, as feminist teachers, what we mean when we ask our students to "discover" their own voice. In my experience, we often do not mean what our students assume we mean. Surely we do not want them to spout whatever comes into their heads. So when they take us at our word, we are often frustrated by their failure to meet our (often unstated) expectations, and they are angry at our refusal to validate their "experience" and to respect their "voice." At some time we have all been puzzled and hurt by such resistance. To understand it, we need to be honest enough to realize that, as feminists, we want our students to fashion a particular kind of voice that corresponds to our own desires as teachers, that which have been authorized by the discursive practices of our disciplines and fields: English, anthropology, history, and more specifically, feminism. To be sure, we might suggest something like "freewriting"as an heuristic strategy. Just as the free associations of the analysand provide the interpretive material for the analyst's hermeneutic method, so the student's first thoughts on a subject will subsequently be shaped by the interactions between teacher and student into a standard disciplinary "narrative." We certainly do not want our students merely to parrot us, to mimic our words mindlessly. However, in feminist classrooms, we tend to privilege certain kinds of "personal" or "experiential" disclosures over others, and we are not satisfied simply to allow students to recount their experience without theorizing how that experience is woven into the fabric of patriarchal social relations, without understanding the ways in which their experience fits into a critique of patriarchy.

To understand more fully the ways in which we, as feminist teachers, desire "voice" for our students, we must assess the relationship between teacher and student. While recognizing that the classroom creates a complex network of both hierarchical and horizontal relationships, both between teacher and students and among students, I have chosen to focus on what follows primarily on the teacher-student dyad because it seems most amenable to a psychoanalytic method. One stratagem by which feminist teachers have attempted to create more egalitarian classrooms is by relinquishing the teacher's traditional position of "mastery." Thus, Janet Robyns writes:

> [Feminist teachers] were not set up as knowers among a group of non-knowers. They were more like part time assistants. They helped as much as they could by giving information about their experiences. . . . The "teacher" did not remain the same person. In sharing our knowledge, our thoughts and experiences, the "teacher" rotated among us. Each functioned as teacher at times because each had something to offer. There was no knower/nonknower, judge/judged hierarchy. (cited in Treichler 1986, 53)

The problem, as Paula Treichler and Constance Penley have pointed out, is that such attempts to eliminate authority serve only to mystify "the hierarchical distribution of power embodied by the university's institutional structure" (Treichler 1986, 71; Penley 1986, 138). The strategy may have been more or less successful during a time when feminist teachers were themselves in precarious and vulnerable positions within the academy, when many were untenured or adjunct faculty. But as feminist teachers have achieved status within the academy, as they get tenure and full-professor status, the fiction of the teacherless classroom becomes harder to maintain. Regardless of our attempts to decenter our authority, as teachers, we must evaluate our students and must do so from the position of a "subject-supposed-to-know." The cultural and institutional structures that dictate power relations between teachers and students are replicated in the psychic life of the students in any college classroom. Our students, who have, after all, already endured a minimum of twelve years of formal classroom education, attribute knowledge and mastery to their teachers whether the teachers accept or relinquish this authority. Students enter the classroom believing that the teacher knows the "right" answer; her refusal to reveal that answer—and feminist teachers quite often claim that they have no "right" answers—can and often does cause more distress than empowerment. Like the analyst, the teacher is the "subject-supposed-to-know."

Students' positing of mastery and knowledge in an "other" creates the effect psychoanalysts call "transference": "As soon as there is somewhere a subject presumed to know, there is transference" (Lacan, cited in Felman 1982, 35). As Robert Con Davis has argued, this transference has consequences for, and indeed defines, the relationship between teacher and student.

> The teacher subject to this transference can still legitimately teach but does so as an imaginary projection, presenting knowledge as a kind of bait (promising everything) that lures the student into the recognition of the unconscious discourse they both articulate so that, ideally, as the instruction succeeds, the student will find a place from which to produce (rather than merely repeat) language. The student in this Freudian model marks the site of the continual possibility of speech, of discourse—initially a suppressed articulation in someone else's language but eventually a site of language with its own relation to the unconscious. (1987, 752)

That an account of transference is psychoanalysis' most significant contribution to pedagogy is hardly a new insight; it has been made by Felman, Penley, Jay and many others. But it strikes me that Davis's description of the student's attempts to find a place from which to produce language may provide a starting point from which feminist teachers may begin to articulate more fully what we mean by "voice." An analysis of transference may enable us to unpack the workings of authority—both real and imagined—in the classroom by moving our attention away from the content of teaching—the exchange of signifieds—and toward the dramas of identification and resistance that accompany the exchange of signifiers.

In the case study in which he first introduced the term, Freud maintained that he failed to complete Dora's analysis because he "did not succeed in mastering the transference in good time" (1963, 140). She remained silenced, a hysteric all her life, unable to find a place from which she could produce rather than merely repeat language (one of the symptoms from which Dora suffered was aphonia—an occasional loss of voice). I would like to suggest that what feminists mean when invoking the concept of "voice" might more accurately be described as the successful mastering of a transference. My choice of the term "mastering," no doubt distasteful to many other feminists, enables me to call attention to the necessary inequity of transference relationships. Lacan writes that "transference is love . . . it is love directed toward, addressed to, knowledge" (cited in Felman 1982, 35). But that love—which Freud argued is originally the love for the parent that is successively transferred to other objects, to teachers or the analyst, for instance—is possible only within a highly unequal relationship; it inevitably involves power, inevitably creates a relationship of imagined mastery and simultaneous identification with, and resistance toward, that mastery. Even as she rejects the role, then, the feminist teacher will be cast as the "subject-supposed-to-know" by the student. The relationship between teacher and student, then, can be no more equal than the relationship between mother and child so valued by many feminists. An analysis of transference will necessarily be an analysis of the power relationships involved in teaching. This inequality—the student's position of ignorance and resistance, the teacher's position of supposed knowledge and mastery—is the "bait" that sets off a process of discovery leading to "a place from which [the student can] produce (rather than merely repeat) language," or to what Belenky et al. refer to as "voice."

At the same time, I wonder whether it is really only the teacher—to whom the student certainly attributes mastery—who masters the transference. Or is the teacher's role as "subject-supposed-to-know" at least in part imaginary and, therefore, as Davis suggests, a "bait" that "lures" the student into "a recognition of the unconscious discourse they both share?" Lacan's rereading of transference in "Intervention on Transference" encourages just this sort of ambiguity. "What, therefore, is meant by interpreting the transference?" he asks. "Nothing other than a ruse to fill in the emptiness of [a] deadlock. But while it may be deceptive, this ruse serves a purpose by setting off the whole process again" (1982, 71). The slippage between Freud's "mastering" and Lacan's "interpreting" suggests something of the nature of Lacan's revision of Freud. The power relation involved is rendered more ambiguous—a "ruse" — directing attention away from the content of the relationship (mastery) to its discursive strategies (interpretation). The "end" of interpretation is less final than that of mastery. The analyst's (or teacher's) acts of interpretation are not the end of the lesson; they are its pretext. Like Katherine's language lesson in *Henry V*, this "ruse" or "bait" reminds us that teaching and the acquisition of knowledge cannot be comprehended merely as the straightforward exchange of information. That exchange is the bait that enables the student's ignorance and resistance to come into play as dynamic forces in the constitution of knowledge in the classroom.

The advantage of thinking of knowledge as "bait" is that it grants the student some agency in the acquisition of knowledge or in the discovery of a "site of language with its own relation to the unconscious." It is the power of the student's resistance that provides the opportunity for this discovery, which, as Felman suggests, calls into question the opposition between knowledge and ignorance and opens up the possibility for a more profound conception of learning. Resistance takes many forms in the classroom, some of which are encouraged and some of which are not. For instance, feminist teachers encourage and reward students' resistance to gender inequalities of all kinds. In a feminist classroom, that is a good form of resistance, one the teacher will attempt to fortify. And although they don't necessarily encourage it, feminist teachers also understand and cope more or less well with students' resistance to their authority as feminists and to feminism's knowledge and insights. Although this is perhaps a less acceptable form of resistance, it is one with which most feminist teachers have learned to cope. Because these forms of resistance in feminist classrooms are enacted primarily at the level of content, I will not deal with them in detail. Rather, I would like to examine one case of a resistance not always as openly acknowledged in feminist classrooms that stress the equality between teacher and students. In this case, the student resists being freed from the teacher's authority; her resistance takes the form of extreme identification that culminates in anger and frustration when that identification is resisted by the subject-supposed-to-know. I find this kind of resistance interesting because it directs our attention away from the content of teaching to its discursive strategies, enabling me to redirect talk about student "voice" to a discussion of how, through transference, a student may find a (provisional) place from which to produce, rather than merely repeat, language.

In my undergraduate feminist theory class, I have begun requiring students to keep a diary on their term projects as they research and write them. The purpose is to focus their attention as much on the process of theorizing as on its products—the theories themselves. This provides them with a space in which to monitor their own relation to the often alienating discourses of theory, which means, quite often, their relationship to the teacher, the subject-supposed-to-know theory. Usually I have a hard time convincing students (especially outside of composition classes) of the utility of writing something that has no direct relation to the writing on which they will be evaluated. Mostly, they tolerate it as busywork, and sometimes it is, but often such writing serves less to illuminate for them the conscious and rational process of writing than to create spaces in which they might glimpse some of the unconscious processes that accompany learning. These diaries have on occasion yielded some insights into the processes of transference I have been describing. For this reason, I would like to look at the diary of one student in a feminist theory class.

E. L. began feminist theory as a last-term senior, a student with a 3.77 GPA (she relates this in her diary), looking forward to graduate school, fully confident of her own sense of "self" and confident that she had found her own "voice." This confidence that she knows what is expected of her is reflected in her first entry, April 14:

> Ever since the first week of classes, when I discovered that I would be required to write a major term paper for each class, I have been searching for topics. I always have plenty of ideas and interests. My problem usually comes when I have to start narrowing the topics down so they will be doable in a few weeks [sic] time. I walk 5 miles a day by myself. This is usually when I kick around ideas in my head. Once I have an idea, I try to talk to someone about it. For me, it helps to extrovert my ideas and get feedback. I almost always learn as I speak.

Yet that confidence was much more fragile than either she or I suspected and was quickly shattered. The experience of writing a term paper for feminist theory created enormous psychic distress, frustration, anger, and resistance. Given her academic history, her difficulties took me by surprise. We struggled together throughout the term to see why she could not complete this paper as easily as others she had written. Her diary provides a record of that struggle. I do not claim that her situation is unique either to this class or to feminist classes. Most teachers will recognize in E. L. students of both sexes whom they have encountered (although in my experience this student is typically female). As I suggested earlier, students' resistance to being freed from authority may at times be as intense as their resistance to authority. I am interested in the particular forms E. L.'s resistance took and in the discursive strategies she used to express that resistance. Her difficulties seemed to be triggered by the supposedly nonauthoritarian context of my feminist classroom, in which I had relinquished certain forms of authority and mastery I ordinarily do not relinquish in other kinds of classes.

In her opening entry, E. L. reveals the first stage of Lacan's stages or "patterns" of psychoanalytic transference by identifying with the "teacher," suggesting, at this early stage, as Ragland-Sullivan notes, that "the emphasis is on likeness and the analyst [in this case the teacher] is perceived as a counterpart" (1987, 37). She assumes that her "ideas and interests," her desires, correspond to those of her teachers and that this correspondence gives her a kind of control or mastery over the process of writing.

E. L.'s reaction five days later to her own first exploratory efforts at producing feminist theory reveals the fragility of her own hard-won sense of identity, of control and mastery: "I think [the assignment to write an exploratory essay on the topic chosen for the term project] distracted me from my original idea. That is fine, I guess—but I don't like being confused. I like knowing what I am trying to say when I write. I don't think I knew what I was trying to say in that essay." This was to become a persistent theme in E. L.'s diary. The harder she pressed me to reveal "what kind of paper I wanted," the more unwilling or unable I was to tell her what she wanted to hear. I say this without complacency because it was both frustrating and embarrassing to realize that perhaps I didn't know myself what I wanted. In the analytic situation, as the ideal "subject-supposed-to-know" is revealed as an illusion, an "imaginary projection," there is a parallel "disintegration of the analysand's supposition of knowing." Ragland-Sullivan describes this process in the analysand as a disintegration of the self. Because the unified *moi* (the ideal ego) gives the subject a sense of "self-cohesion," "any unraveling of the strands that went into weaving that identity as a conviction of 'being' causes a debeing of being: a sense of fragmenting" (1987, 37).

That sense of unraveling, of fragmentation, occurs in the student as well, as she begins to discover a threat to her own very fragile sense of being and reacts to restore it. This position, which feels like a loss of identity, is distressing. E. L. begins to reveal this distress in the same entry: "I don't understand what kind of a paper the final draft is to be. Are we writing humanities-type papers, or social science papers, reviewing the literature, or making up our own theories?" Her growing sense of fragmentation reveals itself in her sense of the fragmentation of knowledge into "disciplines" and the lack of cohesiveness and connection among those disciplines, suggesting that somehow the skills required for writing a social-science paper are useless if one is supposed to be writing a "humanities-type paper" or "making up our own theories." It is as if each of these different "types" of writing requires a different voice and thus a different "self." E. L., then, defines her "self" in terms of Kantian divisions of knowlege, revealing the interplay between the social construction of knowledge and the social construction of the self.

E. L.'s distress reaches a peak with the evaluation of her rough draft. Hardly surprising, this is the point in the term at which students see the teacher not simply as a "part-time assistant," as Robyns suggests or as one who "nurtures" the students' ideas. She has to evaluate—judge—their work as well. At this moment, students most keenly feel the teacher's power. For students who have eagerly accepted as empowering the ideology of feminist egalitarianism—what Evelyn Keller and Helene Moglen call the "romance of women's culture"—this discovery can be painfully disillusioning (1987). As the entries for May 19 and June 1 suggest, E. L.'s frustrations were largely directed at me; I was both failing to validate her usual "voice" and failing to make available a knowledge she could consume:

> May 19: Well, I got my rough draft back. I don't know what kind of reaction I expected—but I was certainly surprised by your comments. Too smooth—read like a final exam. Hmm. Secretly that is quite a compliment. But I have spent a lot of time trying to figure you out and realize that that is not a compliment coming from you. A compliment is what you said about my exploratory essay: provocative. That is what I will aim for in my final draft.

> June 1: Today I talked w/ you in your office. I was in a stupor from staying up all night writing a rough draft of [another] term paper. I must say, it was much simpler than this project—but I did not learn even a fraction of what I am learning doing this.... I realize over and over how I totally write for other people. I know what [Professor C.] wants to hear and how he wants to hear it—so I do it. I have been trying to figure you out—but you are so different from other profs I've had ... you suggested that I start at the end where I thought it was falling apart and you thought it was just getting interesting. How funny.

These two entries begin to uncover the resistance being enacted in this relationship. I commented that her rough draft read like a final exam to suggest that this student repeats language but is anxious about producing it. This student, who thought she already had a "voice" but finds herself suddenly struggling, measures success by her ability to align herself in identification with the teacher. Her inability to fix me with a secure identity threatens her identity, resulting in her sense that things are "falling apart." To her credit, she does at least recognize that she is encountering a qualitatively different kind of learning than she has experienced in other classes. It is more painful because it exposes the fragility of her sense of self, but it is also more productive because it becomes the means by which she interrogates her own relationship to learning.

Ragland-Sullivan could be describing this student's experiences when she describes psychoanalytic transference:

> When the other (analyst) reflects an ideal unity—supports one's *moi* identifications—the narcissistic slope of the *moi* is gratified. When the ideal is shattered, the avatar of aggressiveness arises and shows itself in projected blame, disenchantment, intimations of fragmentation, and so forth. The goal of aggressiveness here is to protect the *moi* from perceiving the tenuous fragility of its own formation. . . . The insistence of the *moi* on retaining its (fictional) unity of individual perception constitutes what psychoanalysts call resistance. From another perspective, however, one might call this stubbornness a survival insistence. (38)

E. L. could feel confident of her identity and "voice" as long as she could stay within the boundaries of her previous experiences with teachers, as long as she was asked only to reproduce those forms of enunciation she had already mastered. I use the term "enunciation" rather than, say, "knowledge" because it seems to me that what is at stake in this case is not knowledge itself, but its signifiers. E. L. had no difficulty understanding the material she was reading; she was not resistant to feminist analysis. Her problem lay in what to do with that knowledge, with how to employ its signifiers beyond merely repeating them, a difficulty of enunciation. When she was asked to explore rhetorical situations that she had not mastered, when her ideal of learning was shaken, she produced what, for lack of a better term, we might call symptoms that included "blame, disenchantment, and intimations of fragmentation." E. L. thought of her difficulties in this assignment in relation to her assignments in another, more traditional class in which her usual repertoire of behaviors were adequate, and this supports my belief that her difficulties lie in the enunciatory, or performative, dimension of learning. At stake here, as Schleifer has argued in another context, is "not the transference of pre-existing feelings from one object to another . . . but the transference of *discursive strategies* from one situation to another" (1987, 805; emphasis mine).

In many students, such psychic fragmentation and distress often produces what I would call "rhetorical symptoms." This is not entirely surprising since the unconscious is "acted out on the surface of discourse" (Schleifer 1987, 804). Freud's hysterics quite often produced symptoms that manifested themselves in linguistic disorders. In the most celebrated case, that of Anna O., the German feminist Bertha Pappenheim who was analyzed by Freud's early collaborator Josef Breuer, Breuer describes the "deep-going functional disorganization of her speech." "She lost her command of grammar and syntax; she no longer conjugated verbs, and eventually she used only the infinitive, for the most part incorrectly formed from the weak past participle, and she omitted both the definite and indefinite article. In the process of time she became almost completely deprived of words" (Cited in Gay 1989, 64). Because the signifiers of knowledge in the academy are primarily written, it seems reasonable that its symptoms of distress, of ego fragmentation, which work on the "surface of discourse," would primarily be manifested in the rhetorical dimension of language, occuring on both the macrolevel, of written discourse—in organizational difficulties—and on the microlevel in such common writing errors as sentence fragments, fused sentences, comma splices, and indefinite pronoun reference. These "writing problems" are more productively thought of as "symptoms" manifesting themselves in enunciation—in the *je*—of the fragmentation of the self, of the *moi*, experienced by students who are in the process of discovering that the "enunciatory strategies" they had once understood as the "truth" are "linguistic strategies inhabited by unconscious desire, by another's desire" (Schleifer 1987, 812).

Curiously, E. L. felt she was losing control of her essay, falling apart—her choice of words is suggestive of her own sense of fragmentation—just as I thought she was glimpsing a locus from which to produce language. We wrestled with this illuminating point of resistance for almost a month. As late as June 5, the resistance was still strongly voiced in her diary; E. L.'s need for control was as great as ever. She could still write: "One thing that I have learned is that I can't do it. I can't sit down and start writing on one thing and end up somewhere else, not unless it is an unguided freewrite or something. I have just been trained too well." She wanted to be in control—of her writing, of her learning, of her life—whereas I wanted her to explore her need for control, which was ultimately what her essay, which ostensibly dealt with eating disorders, was about. To find a place from which she could produce rather than mimic language, E. L. had to situate herself in relation both to feminist and medical discourses on eating disorders. She wanted to resist the characterizations of eating disorders as symptoms produced by the excessive need for control because they posed a threat to her own desire for control and mastery. Yet she lacked any language to articulate that resistance until she was willing to interrogate that desire and her own relation to authority. E. L. also had to realize that her resistance was not simply psychological. It was also culturally produced. She had been "trained too well" to reproduce behavior that in other authoritarian situations had brought her success. She had been taught to desire control, a desire that enabled her to please other authoritative figures from whom she had learned. Her behavior had been adaptive, a "survival insistence."

The process of working through the resistance that her diary records lead E. L. to an understanding that goes beyond specific knowledge of feminist theory or eating disorders to the ways in which learning happens, to its enunciatory framework. The June 6 entry suggests that E. L. has found a place from which to produce language with its own relation to its subject: "I still have no idea if this paper is what you were looking for. I feel better about it than I did about my exploratory essay, and you liked that. I decided a couple of days ago that because I couldn't figure out [what] was being asked of me, I would simply write for myself. What a freeing feeling." This entry suggests that E. L.'s sense of fragmentation, her loss of identity, had been at least temporarily resolved. The process of working through her resistance to the task enabled her once more to reassert the tenuous and fragile coherence of her own subjectivity. To be sure, that assertion may ring a bit hollow, phrased as it is in her diary in the language of "voice" ("I will simply write for myself"). Both her paper and her diary suggest that she has found a "place from which to produce (rather than merely repeat) language." She could use the enunciatory strategies of feminist theory to express her dissatisfaction with both feminist and medical discourses on eating disorders rather than merely mimic their language.

Not all narratives of feminist teaching have such a happy ending. Many students remain stuck either in enunciatory strategies that limit them to mimicking the other's language, as with Katherine in *Henry V*, or in E. L.'s cognitive dissonance, in which the production of language itself becomes symptomatic of the gaps, holes, and scars in the illusory armour of the ego. I offer this case history not to suggest that the resistance E. L. exhibited can be avoided, because, as Felman argues, it is at the heart of any pedagogy worth the name, erasing the very opposition between ignorance and learning. E. L.'s diary—her articulation of her own resistance to writing feminist theory (which was not, I would add, a resistance to feminist theory itself)—provided me with a means of articulating what, as a feminist, I might mean by a student discovering her "voice." My discovery, I admit, was serendipitous, but in retrospect, it makes sense that an instrument designed to enable students to speak about their relation to the discourse of theory might reveal something about the transformation of their enunciatory strategies in relation to a subject-supposed-to-know. I offer this narrative in the hope that other feminist teachers might find in it a means to understand the disruption of the illusion of self necessary to any real knowledge. I do not pretend that it is the only pedagogical practice that could engage the student in such an analysis of transference or of the enunciatory dimension of teaching. There is no one orthodox approach to feminist pedagogy any more than there is a single orthodox approach to psychoanalysis. Feminist pedagogy as a practice is not static. Rather, like feminist or psychoanalytic theory, it is a contested ground, full of conflict and struggle, continually being renewed, recreated, and rethought in light of specific classroom practices—even in relation to such institutionalized discourses as psychoanalysis.

WORKS CITED

Belenky, Mary Field, Blythe McVicker Clinchy, Nancy Rule Goldberger, and Jill Mattuck Tarule. *Women's Ways of Knowing: The Development of Self, Voice, and Mind.* New York: Basic Books, 1986.

Bernheimer, Charles, and Claire Kahane, eds. *In Dora's Case: Freud—Hysteria—Feminism.* New York: Columbia University Press, 1985.

Brooks, Peter. *The Melodramatic Imagination.* New Haven: Yale University Press, 1976.

Davis, Robert Con. "A Manifesto for Oppositional Pedagogy: Freire, Bourdieu, Merod, and Graff." In *Reorientations*, edited by Henrickson and Morgan, 248–67. Urbana: University of Illinois Press, 1990.

———. "Pedagogy, Lacan, and the Freudian Subject." *College English* 49 (1987): 749–55.

de Lauretis, Teresa. *Technologies of Gender.* Bloomington: Indiana University Press, 1987.

Eagleton, Terry. *Literary Theory: An Introduction.* Minneapolis: University of Minnesota Press, 1983.

Ellsworth, Elizabeth. "Why Doesn't This Feel Empowering?: Working through the Repressive Myths of Critical Pedagogy." Paper presented at Tenth Conference on Curriculum Theory and Classroom Practice, 1988.

Emerson, Caryl. "The Outer Word and Inner Speech: Bakhtin, Vygotsky, and the Internalization of Language." *Critical Inquiry* 10 (1983): 245–64.

Feldstein, Richard, and Judith Roof, eds. *Feminism and Psychoanalysis.* Ithaca: Cornell University Press, 1989.

Felman, Shoshana. "Psychoanalysis and Education: Teaching Terminable and Interminable." *Yale French Studies* 63 (1982): 21–44. (Reprinted in this volume.)

Freire, Paulo. *Pedagogy of the Oppressed.* Translated by Myra Bergman Ramos. New York: Herder and Herder, 1968.

Freud, Sigmund. *Dora: An Analysis of a Case of Hysteria.* New York: Collier Books, 1963.

———. *Jokes and Their Relation to the Unconscious.* Translated by James Strachey. New York: Norton, 1960.

Garner, Shirley Nelson, Claire Kahane, and Madelon Sprengnether. *The (M)other Tongue: Essays in Feminist Psychoanalytic Interpretation.* Ithaca: Cornell University Press, 1985.

Gay, Peter, ed. *The Freud Reader.* New York: Norton, 1989.

Graff, Gerald. *Professing Literature: An Institutional History.* Chicago: University of Chicago Press, 1987.

Haraway, Donna. "A Manifesto for Cyborgs: Science, Technology, and Socialist Feminism in the 1980s." *Socialist Review* (1985): 65–107.

Hodge, Robert, and Gunther Kress. *Social Semiotics.* Ithaca: Cornell University Press, 1988.

Jay, Gregory S. "The Subject of Pedagogy: Lessons in Psychoanalysis and Politics." *College English* 49 (1987):785–800.

Keller, Evelyn Fox, and Helene Moglen. "Competition and Feminism: Conflicts for Academic Women." *Signs* 12 (1987): 493–511.

Lacan, Jacques. "Intervention on Transference." In Juliet Mitchell and Jacqueline Rose, eds., *Feminine Sexuality: Jacques Lacan and the école freudienne,* 62–73. New York: Norton, 1982.

———. *Four Fundamental Concepts of Psychoanalysis.* Jacques-Alain Miller, ed., Alan Sheridan, trans. New York: Norton, 1978.

Millot, Catherine. *Freud, Anti-Pedagogue.* Paris: Editions du Seuil, 1979.

Moi, Toril. *The Kristeva Reader.* New York: Columbia University Press, 1986.

Penley, Constance. "Teaching in Your Sleep: Feminism and Psychoanalysis." In *Theory in the Classroom,* edited by Cary Nelson, 129–48. University of Illinois Press, 1986.

Ragland-Sullivan, Ellie. *Jacques Lacan and the Philosophy of Psychoanalysis.* Urbana: University of Illinois Press, 1986.

Rose, Jacqueline. "Where Does the Misery Come From? Psychoanalysis, Feminism, and the Event." In *Feminism and Psychoanalysis,* edited by Richard Feldstein and Judith Roof, 25–39. Ithaca: Cornell University Press, 1989.

Schleifer, Ronald. "Lacan's Enunciation and the Cure of Mortality: Teaching, Transference, and Desire." *College English* 49 (1987): 801–15.

Shakespeare, William. *Henry V.* In *The Riverside Shakespeare.* Boston: Houghton Mifflin, 1974.

Smith, Paul. "Julia Kristeva et al.; or, Take Three More." In *Feminism and Psychoanalysis,* edited by Richard Feldstein and Judith Roof, 84–104. Ithaca: Cornell University Press, 1989.

Tetreaut, Mary Kay, and Francis Maher. "Doing Feminist Ethnography: Lessons from Feminist Classrooms." *International Journal of Qualitative Studies* 6 (1993).

Treichler, Paula A. "Teaching Feminist Theory." In *Theory in the Classroom,* edited by Cary Nelson, 57–128. Urbana: University of Illinois Press, 1986.

Volosinov, V. N., M. M. Bakhtin. *Freudianism: A Critical Sketch.* Translated by I. R. Titunik. Bloomington: Indiana University Press, 1976.

———. *Marxism and the Philosophy of Language.* Translated by Ladislav Matjeka and I. R. Titunik. Cambridge: Harvard University Press, 1973.

6

Disturbing Identity and Desire

Adolescent Girls and Wild Words

HELEN HARPER

It was hard to leave that country, that clean land. Hard to find a way into the
impure, no longer so clearly centred, confusing modern world. Hard to find words
for this wild journey. Hard to become a writer, committing perjury all the time
against the sacred Book. Letting the wildness into the words. Transgressing,
remembering the old fear. Listening to the earth and the women, breathless with
desire, wanting so much the dance and the laughter, the unholy babble of speech.

—Di Brant, *(f)Lip*

This paper explores female adolescent identity and desire and the "unholy
babble of speech" that constitutes feminist avant-garde writing. Specifically,
this paper examines the nature and workings of desire and identification, their
meaning and significance for young women and for the project of feminist
pedagogy more generally. In this, I draw on a study of six seventeen-year-old
high-school girls who were given an opportunity to transgress conventional
school writing practices—to let wildness into their words—using as support
feminist avant-garde literature.[1] What became apparent in this study was that
to read and produce "wild words" using feminist literature was not an easy
task. For the young women in this study, an encounter with feminist avant-
garde writing greatly disturbed the intellectual and emotional structures that
supported their current and more familiar notions of self. The disturbing or
unsettling moments brought about by "wild words" exposed much about
desire and identification for adolescent girls and the limits of a feminist pedagogy that, at its peril, might ignore these processes.

The act of disturbing taken-for-granted assumptions and conventional
practices of society in order to say and "be" what has previously been
unsayable and unthinkable lies at the heart of feminist avant-garde writing

and feminist pedagogy. Such action is informed by a larger project of challenging the processes by which gender as a social and discursive construct, together with other constructs (e.g., race, class, ethnicity), shape and limit the range of identities possible for women. Effective intervention into these processes is dependent on understanding and challenging the social organization of gender identity as well as the intellectual and emotional scaffolding that psychologically supports and limits who one can be and who one wishes to be. What has become increasingly clear is that desire and identification are key to this scaffolding, that is, to the structuring of identity. It is argued from the perspective of psychoanalytic theory that who one wishes to be (identification) and who one wishes to have (desire) organize a play of difference and similitude in self-other relations that define or mark boundaries of recognizable identity.[2] The sharp edges of similitude and difference, of wanting or not, form boundaries that provide a necessary, if provisional, sense of self from which actions are directed. However, the delineation of a self can be limiting in that it demands the exclusion or expulsion of the other possibilities. For example, in the binaries of Western thought, femininity has been organized to include emotionality and to exclude rationality.

The key question for feminist educators is, what forms of pedagogical intervention disturb, the conventional play of similitude and difference in order to break open the range of identities possible? In other words, how do we intervene effectively, acknowledging and utilizing the power of identification and desire, in a project of social and personal transformation? For those who work with female adolescents, the question is, what pedagogical intervention might best serve young women now and later as adults? This is similar to a more general comment by Anna Freud, who suggested that what we most need to know is "which type of adolescent upheaval is best suited to leading to the most satisfactory type of adult life."[3]

As described by Anna Freud, adolescence is a time of upheaval: a time of "developmental disturbance" during which changes in the instinctual drives due to internal and external circumstances disrupt the mental equilibrium achieved in childhood.[4] For the adolescent, the increase in sexual drive and the shift from pregenital to genital sexual impulses runs the risk, in light of the incest taboo, of connecting with the former love objects of childhood, specifically, with parents and siblings. This places tremendous stress on ego defenses. The result is an increase in psychic activity: more repressions, reaction formations, identifications and projections, and more attempts at intellectualization and sublimation. As Freud sees it, the adolescent must, in some form, step away from the family and find substitutes not only for his or her parents but for the ideals that he or she formerly shared with them. Identification, as an act of substitution is key to this process. Identification, as Diana Fuss has described, is a process of substitution and displacement: an ordinary process of "installing surrogate others to fill the void where we imagine love objects to have been . . . a routine, habitual compensation for the everyday loss of our love-objects."[5] Identification, then, is a sign of trauma created by a loss of human relatedness. In the case of adolescents, the loss of connection with parents and the search for substitutes suggests that intense identification may be a central feature of adolescent experience.

For the female adolescent, the rupture between childhood and adolescence involves not only a loss of the connection with one's parents but also a loss or problem of connection with Western culture more generally. Carol Gilligan, in her 1989 study of girls' psychological development, describes this:

> Perhaps adolescence is an especially critical time in women's development because it poses a problem of connection that is not easily resolved. As the river of a girl's life flows in to the sea of Western culture she is in danger of drowning or disappearing. To take on the problem of appearance, which is the problem of her development, and to connect her life with history on a cultural scale, she must enter—and by entering disrupt—a tradition in which "human" has for the most part meant "male." Thus a struggle often breaks out in girls' lives at the edge of adolescence, and the fate of this struggle becomes key to girls' development and to Western civilization.[6]

Young women, indeed all women, particularly those further marginalized by race, class, and ethnicity, must struggle to keep from disappearing in Western culture, from having no identity or, as suggested by Luce Irigaray, from identifying with absence.[7] Language is implicated in this struggle. Drawing on the work of Jacques Lacan, Cora Kaplan suggests that language is key in gender identity and becomes particularly problematic and unsettling for female adolescents.[8] The acquisition of language is, for Lacan, what turns subjects into human and social beings, but entry into the symbolic order is organized differently for females than males. According to Kaplan, in the Oedipal phase, a young girl, in order to identify with her mother, must accept as permanent the missing phallus; and since language is produced in patriarchy such that the phallus is the crucial signifier, a woman's relationship to language is organized negatively or at least eccentrically. At puberty, when adult sexuality is negotiated, there is a reinscription of gender identity played out in relation to language as first organized in the Oedipal stage. Kaplan maintains that in Western culture, women's different or negative relation is expressed in, among other things, the taboo against women's public speech.

Although this taboo has been challenged, it nonetheless continues to exert a powerful influence on women's lives and identities. For women, "the very condition of their accession to their own subjectivity, to the consciousness of a self which is both personal and public is their unwitting acceptance of the law which limits their speech. This condition places them in a special relation to language which becomes theirs as a consequence of being human, and at the same time not theirs as a consequence of becoming female."[9] Although there has been considerable counterargument to traditional Freudian theory and its "missing phallus," what is important here is that Kaplan points to a crucial connection between gender identity and language and its relation to adolescent girls. Considering that young women must negotiate their presence and identity in Western civilization and its language(s) and negotiate the loss of connection with parents and a search for substitute love objects at the time of qualitative and quantitative shifts in sexual impulses, it is not surprising that adolescence is often a traumatic time for them.

Feminist avant-garde writing appears to offer young women alternative grounds on which to negotiate language identity—and identification. This literature is constituted by a set of alternative textual practices, premises, and pleasures organized to subvert dominant language and literary formations through experimentation with, among other things, lexicon, syntax, genre form, plot structure, and image.[10] The promise of this language experimentation (or play) lies in its ability to disrupt the symbolic order, destabilizing similitude and difference, which then might make available space for expanding the range of possibilities. It also provides an example of a community of women writers, readers, and publishers intent on reworking and rewriting women's place in the world through language play. By such rewriting, these communities produce and momentarily stabilize an active presence for women writers not easily negotiated in other contexts. In addition, they appear to offer both in community and in the text alternative (better) possibilities for identification.

Of course, feminist avant-garde writing is inherently disruptive. With its wild words, this literature can unsettle the current identifications and desires that may have secured identity and whatever fragile peace has been achieved as a result. As will be shown, an encounter with feminist literature exposed the struggles of six young women who, at seventeen, have been negotiating female adolescence identity and its "developmental disturbances" for some time. In this paper, I focus on the workings of identification and desire evident in two aspects of the literature that created the most disruption for the young women: its feminist perspective and its subversive language practices.

FEMINISM: DISTURBING SEXUAL IDENTITY AND AGENCY

Predictably, the most intense disruption for students occurred in response to the feminist perspective offered in the avant-garde literature they read. Although they were aware of the kind of literature they would be reading, the young women read the work as radically feminist, and this was simply unpalatable. They saw the project as "too female." Their general reaction was to quickly distance themselves from a feminist identity and claim a distinctly nonfeminist alternative. Rebecca asserted: "I think that you should know that I'm not a feminist. I believe that almost all men are scum and that every woman should have every right, but I don't follow or have any wish to follow all of the feminist issues."[11] Trinh wrote, "I'm really not liking the topics of the poems and am not really inspired to write after reading them . . . I'm not a feminist or even remotely close." Janet commented, "I agree with women getting equal pay, rights, but not just for that but also for equalness among races, that everyone is equal." Although the students agreed with me that one need not hate men to be feminist, they did not seem to be mollified. Janet continued, "When I hear feminism I more or less hear overboard—forgetting all other issues." Denise stated: "I think feminists get carried away at points. Everything offends them."

"Disturbance" was evident as well in the strong efforts of the young women to avoid naming or referencing gender even when it seemed appropriate to do so. Rebecca, for example, in replying to a question about what she learned from the project, commented: "I like to know what other people in Canada are writing and I like the idea of just experimenting with the form and knowing that there are other forms you can use. I learned things like that." Although the project was explicitly about "women" writers, a fact highlighted throughout the project, Rebecca resisted naming it as such, instead using the nongendered term "people." This occurred again in an instance when she was speaking about her film-arts class. Rebecca began: "Almost my whole class is boys. There are a couple of girls but they skip a lot." But then she continued, "So I was trying to run this film but people won't show up, and things like that, and they were really acting immaturely, like, they fool around and we never got the film finished." Despite initially admitting that gender was important in understanding her experience—the only time she did so—Rebecca quickly switched to using the words "people" and "they" rather than continuing to highlight gender. It seemed as though she recognized a mistake in such naming. This occurred with the other students as well. For example, in response to a question about parental expectations, Zandra dismissed the possibility that gender might factor into different expectations for her brother, commenting, "It's an age thing."

When I mentioned I had overheard a young woman explicitly state that there was little gender "oppression" in the world now, Zandra and Janet in response shifted the conversation quickly away from gender. Zandra began by commenting on the young woman who expressed the opinion:

> Zandra: This person is living in a bubble.
>
> Helen: But you tell me that you don't think about gender oppression, that you don't feel oppressed in your own lives. Is that right?
>
> Zandra: Yes, but it still happens in other people's lives. You see it but—
>
> Janet: *We just happen to be lucky.* [my emphasis]
>
> Zandra: Yeah.
>
> Janet: But I think we realize that people struggle. This school for instance, a fair number of these people can't afford to go to university, can't afford a decent meal. We see this.

Issues of class ("People can't afford a decent meal"), race ("All races are equal"), and even age ("It's an age thing") were used to eclipse any reference to gender. And gender was quickly rendered invisible here once again in the acknowledgment that "people struggle."[12]

There were a number of things that seemed to underlie and anchor the students' reactions. It is possible that the "backlash to feminism" reported in the popular press and media may in part have produced or affected the students' responses.[13] In the context of identity, desire, and identification, this could be understood as a reaction to a history of failed identification with feminism. Related to this, the students' reactions may simply have been reflecting the liberal humanist discourses that often underlie much of educational philosophy and school practice. Such discourses construe fairness and equity as equal numerical representation, so maintaining a balance of perspectives is paramount. Feminism, and more specifically, the design of the study, with its singular focus on female students, writers, and experience, runs counter to these notions. Disturbed by this alternative perspective, students worked to prevent the project from becoming any more female and certainly not more feminist in order to create a balance—in order to be fair. But there seemed to be something more intense fueling their responses.

I suspect that the "wild words" of feminism were disrupting the fragile renegotiation of sexuality required of adolescents. As stated previously, one of the developmental disturbances of adolescence is the shift away from the family to an "other," in response to qualitative and quantitative change in sexual drives. What appeared to be intensifying an urge toward a "balanced" perspective was a fear of risking a newly focused desire for an "other": in this case, heterosexuality.[14] The feminist literature, with its overt articulation of women's oppression, was disturbing because as the students saw it, men were being ignored, dismissed, or denounced in this experience. But their concern was not about ignoring or dismissing fathers and brothers. Fathers and brothers were rarely mentioned by the young women in this study; instead, what ran through the transcripts and the students' writing were references to heterosexual relationships—to boys and boyfriends. Indeed, the young women initiated a kind of "rescue" mission for men who might be lovers. Dispersed throughout the project were comments like Trinh's "I don't find anything wrong with the guys I know" or Lauren's "I just admire men . . . escially [sic] tall, dark, masculine men with sexy voices."

The students in this study seemed to define themselves as women largely in terms of heterosexuality or "heteronormativity."[15] Lauren was clearly explaining this when, after describing various men she would like to have in her life, she wrote, "Don't worry, Helen, I'm not sexually obsessed, I'm just a teenage girl." Lauren was evoking a notion that to be a teenage girl is evidently to be obsessed with men, an obsession that is "normal." Similarly, when Janet wrote a poem about a female friend, she also referenced heterosexuality. A section reads:

> Selena talks, listens, cares, shares
> double-dates, shopping trips, shared sports,
> shared men, shared dinner.

I am not sure what Janet meant by "shared men." It may be that Janet was saying that she and her friend like the same kind of men but are not competitive or possessive about them. Taken more metaphorically, the phrase suggests that part of what may bind Janet and Selena together is that they share an interest in men. They share men. This second possibility suggests that what Janet and the others may be using primarily to define women as women is an interest in, or more accurately, a desire for, men. It was evidently a very important definition that the feminist avant-garde writing disturbed.

Feminist avant-garde literature is not often constructed through heterosexual desire. Apparently, for the young women in the study this precluded such desire operating in their reading and writing practices. If working with the literature requires some degree of identification with the woman as both subject and writer in feminist avant-garde writing, students needed to relax the prescription on woman or "teenage girl" as constructed through a desire for men. Relaxing this regulation opens up possibilities of other desires being narrated into existence (for example, women loving women), thus unsettling an identity constituted largely and perhaps precariously by heterosexual desire. The strong efforts of the young women to reinsert heterosexuality into the discussion and into their writing speaks to the incredible power and pleasure of this desire. This study consisted of only twelve sessions, which, in light of the students' entire school program and their lives outside of school, represented only a small amount of time and energy, and yet the students made intense, indeed urgent, efforts to work heterosexual desire back into the project. The tension in engaging even briefly in literature that excludes heterosexual desire speaks to the power of this desire and perhaps as well to its vulnerability, even fragility. The energies marshaled together to ensure that heterosexual desire stayed in the discussion suggest that there may be a serious threat from other, evidently powerful and potentially disruptive knowledges or desires. The question then concerns what knowledges and desires threaten female, heterosexual, adolescent identity.

The literature did provide a place to speak of a same-sex Eros—that is, the pleasure of female relationships. It also provided a place to speak of the "problem" of male relationships. Occasionally, students spoke from these spaces. Despite the fact that the study and the literature were seen as "too female," the students did take the opportunity to write and talk about their female friends and family relationships—with sisters and mothers—with enthusiasm, perhaps with some relief. Although they wrote about the problematic nature of some of these relationships, their poetry, by and large, celebrated their female friends and maternal relationships. Since they perceived these relationships to be platonic, this did not threaten their investment in heterosexuality. Also, although the young women did expend a great deal of energy inserting heterosexuality into the project, there were a few occasions when the girls admitted that men were not necessarily worth the effort. Rebecca's comment "I believe that almost all men are scum"; Lauren's statements that "boys are too stupid to do the dishes"; and later: "I was really upset. I don't know why, probably over a guy, as usual . . ." —speak to the problem of heterosexuality as experienced by the young women in this study. Their discussion of the pleasure of female friends and maternal relationships and the problems of male relationships suggests that defining oneself outside of a male referent, outside of heterosexuality, was possible, even enticing, and yet at the same time, confusing and dangerous.

However, it is also possible that this encounter with feminist avant-garde literature may have served to further fuel heterosexual desire. For these young women, who constitute men as objects of desire and as central in their identity as women, ignoring or dismissing or admitting that the real men in their lives are problems, may feed the desire for the ideal man who inhabits their dreams and fantasies—men who existed in the various other school and popular texts they were reading at the time. The feminist avant-garde literature may serve to heighten the difference between real (and dismissible) men and the ideal symbolic men, thus increasing the desire for ideal men. Ironically, the feminist literature may have intensified students' investment in heterosexual desire and its search for the ideal man.

The feminist perspective offered in the literature also provoked concerns about agency. One of the strongest desires expressed by many of the students was to see and produce themselves as unaffected by gender, race, or class oppression. As mentioned previously, Zandra and Janet spoke of being "lucky" in this regard. The feminist literature offered a belief that women's lives are or have been constrained by social expectations and "oppressions" beyond an individual's control. Agency is possible but only through collective action, which begins with an acknowledgment of gender oppression. It was a position the young women in the study found unappealing. Janet, for example, refused to show sympathy or empathy for female characters in "oppressive" circumstances. She stated flatly: "All I want to say is that they [the characters] deserve it 'cause they're stupid and they should know that isn't the only way—that they can get out of it. It doesn't matter where you live, and there's a way to get out of it. Come on, girls."

The students insisted on the control women might have over their lives, resisting the victimization of women, perhaps, and denying the material circumstances that prevent women from walking away from oppressive conditions. They preferred to read about individual women in powerful, positive circumstances, freely and independently changing their lives, if need be. The literature was at odds with the optimistic belief the young women had in their own power to control their lives.

In part, their optimism may be a response to the loss of their parents as love objects. The loss of this particular relationship with parents, although difficult, opens up other exciting possibilities—for example, desire for another. It also frees the child and parent from the tensions that inevitably result when love objects fail to satisfy desire. But to acknowledge that women may be oppressed suggests that these young women are not themselves free agents in the world and that that world, even without parents, is not free of constraints or problems. Clearly the fun of flirting with boys, of "sharing" men, and the pleasure and power in thinking that the world is yours, that you are indeed lucky, seemed to be placed at considerable risk in this encounter with feminist avant-garde texts.

It is important to acknowledge the complexity of this encounter. Students brought their personal history and past identifications to their reading. They also had to contend with my previous identifications with the "woman" constituted in the literature and with my pedagogical desires to create a feminist haven in the context of patriarchal academe and to "rescue" my female students.[16] These dynamics, together with the particular social and historical times, affected what was possible at any one moment. However, since heterosexuality and agency were important issues to the young women in this study, I want to consider these concerns in terms of the major psychic/social project of adolescence, that is, separation from parents and the search for substitutes. The knowledges and desires that threaten female heterosexual adolescent identity might well be the powerful identification and desire for the mother and, to a lesser degree, the father. Considering that adolescents seek to distance themselves from their former love object—their parents—yet at the same time remain in a dependent relationship with them and considering that any love object will invoke but ultimately fail to satisfy desire, it follows that child-parent relations will be complex, volatile, and fraught with contradiction. It is not surprising that adolescents will love and hate their parents, and both love and hate their substitutes.

Sexual identity, according to Sigmund Freud, is organized in relation to the nature of parental attachment. The attainment of heterosexuality is dependent on the child identifying with the same-sex parent and desiring the other as love object. For Freud, female heterosexuality means identifying with her mother and transferring her desire from her mother to her father. In this, I believe Freud falsely assumes a strict separation between desire and identification and a rigid polarity between what mothers and fathers offer their children.[17] As Diana Fuss and Jessica Benjamin, among others, have pointed out, identification and desire may operate with both parents.[18] For the young woman who is claiming a heterosexual identity, the task, it would seem, is first to ensure a focus on the father as a primary object of desire and second, to secure a substitute for the father with a male (real or symbolic) from outside the family. This task is attempted in a complex and shifting context of maternal and paternal desire and identification. If desire and identification are not entirely separate and if identifications and identities (including sexual identity) are fluid, partial, social, contradictory, and nonunified, then this task is immensely complex.

One route through this quagmire of desire and identification for young women might be to first ensure the mother's unavailability as a love object by insisting on her heterosexuality. If the mother is named as heterosexual, then the daughter's desire for the mother is thwarted. This desire is then redirected to the father. In this way, the "good mother" might be seen as one who insists on her own heterosexuality, thus pushing the daughter, despite herself, to the father and to heterosexuality. The feminist literature did not act as the "good mother" through such an acknowledgment. Instead, the writing reminds readers of the pleasure of identification/desire for women and of the first woman we knew—our mothers. This might in part explain the hostility of the students toward the feminist literature and their intense efforts, in the absence of their "mother's" affirmation of heterosexuality, to affirm their own heterosexuality so stridently.

The daughter's second move must be to deflect her attention away from her father as love object. She must find her sexual object choice outside the family. Possibly, this might be achieved by intensifying her identification with the father, who would then diminish his status as a love object and force the search elsewhere. If agency is one quality that safely distinguishes the father from the mother in a patriarchal society, it could serve as an important and very attractive basis of identification with the father. The "good father" will insist on his agency and on his daughter's, as the daughter will stress both his and her own agency. Since the patriarchal power and agency of the father is challenged in feminism(s), it is not surprising that the young women claiming heterosexual identity find the literature unsettling. The more maternal identification, desire, and agency are promoted—as the "said" of feminist avant-garde writing—the more impossible it is to claim agency as the grounds for paternal identification. The more gender polarity is challenged, the more precariously gender and sexual identity may appear and the more disturbing the experience with the feminist avant-garde may be.

Even at best, there are serious complications in identifying with the father. If the daughter identifies strongly with the father, she runs the "risk" of incorporating his desires—including, presumably, his heterosexual desires for the mother. As Diana Fuss comments, "What is identification if not a way to assume the desires of the other?"[19] This threatens the daughter's heterosexual desire, revealing its fragility and rendering her ambivalent about identification with the father and his agency.

The young women in this study do reiterate their agency throughout the project, but they are not unequivocal. They spoke of being "lucky" compared to other people: other women and their oppressions. The word "lucky" is an amazing designation. It allows the young women to identify with their fathers in terms of agency and to disconnect themselves from their "unlucky" mothers. Moreover, the identity of a "lucky woman" occurs by chance rather than by deliberate political action, so the young women need not claim the identity of the feminist.

The same as her father in terms of power and agency, the same as her mother in terms of heterosexuality, the heterosexual adolescent daughter shifts to one who is different—to a male (symbolic or actual) from outside the family—to secure heterosexuality. This love object is socially outside the family but in every sense created by the family. This route or pattern, though not unproblematic itself, may be sufficiently helpful in securing sexuality for the young women to insist on it. But it is precarious, disturbed even by a brief encounter with feminist avant-garde literature, even with young women who, nearing the end of adolescence, have struggled for some time with the issues of adolescent identification and desire.

I do not wish to suggest that this is the only explanation for the responses of the young women in this study. Nor do I wish to suggest that this is the only pattern or route of identification and desire that is occurring for heterosexual female adolescents generally or for those in this project specifically. Instead, I offer this interpretation as one place to begin to understand the complex psychic and social environment of female adolescence.

Feminism was only one aspect of the literature that disturbed the young women in the study. The sabotage of conventional language and literary practices that characterizes feminist avant-garde writing was also unsettling for them and this, too, seemed related to the workings of desire and identification evident in the "developmental disturbances" of female adolescence.

DISTURBING LANGUAGE: UNSETTLING "GOOD GIRLS" AND "GOOD STUDENTS"

Feminist avant-garde writing offers experiments with language and literary forms. It celebrates the woman writer/reader/subject as a linguistic and literary rule breaker. As discussed at the outset of this paper, this writing appears to offer an alternative to young women for whom language poses a problem in relation to gender identity. However, the disturbance offered by this literature seemed to evoke, and at the same time threaten, the social identities of "good girl" and "good student/writer." Valerie Walkerdine, Carol Gilligan, Michelle Fine, and Nancy Lesko, among others, have described the qualities that constitute the good girl/good student: conformity; compliancy; control of the body, voice, emotions; and physicality.[20] The "good girl" appeared to be an important identity for the young women here. Their identification with this construct compelled them to remain in the study and attempt to work within its parameters even when they were not necessarily willing or happy about doing so. Denise explicitly evoked this identity when she described why she finally submitted some writing: "I thought, 'I've GOT to do something for her [Helen] or she'll think I'm totally ignoring her.'" Denise, embracing the image of the good girl, felt the need to express concern about offending or ignoring me. Rebecca, too, expressed this concern when she wrote, "I think I should let you know I'm not a feminist." It would seem that in order to be fair, Rebecca believed she "should" let me know her politics. In a different vein, Trinh explicitly described herself as a "good student" and then, fearing she sounded conceited, felt she must explain: "I meant good, not only in English but in all my classes, in the sense that I do my homework every night and pull off good enough marks, like, I don't have a problem with whatever my teachers assign. I didn't mean good in the sense that I get awesome marks." For Trinh and the others, to be a "good student" or more specifically a "good girl" refers to someone who is conscientious, compliant, and modest and who certainly doesn't offend. These qualities are at odds with the brash and subversive woman writer in feminist writing. ·

A poem entitled "I'm a Dangerous Woman" evoked the image of the "good girl" for Zandra. Zandra listed the poem as one of her favorites, and during an interview I asked her whether she would like to be a dangerous woman:

> *Zandra:* Sure, why not. Everybody wants to. Because I'm suppose to be
> the goody-goody—my sister is the wild one ... but I'm like—I'll
> do what I'm told, it's okay, I'll do it, kind of thing.

Yet Zandra later spoke of her ability to be dangerous when describing why the poem was her favorite:

> *Zandra:* I don't know. I find that some parts of it are true.
> *Helen:* Are true—Which parts?
> *Zandra:* Her brain, not her body is dangerous. I think that people don't
> believe it or buy it but that it is, like, a real weapon ... I've always
> been interested in the FBI, CIA, and stuff like that and usually
> they use women as decoys—but to actually think they could do
> more that just that. I like that—strange. I really like the idea....
> A lot of people think "she [referring to herself] wouldn't go hurt
> anyone, she wouldn't do anything," but I could [laughs].

Zandra was able here to see herself as possibly breaking expectations—playing with the possibilities of being dangerous. Clearly she wanted an alternative subject position to the good-girl image, the "goody-goody," and the "decoys" that she reads and writes about in spy mysteries. Clearly, she wanted to be "dangerous" in the way a man can be dangerous, physically as well as intellectually. It was a strange and delightful idea. She laughed at the thought.

Feminist avant-garde writing promotes and celebrates the woman writer as a rulebreaker, but Zandra struggled with this position. She defined herself as a compliant person who is not dangerous but who could become dangerous if she were to take up the position of being male or, possibly, if she entertained an imaginary identification that establishes a new position for women. The former allows for a kind of cross-dressing—that is, a woman who becomes a man and breaks the rules; the latter calls for redefinition of woman to encompass danger, aggression, physicality. The possibility of cross-dressing insures that the opposing characteristics that constitute the categories of maleness and femaleness, (e.g., active/passive, reason/emotion) remain intact rather than redefined. The "good-girl" image stays intact; she merely masquerades as a male. If "cross-dressing" means identification with a man and his desires (who in the context of this study might be presumed heterosexual), then this means assuming his sexual object choice—woman. This would be disturbing but also perhaps enticing and pleasurable to heterosexual women, knowing that cross-dressing is a temporary state and that there is a "real" identity to which one can return. Redefinition of women to embrace activity and aggression means the loss of the "good-girl" identity. The desire to be dangerous, to be wild, physical, and intellectually aggressive, both generally and in the context of writing and reading acts, tempts this redefinition or at least a kind of cross-dressing, if only in this one instance.

The subversiveness of the feminist avant-garde writing disturbed the students' definition of literature and the identity of "good writer." The disruption was evident in Rebecca's description of one of the selections:

> It was just, like, it didn't really seem like a poem. It was like she just picked a bunch of pictures and then typed the words out. . . . It did seem like she kind of threw it together. It almost seems as though she had taken someone else's work and just written something over it. She's, like, manipulating their words. . . . It seems like for women's liberation or something. It's something you might see—the wall and the graffiti and all that. Well, I guess some poems—poems don't seem like they should be political, I don't know why.

For the students, the feminist poetry recalls a definition of "literature" as serious work, reverent and respectful of language and literary conventions, transcending its situatedness and political interests. To be the "good-girl" writer/reader within this conventional notion of literature means refusing to mark oneself as gendered or to highlight gender oppression. Hilary Davis describes the marking of "the good and bad girl" reader in reader-response theory:

> Mainstream reader-response theory dichotomizes the woman reader as either "disembodied" or "embodied" either a good girl or a bad girl reader. Women readers are viewed as angels, monsters, or amazons. Yet these images require that patriarchy acknowledge the reader as a woman thus violating its own definitions for "woman" and "readers." Within androcentric reader-response theory the majority of women readers are invisible. Women readers masquerade as disembodied in an attempt to "pass" as legitimate readers.[21]

To be seen as a legitimate writer/reader, Rebecca and the others must avoid becoming embodied in their response to the literature, thus it is difficult to identify with the subject position in feminist avant-garde writing, which conspicuously highlights the presence of the female body. Also, since it is a body that does not usually reference heterosexual desire, it means highlighting a "wrong" female body for these student readers.

In addition, to avoid embodiment in their reading and writing practices, the students invoked notions of creative writing as a matter of personal style rather than a social convention. Denise explained: "I'm glad they [feminist writers] can write like that, but I don't think I can. It's great. I appreciate it, but. . . . it isn't really my style. I kind of write—I don't know how I write—I just write." Strongly committed to writing as personal style, Denise couldn't identify with the avant-garde writing. Several of the students also spoke about their pleasure in writing "spontaneously." Trinh commented, "When I write poetry, usually I'm just writing down what I feel, and so I'm not really thinking about the form that its taking but rather the words that I'm using." Later she wrote: "I was just distraught, I guess, and angry over something and so I wrote it. I wasn't thinking about what kind of form it was taking or anything. I was just writing it."

In a similar vein, Rebecca spoke of the intrusiveness of the project. She described her writing as a form of escape:

> When I write, I try to escape from my problems and worries or the usual boring things which occur my life . . . I find I can't write about myself or other people I know personally and truly escape into that other world and enjoy it . . . Well, I was trying to use the forms of the poems you gave me, so I was trying not to like copy them but to use the same kind of writing and then use maybe a slightly different theme, so I couldn't really escape because I was using a certain form, so I don't know.

For Rebecca, writing is a form of escape and offers the pleasure of being "swept away," which is not available since feminist avant-garde writing draws attention to literary and linguistic convention. It demands self-consciousness. Students also spoke about how they wished to write about their emotional life. Rebecca, for example, wrote in her journal, "I find that I write more powerful poetry when I'm depressed and angry" and later, "I released some of my anger and frustration when I wrote this." Zandra commented that she wrote at times "to get my anger out." This therapeutic use of writing was addressed only in terms of individual feelings unconnected to larger social or political conditions.

The wish to "just write" and not to think about it, to be just "swept away," to "escape," to be written and be released from one's emotions suggests a very feminine writing defined by the emotional and irrational. Further, creative writing was at times viewed by the students as something very personal and private: writing done in their bedrooms, written literally "lying on the bed," Denise would tell me. Rebecca described her writing as a hobby: an important hobby but only a pasttime. It would seem a very gendered image of writing. Women, particularly white, middle-class women, have a history of such writing, and this history and the ideology that supports it was directly reproduced in the writing curriculum of the late eighteenth and early nineteenth centuries. It is an image that is also strongly supported by an emphasis on the psychological and therapeutic conception of creative writing that ensured its place in the school curriculum. It maps neatly onto the traumatic experiences that underlie adolescent life. It is writing that does not threaten femininity, and it is certainly at odds with feminist avant-garde writing, which looks to the pleasures of writing publicly and politically subversively.

As described at the outset of this paper, women have a difficult, if not outright problematic, relationship to language. The oxymoron of the "woman who writes publicly and subversively" may be particularly traumatic for young women at the edge of adulthood who face separation from their parents and a difficult entrance into the more public sphere of postsecondary education and eventually the world of paid work. The strategy of disembodiment, of masquerade, and feminine writing permits some way of resolving the tension between femininity and public voice. The question remains as to why the feminist writing does not offer a more attractive possibility.

I suspect that the reason feminine and disembodied writing is so difficult to disrupt is that it, in part, supports and is supported by a nexus of passivity, pleasure, femininity, and heterosexuality. Particularly disconcerting was a connection between passivity and heterosexuality made by several of the students.

Rebecca connected feminism and anti-male sentiment by indicating that although she sees "almost all men are scum," she isn't a feminist. This was immediately followed by a statement by Trinh, which, however seriously she meant it, introduced the notion of pleasure: "I am not a feminist. I don't find anything wrong with the guys I know. I am very indifferent and passive. I don't care about equal rights or wages. I would be completely happy to grow up and get married and be a housewife. I would love that. I am just indifferent to it all." Trinh carefully connected passivity and indifference to pleasure. Specifically, she linked pleasure (being "completely happy") to heterosexuality ("being married and a housewife") to a nonfeminist position ("I am not a feminist"). Forging this connection among passivity, heterosexuality, and femininity results in a feminine writing or at least a disembodied writing, which the feminist writing with its active, subversive, and lesbian sensibilities disturbs.

Moreover, if one of the major disturbances of female adolescents is the separation from parents and the search for an "other" outside the family, then feminine or disembodied writing functions in complex ways. The father can be seen as representing the status quo, culture, and civilization, since, in the traditional organization of the family, it is the father who comes from the public sphere to the family, and back again. In Western cultures, he provides a route away from the family and independence from the family. Feminist writing would appear to offer separation from the family but also from Western civilization, rerouted through a mother who writes publicly and subversively. Either of these options require strong acknowledgment of, and identification with, the public life of the father or mother. In the case of the father, if identification with him organizes a route away from the family and if identification is also needed to divert (however incompletely) desire for him, then a young woman's independence and her search for someone outside of the family are placed at some risk if identification is thwarted. And even in these times, strong identification with fathers is still not encouraged in daughters. In the case of the mother, strong identification is encouraged but in the case of traditionally organized families, it is the mother of the home with whom one is expected to identify. Identification with the public mother—the feminist mother—provides separation but also subverts the order of the world which promises among other things, pleasure in passivity. The strategies of feminine writing or disembodied writing may offer the young women in this study a far less risky means of reconciling femininity and public voice and of affirming heterosexuality and the separation from parents. The costs of identification with the woman in feminist language may simply be too high, too dangerous, to a current identity that already seems too precariously constructed.

DISTURBING INTERVENTION: FEMINIST PEDAGOGY

The two major social/psychological tasks of adolescent girls seem to be (1) to distance oneself from parents and siblings and to affirm a sexual identity outside the family, and (2) to reconcile femininity and public voice and more generally forge an identity in a society where female is viewed as aberrant. The desires featured strongly in the voices of the young women in this study are (1) the desire/pleasure in heterosexuality, (2) the desire for agency and, (3) the desire to please, to be compliant. These desires, I would suggest, are interconnected and in conflict, a conflict that confounds easy solutions to the two major social/psychic tasks of adolescent girls. Effective feminist pedagogical interventions, it would seem, cannot rely on a simple and positive correlation of feminism and on the desires and identifications it makes possible; nor can they depend on the destabilizing effects of language and literary avant-garde practices. Instead, they must find some way to work within the desires, identifications that play themselves out in the feminist classroom.

Diana Fuss asks "how the power of identification might be utilized in the service of a non-violent, progressive-thinking politics."[22] For feminist teachers working with adolescent girls, the question is, How do we intervene effectively, acknowledging and utilizing the power of identification and desire in ways that will expand the range of possibilities for young women in a project of social transformation? More effective intervention will depend upon understanding and learning to work with the power of identification and desire. This has been expressed as working with resistance, although I am now renaming it "working with identification and desire." As evident in this study, identification is a process that will not orient a student easily or necessarily positively toward feminism. The possibilities and processes of identification and desire may indeed create struggle. Acknowledging this and having students and teachers work with theories of identification and desire have the potential to enrich students' experience with both traditional and avant-garde texts.

For the young women in my study who are invested in heterosexual desire and personal agency, better pedagogical intervention may mean providing texts that offer neither the traditional heterosexual sensibilities of standard-school literary fare nor the lesbian sensibilities offered in the feminist avant-garde literature but, instead, a plurality of sexual identities including female bisexuality and a reconfigured heterosexuality, perhaps symbolically inscribed as motif, metaphor, image, character, or story line. Feminist science fiction, for example, may offer greater play with identity and desire. Works like Joanna Russ's *The Female-Man* or Marge Piercy's *Woman on the Edge of Time* offer fantasies in which bisexuality or pluralities of sexualities are organizing themes or motifs. Related to this, the gender polarity organized in the identities of mother and father needs to be broken. An emphasis on the public lives of mothers and the family lives of fathers and on the reorientation of family as both private and public might refigure the range of identifications and desires possible. In particular, the independence and autonomy of the mother within the family still needs to find cultural expression. This may allow young women to more effectively utilize the power of identification and desire as they negotiate themselves through the quagmire of female adolescent experience and beyond in an expanded horizon of possibilities.

In other words, there needs to be more "wildness in the words" than there is in feminist avant-garde writing, in feminist pedagogy—particularly for girls and young women, but perhaps ultimately for us all.

NOTES

1. The young women who participated were enrolled in a grade twelve creative writing option class in a large multiracial, multiethnic, coeducational high school. Four of the young women were white, one was of Asian background, and the other South Asian. With the exception of one student, all were avid readers and writers who wrote creatively in their spare time. The six young women in the study met together as a group during class time once or twice a week for a period of two and one-half months. Twelve sessions were held. Under my direction, the young women read and discussed eighteen literary works and produced their own creative writing. They were also asked to keep a journal to reflect on their poems, the literature, or any other issue or concern they wished to raise. Each of the students participated in an individual interview at the end of the project. The literature selected for the sessions included works by contemporary writers featured in the 1989–1991 issues of three Canadian journals, *Fireweed*, *(f)Lip*, and *Contemporary Verse*, all well known for publishing feminist, avant-garde writing. All literature selected for the study was written by women for women and offered a wide range of unconventional uses of language and literary form. Some works we studied blended traditional forms of poetry and prose, some poetry had strong visual components, some transgressed rules of orthography and syntax or semantics, some displayed unconventional arrangements of line and verse. Themes in the literature included mother-daughter relationships, sisterhood, female childhood, women's immigration experience, female friendships, alcohol addiction, the homeless, and urban violence.

2. For a more detailed description of identification and desire, see Diana Fuss, *Identification Papers* (New York: Routledge, 1995), especially 1–14.

3. Anna Freud, *The Writings of Anna Freud*, vol. 7, *Problems of Psychoanalytic Training, Diagnosis, and the Technique of Therapy: 1966–1970* (New York: International Universities Press, 1971), 47.

4. Ibid.

5. Fuss, *Identification Papers*, 6.

6. Carol Gilligan, *Making Connections: The Relational Worlds of Adolescent Girls at Emma Willard School* (Cambridge: Harvard University Press, 1989), 4.

7. Luce Irigaray, *The Sex Which Is Not One* (Ithaca: Cornell University Press, 1985).
8. Cora Kaplan, "Gender and Language," in *The Feminist Critique of Language: A Reader*, ed. D. Cameron (London: Routledge, 1991), *passim*.
9. Ibid, 68.
10. For a more elaborated discussion of feminist avant-garde writing, see Wendy Waring, "Strategies for Subversion: Canadian Women's Writing," in *Work in Progress*, ed. R. Tregev (Toronto: Women's Press, 1987). An excellent text describing feminist avant-garde work and community in Quebec is Karen Gould's, *Writing in the Feminine: Feminism and Experimental Writing in Quebec* (Carbondale: Southern Illinois University Press, 1990).
11. The six students have been given pseudonyms: Rebecca, Denise, Zandra, Trinh, Lauren, and Janet.
12. I remember now that at that time I wondered about the "truth" of their statements and the question of false consciousness and my role, which to them must have seemed like Iago whispering some nightmarish story in their ears. I remember getting caught somehow, wanting, despite all I know, to believe their words—*"We're just lucky"*—to ignore what I know and to ignore some of their stories in which they weren't so lucky. My desire to imagine their escape, and thus perhaps my own, from a patriarchal world seemed to suppress momentarily, at least, wild words and their other knowledges.
13. Susan Faludi, *Backlash: The Undeclared War Against American Women* (New York: Doubleday, 1992).
14. All of the students in this study claimed, if indirectly, a heterosexual identity.
15. *Heteronormativity*, as the word suggests, refers to the notion that heterosexuality is assumed as a universal experience. As the standard or norm, it is expected and valued. See Michael Warner, *Fear of a Queer Planet: Queer Politics and Social Theory* (Minneapolis: University of Minnesota Press, 1993).
16. My desire as a feminist teacher is captured in a paragraph by Alison Easton: "Like many a feminist critic before and after me, what I most wanted to do at first was set up a Women Writers course. Such a course resembles Charlotte Perkins Gilman's utopian Herland—a feminist enclave at the edge of the patriarchal academic empire, a utopia probably without male colleagues and possibly even without male students, where only texts by women are discussed and by a kind of critical parthenogenesis women without the aid of men produce analyses of the writings of women." Alison Easton, "With Her in Ourland: A Feminist Teaches Nineteenth-Century American Literature," in *Teaching Women: Feminism and English Studies*, ed. A. Thompson and H. Wilcox (Manchester, England: Manchester, 1989), 149.
17. Sigmund Freud theorizes the relationship between desire and identification in a number of his writings. See, for example, *New Introductory Lectures*, vol. 22 of *The Standard Edition of the Complete Psychological Works of Sigmund Freud*, ed. James Strachey (London: Hogarth, 1964) and *Group Psychology and the Analysis of the Ego*, vol. 18 of *Standard Edition*.
18. See Fuss, *Identification Papers* and Jessica Benjamin, *The Bonds of Love* (New York: Pantheon Books, 1988).
19. Fuss, *Identification Papers*, 12.
20. See Gilligan *Making Connections*; Valerie Walkerdine, "Femininity as Performance," *Oxford Review of Education* 15 (1989), 267–79; Nancy Lesko, "The Curriculum of the Body: Lessons from a Catholic High School," in *Becoming Feminine: The Politics of*

Popular Culture, ed. Leslie Roman, Linda Christian-Smith, and Elizabeth Ellsworth (London: Falmer Press, 1988); Michelle Fine and Pat Macpherson, "Over Dinner: Feminism and Adolescent Female Bodies," in *Disruptive Voices: The Possibilities of Feminist Research*, ed. Michelle Fine (Ann Arbor: The University of Michigan Press, 1992).

21. Hilary Davis, "Recuperating Pleasure: Towards a Feminist Aesthetic of Reading," Ph.D. diss., Ontario Institute for Studies in Education, 1993, 4.
24. Fuss, *Identification Papers*, 8.

Part 4

Desire and Re-Signification

7

Desire and Encryption

A Theory of Readability

GAE MACKWOOD

We are accustomed to approaching symbols as an archaeologist struggles to decipher documents in an unknown language.... We live with the handy prejudice that all one has to do is attach the meaning to the thing, ... join the semantic significations to the hieroglyphics, in order to pride oneself on one's success in the act of decipher-ing. But all this process really accomplishes is to convert one system of symbols into another, which then in turn becomes accountable for its secret.
                                                    —Nicolas Abraham, "On Symbol"

Some would be tempted to appeal to a phenomenological description ... [but] ... psychoanalysis stakes out its domain precisely on this *unthought* ground of phenome-nology. To state ... the problem which faces us: how to include in a discourse ... that very thing which in essence, by dint of being the precondition of discourse, escapes it? ... Pleasure, Discharge, Unconscious ... cannot strictly speaking signify anything, except the founding silence of any *act of signification* ... instead of re-signifying them, they strip words of their signification, they *de-signify* them, so to speak.... These fig-ures of antisemantics ... require a denomination ... we shall propose ... by the neol-ogism *anasemia*.
                                          —Nicolas Abraham, *The Shell and Kernel*

READING DESIRE

"Reading desire." In a significant way, this phrase seems contradictory. Gilles Deleuze offers the following: "Desire never needs interpreting"[1] and "desire is no more symbolic than figurative, no more signified than signifier."[2] Indeed, some have suggested that the cultivation of desire, as an engagement of one's conscious and unconscious psychic aspects, can function as an antithesis to a modernist "cult" of reason and rationality.[3] As many of our reading practices carry at least the vestiges of modern logic and reason, *reading desire* seems a difficult and unstable possibility, at best.

Reading desire is a complex practice for another reason. Among other things, desire seems to be named for its function as a *directional signal*, pointing to *the body*, to "things" *erotic* (love/sex), to a *lifeforce* ("life instinct" or "life drive," in opposition to a Freudian death instinct), to *affect* or *emotion*, to the *corporeal* or *material*, and in the case of pedagogy, to *what has been crucially denied* in formulations of knowledge, learning, and pedagogy (i.e., the irrational, emotive, somatic, fleshy sensuousness of the teaching-learning scene). Conceived in this manner, learning desire *teaches us* to interrogate how we practice, pedagogically, what our desires point to: Am I teaching in ways that deny the body? Should I be teaching in a way more consonant with the body/affect/ senses? Is my teaching disembodied? These questions lead to categorizations of pedagogy: teaching "minds," *or*, perhaps, teaching "bodies." But if the body "interrupts" the mind or the mind seeks to become "disconnected" from the body, is desire something we *need* to read? Is desire even something that *can* be read?

As many conceptualizations of desire, identity, and subjectivity come from within the framework of psychoanalysis, it seems significant (particularly for pedagogy) to understand how psychoanalysis performs pedagogically in teaching us how to read. By definition, the reader does not exist, at least not "before" or prior to the text, even the text of desire. Texts "teach us how" to read them, and in doing so, they construct who we are as readers; texts desire and construct us as we desire and construct them. If desire indeed functions to point us in particular directions, then this function is inseparable, if in difficult and uncommon ways, from certain conceptualizations of reading and readability. And if desire is tied up in reading and readability, then by some process we must learn to *read* desire. It is to these interconnections that we now turn.

READING TALES FROM THE CRYPT

Psychoanalysis and the detective genre have much in common: Freud himself was said to read Sherlock Holmes mysteries for insight into analytic practice.[4] In both genres, there is a quirky double moment in how our reading desires are satiated, a double and seemingly contradictory desire for deduction to follow *both logical and emotive dimensions*. On the one hand, we need the detective to perform analytically, transporting us from a seemingly incomprehensible maze of clues at the crime scene to a clearly reconstructed narrative solution. On the other hand, this drive for logic must envelop the intersubjective relations between detective and murderer, satiating our desires to see the murderer caught in his or her own web of deception, which, although cast to "save," instead leads to the murderer's downfall. This double moment of deduction *and* deception, our desire to trace the symbolic structure of clues to their conclusion *and* in doing so, to expose deception from truth—is characteristic of much of what in ordinary language we call *reading*. The text's ability to be read, its *readability*, can be thought of as its decipherability, comprehensibility, intelligibility, *legibility*, but can also be though of as its ability to engage the affect, to fascinate, appeal to, enthrall, stimulate, and satisfy our desires for justice. This is nowhere more evident than in the contradictory desire activated by the anticipation of ending in the detective story: the desire to finish and reach the penultimate logical ending, but also a desire to resist ending and continue the enjoyable puzzling chase of the murderer. Hence, we could speak of a double interest in reading: to satisfy a desire for clean analytical or logical meaning and also to gratify our emotional and sentimental desires, an affective satiation of desires for revenge, justice, truth, triumph, conquest.

Readability is also about safety and risk: about guaranteeing a world and ourselves in that world—both referentially and intersubjectively.[5] The detective-story quality of many psychoanalytic cases provides a tightly controlled narrative sequence guaranteeing the desires and identities of the detective and criminal, as well as the logical procedure of assembling clues toward an expected final solution. Unlike such a Freudian *fort . . . da* game, however, the movement from structuralist to poststructuralist theories of signification highlight a movement from a *readable* text to a *writable* one.[6] Roland Barthes's *S/Z*, for example, suggests a shift from *consuming* a stable *work* by linking determinate symbols to decipherable meanings to *producing a text*, writing in and through an indeterminate, intertextual universe of signifiers and signification. The text becomes less a structure that can be controlled safely (by *anyone*) and more an open-ended process of "structuration" within a realm of play and flux. Such poststructural texts question and destabilize the idea of reading as an exercise in safety; to some it may even seem there are no safe zones of meaning or intelligibility but rather an endless playing field of ever-increasing risks and dangers.

Such a poststructural turn on processes of reading and readability questions the production of desires, identities, subjectivities, and the social as a "safe" venture in a manner the detective story seeks to create. As a teacher and writer, I also want to interrupt the "safety" of reading to consider other questions and possibilities beyond simply guaranteeing safe boundaries between self and other and safe structuring of the social field, where desires and identities settle neatly into place.[7] What conditions the possibility for desire, desiring, identification, identity, and subjectivity to become *readable*? By others? By the self? By what criteria are certain identities, subjectivities, and desires rendered or judged readable? What, then, are the limits of readability? What desires are activated in the process of reading safely? Or "unsafely"?

Structures of reading and readability, desire, identity, and subjectivity do not operate outside the boundaries of the social, nor are they devoid of the struggles and resistances characteristic of discourse in general. The importance of reading and readability become even clearer in consideration of how desires, identities, and subjectivities are read within the social sphere.[8] Although psychoanalysis and poststructural literary theory suggest and articulate how the formation of desire and identity is an indeterminate but functional fiction, this does not mean, as Barbara Johnson notes, that these fictions do not have real historical effects.[9]

In light of this, questions of reading and readability seem important to both stage and respond to in transformative education. Although psychoanalysis and poststructural literary theory articulate the vicissitudes of desire, identification, and self-fashioning, a significant effort to "transform" social spaces must include creating new possibilities not just for self-making and self-articulation but also for the readability of the social space and social imaginary. Identity politics do provide such a theory and practice of reading the social sphere, but in that reading social location serves as the only, and *literal,* marker of intelligibility. Are there other possibilities for readability, in which individuals and their desires are not "read" as personifications of readable traits based upon social location? And what of the reading of social location itself? Can a reading be performed that does not reduce the readability of the social to a guarantee of safety, a guarantee of fixed and stable social relations?

The question of reading and readable sources of meaning for desire and identity is a central theme in the work of psychoanalysts Nicolas Abraham (1919–1975) and Maria Torok (b. 1925). Although their theories of self-fashioning and self-articulation are not constructed directly with attention to social difference or change, they do develop a theory of self-creation and enunciation sensitive to the fragmentary and transformable self that is articulated in poststructural theory and that is vital to any theory of reading that links this self to the dislocations and displacements of the social imaginary and social field. Abraham and Torok provide commentary on the nature and process of self-transformation and change, hence a theorizing of *reading* these changes; but their clinical studies also articulate the ramifications of blocked or absent desire(s) in the process of self-fashioning, leading to a theory of *encryption,* or the limit conditions of reading and readability. For Abraham and Torok, a topographical space designated as "the crypt" interrupts regular psycho*analytic* readings of desire and identity. Such "tales from the crypt," or the limit of readability, allow transformative pedagogy to consider cases where desire does not map nicely onto identity, and therefore the vicissitudes of identity themselves interrupt any synecdochal relationship between "safely" readable individuals and social groups.

For Abraham and Torok, *anasemia* names the reading process of a radicalized semantics in which meaning is not directly or easily substituted for a decoded or deciphered symbol, in which phenomenological belief that when a "thing first became sign its being was retrieved in the proper name" is found to be questionable.[10] In reading psychoanalytic concepts, Abraham and Torok discern difficulties with the assumptions of "safe" reading: namely that key psychoanalytic concepts do not relate directly or immediately to an object or a collection of objects and therefore a "safe" reading based upon a simple translation of "things" to "words" cannot be guaranteed. Similarly, I would like to suggest that some forms of critical pedagogy have taken up an understanding of identity politics that may not "guarantee" a safe reading of desire as mapped onto certain corporeal characteristics, nor can individual identity be inscribed into social group identity in any "safe" or permanent reading. Clinical demonstrations from Abraham and Torok's cases of how "the crypt" interrupts identity formation suggest that anasemic reading may engage us pedagogically to discover alternate reading practices useful to transformative education.

THE WOLF MAN'S SECRETS:
ANALYSIS OF A NIGHTMARE/A NIGHTMARE FOR ANALYSIS

The architecture of Abraham and Torok's psychoanalytic insights into readability is framed primarily from their rewriting of Freud's occult "Wolf Man" case. Nicknamed for his phobias and principal dreams of wolves, Russian-born Sergei Constantinovitch Pankeiev (1887–1979) dwelt in analysis most of his adult life. From the early stages, the Wolf Man's case was to prove a nightmare for Freudian psychoanalysis *itself*: while Freud sought to use it as irrefutable evidence for his theories, the Wolf Man continued to suffer his entire life and became an anomaly, subverting every attempt by Freud to explain his condition as having an origin in childhood Oedipal desires and fears.

Abraham and Torok offer a rewriting of this puzzle that is paradigmatically different from Freud's obsessive revisions of the Wolf Man's seemingly unreadable material. They recast Freud's insistence on the *reality* of the primal scene, the importance of childhood sexuality as the *origin* of neurosis, and the necessity to *read symptoms at face value* rather than as signifiers of their own production. This *rereading* of Freud's case in particular announced a *disjuncture* between the "I" registered as the *identity* of an individual, and desires supposedly *claimed* by that "I." Freud himself had observed in 1913 that although a woman patient had abreacted (discharged) her troublesome experience, her daughter retained the *mother's* experience *as if it had belonged originally to the daughter*.[11] Yet he could not, in the Wolf Man's case, free himself of the conviction that became the antecedent and subsequent focus of Abraham and Torok's reinterpretation: the prejudicial reading practice of attaching *directly and only to that individual* all desires, events, feelings, and fears registered under the pronoun "I." The "I," in fact, cannot be articulated as an essence; rather, its identity is always that of a relation, properly *relational*. Abraham and Torok leave open the possibility that desires or activities recorded as the possession of "I" or "me" might instead refer to, or be the possession of, another person or persons. As Derrida suggests of their work, "the *signature*, if one could still use the expression, vacillates between the names."[12] This discovery forces a radicalization of the structure of psychoanalysis itself as perhaps beyond its "definite, possessive, and personal" roots in Freud.[13] Thus, Abraham and Torok's work hints at a gap between identity and its discontents, particularly, of a gap between desire and identity.

THE PSYCHIC LIFE OF MAKING AND MASKING:
INTROJECTION/INCORPORATION

Abraham and Torok's reinterpretation of Freudian psychoanalysis offers insights into the relationship between desire and identity through the key processes of *introjection* and *incorporation*. For Abraham and Torok, these together constitute the sum total of self-fashioning. Although Torok in particular takes great lengths to distinguish the two as radically different processes, this means less that the two are opposed in function than that incorporation operates or intervenes at the limits of introjection itself, when introjection fails.[14] The two are thus coimplicated in a relationship of supplementarity in the formulation of the self.

The term *introjection* has undergone several transformations in psychoanalysis.[15] But it is only through Abraham and Torok's careful refinement of the term that *introjection* has come to denote specific clinical characteristics *and* outline a more generalized approach to psychical development, that of "broadening and enriching the ego."[16] The *object* of love itself is not "introjected" but is properly given the role of mediator toward the unconscious.[17] Thus, introjection as a process "transforms . . . desires and fantasies of desire, making them fit to receive a name and the right to exist and unfold in the objectal sphere."[18] In this sense, introjection can be considered *metaphorical* in nature, for as any loss of a loved object is introjected, libido is successfully displaced by the substitution of words for and about the lost object in a potential *associative* relationship.[19]

Rand suggests a reading of introjection in Guy de Maupassant's short story, "At Sea" (*En mer*).[20] In the story, two brothers aboard a fishing boat encounter stormy seas. The elder brother must make a choice between capsizing the boat or saving his younger brother's arm, which stays a rope keeping the boat afloat. A decision is made to save the boat, requiring amputation; the younger brother decides to preserve the cadaverous appendage despite the elder's wishes to dispose of it immediately. The arm is shown to the family, then given proper burial at the church. Rand suggests that the story illustrates how the loss of the arm is acknowledged through public and private suffering and how the object mediates both the loss and transformation from the old body-arrangement to the new. By refusing to hide this loss or experience it as shameful or secret, the younger brother was able to fully mourn the amputation and *name* his loss publicly. In this sense, the younger brother remained *in connection* with himself and his landscape, experiencing a touching-touched adaptation and self-fashioning with his world.[21]

Introjection is our lifelong activity of self-fashioning. The guarantee that introjection has taken place is the metaphorical replacement of the lost object's presence with language. Initially, the loss of the object acts as a prohibition to introjection, halting the process.

The ego then faces the painful but necessary work of mourning the lost object *as lost*, thus introjecting the loss and freeing libidinal attachments to be recovered and available for reinvestment with other objects. The "hinge," or connecting experience between introjection proper and *incorporation*, resides in how the self copes with the *loss* of the object of love. If the loss is unrecognized, refused, or unfelt, introjection is thwarted and *incorporation* of the lost object may occur. Although introjection can be said to be a true process of self-fashioning, *incorporation* is a mask or concealment, a *fantasy or desire for* introjection, even a claim introjection *has* occurred, but in all cases, it is a detour around the actual process of introjection.

Incorporation marks the hostility or unwillingness to undergo the painful process of mourning the lost object of love: the loss is instead considered unacceptable and is denied by the ego. Following denial, the ego magically creates a fantasy object in the attempt to contain and continue the pleasures originally experienced by the real object. Rather than accept the loss and transform it into words, the object is "reconstructed," now as a *fantasized* object and "kept" in, contained by a whole constructed architecture Abraham and Torok label "the crypt."[22] These fantasies are not without a price. Desires attached to the (previously) lost object remain attached to the fantasy object, *buried and kept secret* within the ego to preserve the fantasy that loss did not occur, so the fantasy-object can continue as a desired source of pleasure. These concealments render individuals' identities enigmatic, all in order to conceal and continue the new incorporative self-architecture.

Abraham and Torok point out on several occasions that incorporation can be performed in differing ways: the ego and the "fantasy" object act collaboratively against some external force or act oppositionally and aggressively toward each other. Two clinical cases illustrate the workings of incorporation.[23]

A woman suffering from depression expresses moods of self-depreciation, despair, and worthlessness; she conveys an incident from youth in which her father deserted the family for unexpressed reasons and his whereabouts remain unknown—but she wonders if he is still alive. Transference does not occur, amid lengthy analysis. It is only when the analyst relinquishes a prejudice in favor of only one "I" speaking that the meaning is clear: she is fantasizing the afflictions of *another* as her own. The lost father becomes incorporated within her as a fantasized presence—she lived as if she were *her father*, suffering because he was separated from her, crying over her, accusing himself of his neglect of her, happy in overzealous moments of pursuit but feeling worthless in his abandonment of her. She, in turn, "protects" this incorporated entity, due to her empathetic identification with his supposed/fantasized "guilt." But no outward manifestation of this habitation is apparent. She neither dresses nor acts as a man, nor does she speak about him.

"Victor" is married and works at a good job but describes himself as constantly embroiled in conflicts with his superiors at work and as feeling unsuccessful; he complains that his wife is jealous, possessive, and frustrating, yet he remains with her. He recalls a past car accident, after which he stumbled around the scene, searching for the young friend who was with him. He makes a statement, strangely replacing the name of the friend with his own name: "Where is little Viki?" He is (has incorporated) his older brother Gilles. Victor had idealized Gilles as his protector since childhood but was thwarted in his desire for Gilles as a lover. After the car accident, Victor *is* Gilles, once again "searching" and "protecting" little "Viki." But "where" then is Victor? He abandons himself to becoming embodied in his critical wife: she speaks all of "Victor's" complaints to "Gilles" and berates "Gilles" for abandoning Victor. Thus "Gilles" can be punished and thwarted for having rejected Victor's love *and at the same time* "Gilles" retains his status as protector for Victor. The topography is tortuously twisted. "Gilles" is kept, retained, *encrypted*, as the object of Victor's affection *and* condemnation. Sorting out desire and identity in the process of incorporation thus becomes an antimetaphorical process, no longer a process of replacing a "lost" object with a "name," but rather a *designifying* process, in the sense that the object remains (even though as "fantasy") and cannot be named/read in any usual manner.

READING THE PSYCHIC LIFE OF MAKING AND MASKING: DESIRE AND IDENTITY

A comparison of the processes of introjection and incorporation yields very different topographical surveys of the self. Through introjection, the lost object is displaced into language and libido is released to become possessively attached to new objects; the landscape is reconfigured through its bond with the new object. Testimony to identity here is a relatively simple affair: the self is articulated on the basis of a foundational attachment to a loved object or objects. But in incorporation, the landscape is overrun with conflicting architecture designed to confuse and protect, to render empty any attempt at self-articulation. Contradictory voices emerge because of desires secreted away in the crypt: encrypted selves display what can best be described as all the drama of a courtroom trial. "Witnesses" testify to differing desires, identities, and events; "secret" witnesses must be indicted to give testimony to their existence within the self; the ego "proper" and the fantasized love object make statements as respective counsels; all are engaged in the business of *both* truth and fiction. The incorporated self functions like a trial that never concludes, or more properly, like an *endless pretrial*, in which the contradictions and oppositional accusations are still fresh and operative, *before* judgment or resolution on any unitary identity is passed or even posited as the end of a linear narrative. It is as though the *contradictions themselves* create the architecture, as if a simple, singular testimony of "truth" could produce no self at all. As Derrida suggests, incorporated entities exist through "what architects call 'the resistance of the materials' that balance the pressures, repel intrusions, foresee collapse, or in any case delay it."[24] The tensions and frustrations that provide this balance arise because the incorporated object is a heterogeneous "inside" to the inside of the self, a foreigner lodged within the self, feigning introjection. Freud's Wolf Man, for example, could neither be understood as an identity developed from an originary event, nor even as a narrative fictionalizing such an origin to provide comprehension—or *readability*.

From these divergent topographies, questions about the relationship between identity and desire arise. In the process of incorporation, desire seems almost a disruptive force to the metaphoric displacements of "lack" and "law" in Abraham and Torok's introjection: in incorporation, the desire to continue the relation with the lost object swells to the point of fantastically constructing it as "never lost." Introjection, in contrast, seems to accept loss and reconstitute the self by fixing identity through a relation with a new love object. If anything, in incorporation desire seems to overrun any law that may attempt to dictate strict boundaries between truth and fiction, reality and fantasy. Similarly, although desire seems to be in response to the "lack" of the missing/lost object, the "lack" does not always create an empty space that becomes the cause and condition of a speech to "fill" it: as Abraham and Torok suggest, incorporation names the process by which signification by metaphor becomes *unattainable*. Further, in Abraham and Torok's clinical cases, desire seems to thwart any attempt to *articulate* identity, or to render itself readable as a symptom that could symbolically trace/be traced to identity, because of its encrypted nature: identity becomes unspeakable because of the secret nature of the encryption. There are no words that can be spoken, and no desire can be revealed because the fantasized object is enclosed within the complex and contradictory architecture of the crypt. Thus, in incorporation, no symptom seems to exist, and therefore reading is blocked. In this sense, Abraham and Torok's topographical reading of the self is somewhat akin to Gilles Deleuze's, when the latter claims that "[desire does not function as a] bridge between a subject and an object."[25] Abraham and Torok's subject of incorporation is most certainly "split" by the crypt, and even though desire is directed toward an "object" of love, it finds it must *create* that object, phantasmically.

Judith Butler provides a lucid example of the convolutions of desire and identification created in the process of incorporation. For Butler, the "fantasized object" created to be contained in the process of incorporation becomes thought of as so *literal* that, for example, a desired homosexual object could be incorporated as a *literalized* sexual anatomy, thus seeming to constitute a heterosexual identity. In this example, Butler claims, identity is developed through a conflation of desire with a type of "literalized" reality: the melancholic (incorporative) heterosexual male states, "He never loved another man, he *is* a man, and he can seek recourse to the empirical facts that will prove it."[26] Encrypted homosexual desire thus leads to *identification*, but in a very strange way. The difficult question from these examples, however, is how to *read* this: if desires are encrypted such that they appear *erased, unreadable,* and *no symptom is present,* how can readability exist?

READING AND PEDAGOGY:
DETECTIVE FICTION, OR ANASEMIC TRANSLATION?

I began this essay by discussing the queer similarities between psychoanalysis and the detective story, noting how both entail a doubled desiring code of decipherment and affect. Abraham and Torok's theories of introjection and incorporation elicit a different practice of reading, caused by seemingly unreadable, *encrypted* desires. From such differential theories of reading, the practice of pedagogy itself might be re-cast.[27] As an interpretive and relational process, reading has a great deal in common with pedagogy. Practices and performances of reading, like practices and performances of pedagogy, produce desire, identity, and knowledge as they stage possible scenes for these performances. Both pedagogy and reading offer and perform techniques of making sense. By weaving pedagogy and reading intertextually, I hope to outline the important implications that result from these differing practices of reading (reading/pedagogy) as *"detecting,"* versus Abraham and Torok's *anasemic reading* (reading as anasemia).

GOING TO DETECTIVE SCHOOL

One of the foundations bequeathed by Freud to modern psychoanalytic writing is the performance of reading as the *seductive, interrogative solving of a puzzle* with a *determinate, empirical* solution. It is easy to see how many pedagogical performances could also fall into the category of detective work or puzzle solving. Students quite frequently puzzle us by the nature of their activities in the classroom. Why did she do that? Why doesn't he care about this class? Why can't he learn how to read? These are common enough figurations of pedagogy as puzzle solving—one has to think only of staff-room conversations: it must be his/her family situation, it must be hormones (s/he's "at that age"), it must be the neighborhood influences. Lest we too quickly object that not all teachers view students or student behavior as a sort of (troubling? troublesome?) *empirical puzzle* or *problem* to be solved, even more relational or dialogic pedagogical relationships involve moments of puzzlement and potentially lend themselves to deductive framing. Why does she desire to be like with this particular social group? Cultural status? Who is s/he in this relationship with me, the teacher-authority? Who is s/he in relation to this school, this community? Who am I in this relationship? In the face of uncertainty or a seeming lack of knowledge, the desire for deduction toward a causal, originary answer, "fixing" identity in a safe reading, is both a common and an enduring response. What is responsible for the seductiveness of such a practice of reading/pedagogy?

The compelling lesson we learn in detective school, which comes to hold such a place of prominence in our reading (and, I would argue, our pedagogical) practices, is the seduction of a Sherlock Holmes identity that exists "before the crime." The seduction of solving a puzzle involves the construction of the detective as a determined identity, *independent* of the crime scene and suspects. If the subject is in this way "removed" from any *relation* to the scene, it becomes that much easier to construe the "solution" to the mystery as an object or "other" to be traced, detected. After all, what else could a thoughtful, rational detective—"subject" expect to find but the "object" of his/her own creation?

Detective school has at least a three-lesson curriculum in mind to create us as detectives "before the crime": *independence, objectivity,* and a certain notion of *ethics.*

Since the detective story demands *from the beginning* that the reader suspend belief or disbelief in all elements of the case, detective-school-as-text invites us to create and fill our own interpretive gaps, to *create the readability* of the text for *ourselves,* as highly independent and intelligent thinkers. Through this sense of independence, coupled with a complete disrespect for transcendental truth or social convention, detective school also compels and entices us as readers/teachers to consider ourselves as *objective* detectives, unswayed by easy solutions to simply scapegoat a likely suspect or by logically unsatisfying solutions that omit clues or fail to explain all events. But perhaps detective school's greatest lesson is in its interpellation of the subject as someone charged with an *ethical* imperative to find the truth. By highlighting how truth is neither transcendental nor determined by social convention but rather *hidden* by coercion and violence (of others, self, or language), the detective text drives readers forward toward the solution, charging them with an ethical imperative to "right" the wrongs of the intersubjective situation. Lest we begin to feel detective school prescribes a rather coercive or *contrived* curriculum, we could note how these elements strangely parallel those of "critical thinking" about the social realm found in critical and radical pedagogy, not to mention the ethical readings of certain poststructural and deconstructive criticism. This is not to suggest such readings cannot be put to ethical ends but rather to question the performances of "independence," "objectivity," and "ethics" referenced to them. Pedagogically, we must pay attention to the power of these texts to have us co-construct their narratives and ask, as Derrida has, Is there an "impulse of identification which is indispensable for reading?"[28]

Learning to read and teach in detective school is not just a matter of constructing the detective but also concerns conditioning the nature of the answer the detective seeks. Although detectives are seemingly "free" to create the path toward readability and solution, detective school dictates that it must indeed be a "path" one follows, always toward an *origin* or *originary text* for solution. The desiring mechanism that impels detectives on in their quest for origin is the *secret.* Without a secret or presumed secret, the likelihood of a causal origin would significantly decrease, for the knowledge of a secret's existence and the presumed knowledge (and guilt) of one who has hidden the knowledge guarantee both the origin's existence and the desire to achieve it. Even though Abraham and Torok took great pains to outline a theory of reading and readability *other* than the detective story, their belief in one *secreted* identity within another formed the basis for the theory of incorporation. The desire for detection becomes that much more powerful when a secret or perceived secret is involved. Again, the teachers in the staff room wonder: "Why haven't we heard from the parents? It seems so strange. I don't think this student is telling us everything about why s/he's missing so many classes." The secret *must be traced*, the referent must be found, whether it is potentially found to be truth, fiction, or something in-between. Without the origin, the clues would not fall "into place," constructing a readable narrative and satiating our need to settle intersubjective relations in the story, to close the case.

PEDAGOGY AS TRANSLATION: ANASEMIA

In contrast with "going to detective school," pedagogy might instead engage in Abraham and Torok's differential strategies of readability, formulated through their psychoanalytic narratives of introjection and incorporation and collectively termed *anasemia* or anasemic reading. Derrida describes this project as follows: "How to include in a discourse, *any* discourse, that which, being the very condition of discourse, would by its very essence *escape* discourse."[29] In such a reading, words must be taken neither literally nor figuratively but as an "allusion to that without which no meaning—neither literal nor figurative—could come into being."[30] Clearly, we are not talking here about a simple strategy of linking a "word" to a "thing," a name to an object, signifier to signified. To unpack the strategy of anasemia, we need to consider it as both a practice and a question of *translation*.

Generally, we understand translation as a process of movement from one language to another. Anasemia as translation also implies a translation or transportation from one language *into itself,* describing the way words flow beyond themselves yet still allow their initial reading to *coexist* even though the reading is also *exceeded*. This is possible because of Abraham's claim that psychoanalysis itself imposes a "radical semantic change," a de-signification of words used in their ordinary sense that allows the word *both* the ordinary sense *and* a translation into a whole new language. But in doing so, an anasemic translation, anasemia *as* translation, will have to translate into discourse that which escapes it, in other words, what Derrida calls "non-discourse," "the untranslatable," "the unpresentable."[31] This unpresentable is the condition or possibility of translation, of readability: it must paradoxically be made present in a way that does not betray its existence as unpresentable. An anasemic reading is not, then, a translation involving the formal logic of relating a concept to an object.[32] In essence, an anasemic reading manages to make the law by which a method constructs its object *apply to the method itself.*

In performing this enfolding process on the structure and text of *psychoanalysis*, Abraham advances a particular figure, that of a shell and a kernel, to designate the *agency* of the Ego (and in doing so, he identifies the agency and figure of psychoanalysis itself). For Abraham, the Ego is "fighting on two fronts: turned toward the outside, moderating appeals and assaults, turned toward the inside, channelling excessive and incongruous impulses. [This agency is] a protective layer . . . a shell."[33] What is located within the shell is designated as the *kernel*, that which is unpresentable (in the case of psycho-analysis, the Unconscious) but is "presented" in a strange way because "the shell itself is marked by what it shelters; that which it encloses is disclosed within it. [The kernel's] secret and elusive action is nonetheless attested to at every step."[34] But although the shell is said to "shelter" the kernel, in no way can these two images be said to be identical to each other, nor do they "pos-sess" or control each other. It is not as if the shell, peeled back, "reveals" its kernel as an accessible surface. The kernel is "presented" only anasemically; it never passes *through* the shell to be made visible, but its activities are inscribed in and by the shell. Derrida calls the action of the shell and the kernel a trans-lation "otherwise"—"[a translation] into itself outside itself."[35]

As a theory of translation, anasemic reading (anasemia of reading) explains the process of reading used in Abraham and Torok's clinical work with cases of encrypted desires. Recall that neither desire nor identity is easily deci-phered in incorporated individuals, due to the confusing architecture of encryption. In the case of the young woman who "was [had encrypted] her father," no symptom was obvious to the analyst. This was because of the young woman's *protection* of the encrypted father from outside forces (i.e., the analyst) but was also caused by her "protection" or *enclosure of* the missing father *within* herself. The woman thus "displayed" the action of the father through her own activities and words, but without "revealing" him as an incorporated entity. Likewise, the shell "encloses what it discloses"; it encrypts the kernel and, in doing so, "discloses" the activities of the kernel acting *through* the shell.

Although Abraham and Torok's anasemic reading of *psychoanalysis* reveals a different mode of reading than "going to detective school," this reading as translation also has the potential to recast relationships among desire, identity, and the social in pedagogy, particularly in transformative pedagogy. As detec-tive school teaches us to search for the causal *origin* of desire and identity and identity politics insists on a synecdochal mapping of desire and identity, onto social groups, both these reading strategies fail to escape a simplistic represen-tational reading scheme that attaches a referent (material "thing") to an intending sign (possessed by an author) that points to the referent. An anasemic reading of social groups and social-group identity no longer metaphorically attaches the name of the group to certain corporeal individuals or empirical characteristics of individuals. Rather, anasemia names the translation process by which messages are sent not from subjects to objects but travel on the anasemic plane between the shell and the kernel, an image that helps explain the *agency* of such a reading. Such an image configures different answers than the detective's recourse to originary or essentialist explanations for particular group identification.

Anasemically, we could ask how it is that a social group identity (fantasized or otherwise) can mobilize empirical bodies into sexually desirous, gendered, or racialized bodies. Whereas the detective finds recourse only in tracing "originary identifications," anasemically we have the image of a somatic kernel behind a shell of social desire and identification. The somatic (of which the body is a part) cannot be directly presented[36] but is instead enclosed within a shell of social positioning and naming that both camoflages *and* speaks its activities. This somatic, which never becomes an accessible surface, is *behind* the shell, *delegated* by the social group/shell that receives and articulates this unpresentable somatic through the shell's various "modalities of reception."[37] The detective's efforts to construct the somatic (or even just the body) as *referent* and social-group identity as *intentional sign* go awry because of the frailties of representation: the somatic/the body is always more, excessive to any sign. Anasemically, however, the somatic is acknowledged as the unpresentable, the condition for reading, and hence, social group desire and identification become much less (but much more) than an attached sign.

Anasemic reading also implies much broader effects upon the manner in which we understand pedagogical practices and pedagogy itself. Anasemic reading also helps explain what Abraham and Torok term the "phantom effect," a type of incorporative architecture similar in effect to the crypt but parallel to more traditional scenes of pedagogy. Although in the crypt of the self, it is the self that has created its own prohibition and secret to keep (although the secret may involve a scene with other individuals); in the crypt of the phantom, it is *another's* secret, another's failed introjection that comes back to haunt, particularly an *adult* (a parent's or perhaps a teacher's) secret: this creates a *transgenerational* "haunting" by a *transgenerational phantom*. This "haunting" produces the same traumas of rejected mourning and unreadability that occur in the crypt of the self, as they are effects of a similar prohibition toward silence and secret-keeping. But the transgenerational phantom expands the realm of psychoanalysis beyond individual diagnosis to the diagnosis of familial, social, historical, and (I would add) *pedagogical* patterns and movements. (Nicolas Rand and Maria Torok, for example, utilize this theory to diagnose some of the "illnesses" within the history of psychoanalysis itself.)

Abraham describes Shakespeare's *Hamlet* as a classic example of transgenerational haunting in which Hamlet's lack of desire and courage to avenge his father's death is caused less by Hamelt's being a weak-willed academic than by the effects of the dead king's secret that "haunts" his son.[38] (It is, of course, convenient that an actual "ghost" character "haunts" Hamlet; in clinical cases of cryptic identification, the term "ghost" or "phantom" is entirely figurative.) Abraham suggests it is the ghost and not Hamlet who is more in need of analysis, for it is not the child who has lost a loved object but rather the parent/other whose own failed introjections (of whatever nature) are unmourned. For Abraham, both Hamlet's "investigative" activities and his apparent lack of desire to seek revenge *cannot* be explained because they are *beyond* Hamlet's character, and *beyond the play itself*: Hamlet is a pseudocharacter, a mere tool or puppet for the activities of *another* agent—the phantom. Hamlet's admonishment to Horatio to "tell my story" is carried out by Abraham as he writes a sixth act to the play in which the phantom's secret is spoken, allowing Hamlet to discover his father's unintrojected trauma and to himself be storied and become a character.

Although the dead King Hamlet's "pedagogy of secrets" describes a parental and pedagogical scene of incorporation, transgenerational haunting also applies to theorizing education as a wider social and cultural practice. Because the theory of the phantom implies the unconscious transmission of a previous generation's secret to the next generation, it could be generalized into a theory of education, an *infected pedagogy* or even an anasemic pedagogy (anasemia of pedagogy). The *mark or symptom* of such an infected pedagogy would be childrens' unwitting repetition of uncanny, unresolvable investigations occasioned by secrets that cannot be revealed because they belong to a previous generation and a previous history.

Rand suggests that the phantom can help to explain, for example, the repetition of past political ideologies in youth who have had no previous experiential contact with such ideologies. Any shame or embarrassment to a nation or political ideology that is secreted by a generation may easily be handed to the next generation, creating a phantom effect of *infected pedagogy* posturing an *infected politics and history*. Such may be the case, Rand argues, in the neo-Nazi movements of the 1980s and 1990s in which youth appear fascinated with, and in some cases desire to take on, past ideological positions, while never having possessed any direct experiential contact with the Nazi wartime regime.[39]

How is it that past ideological positions can mobilize the bodies of youth to desire and perform violent acts, years later? Again, the shell-kernel image comes into play. The kernel (here described as "the phantom") is unpresentable but noticeable through the actions of the shell. Although antiracist education may be directed at the "new" young Nazis and "*their*" actions questioned, it is perhaps the ghosts of World War II Nazi Germany who are in need of analysis. In confronting the ghosts of Nazi "fathers"—their unmourned lost objects, their failed introjections—the activities of neo-Nazi youth may be explained.

PEDAGOGY AND ANASEMIA: READING CASE STUDIES IN DESIRE AND IDENTITY

Anasemic readings of pedagogical scenes and events represent a reading of desire and identification quite far removed from tracing the causal, originary solution to the detective's case. Although these reading performances explain differently the relationships between desire and identification, between children/students and parent/teachers, anasemic readings may also help to develop new areas of research in curriculum studies and in studies of pedagogical desire and identity.

School curricula are by nature selective pieces of culture designated for the purpose of transmission to the young and as such may manifest phantom effects in themselves. Given the textbook's important function as *the* cultural artifact of choice for teaching, the secrets/potentially embarrassing elements of a culture may be encrypted into these texts and unwittingly passed onto future generations.

Toni Morrison's *Playing in the Dark: Whiteness and the Literary Imagination* is an important work for teachers of upper-level grades that in its own way alludes to similar textual effects of incorporation described by Abraham and Torok.[40] Morrison describes what she terms "linguistic responses to an Africanist presence" in American literature that manifest white social unease with black Africanist bodies and presence.

> The linguistic responses to an Africanist presence complicate texts, sometimes contradicting them entirely. A writer's response to American Africanism often provides a subtext that either sabotages the surface text's expressed intentions or escapes them through a language that mystifies what it cannot bring itself to articulate but still attempts to register.[41]

These "afflictions of the text" would for Abraham and Torok signal the fantasy of introjection or incorporative effects, which disrupt and deliberately obscure the reading of the text. Morrison describes some of these afflictions as "metonymic displacement" and "patterns of explosive, disjointed, repetitive language," which for Abraham and Torok are indicative of the subject's effort to complicate and convolute speech in order to disguise and hide incorporated entities. The disruptive language of Morrison's "linguistic responses to an Africanist presence" cannot be explained within the text themselves because they are beyond these texts, as Morrison points out, with previous generations' hidden embarrassment at the history of black slavery in America. Performing textual analyses such as Morrison's on curricular materials could reveal phantasmic effects of generational secrets and could serve as a vital part of multicultural, antiracist and postcolonial efforts in curriculum analysis and development.

Concepts of incorporation and anasemic reading also provide a general *mechanism* by which individual teachers' and students' border crossings over trauma and change can be negotiated. In this sense, cultural, linguistic, personal, professional, or psychic adaptation in bi- or multicultural settings could be investigated anasemically.

Because the basic structure of introjection requires the mediation of desires from the lost object and onto language "about" the object, any traumatic event that is silenced or prohibited and thus left "unsaid" could subject the individual to an "illness of mourning," or incorporation. *Student-teachers* negotiate border crossings that may be fraught with trauma: the student-to-teacher-authority passage; the adolescent/young adult-to-adult or perhaps parent-to-professional passage; the transition from lay person to licensed craftsperson, from student to employee, from tuition payer to breadwinner; and for some, the uneasy negotiation of ethnic and racial differences between one's own culture and the culture of what can be a new and different community and school. As the passage of development from student to teacher may involve traumatic losses and many psychic adaptations to the new role, case studies of student-teachers may reveal encryptions of the self if these losses are not properly introjected.

The negotiation of social differences may be of particular difficulty for a student-teacher crossing the borders of a home-and-family setting racially different than that of the school culture.[42] Because race and racial identities are issues of difference and potential disparity, a traditional liberal response seeks to erase race significations altogether, trying to "bridge" such crossings by exhorting "racelessness." Similarly, the universality and invisibility of "whiteness" is a further, and related, denial of racial investments.[43] But because race *is* an economy of desire and investment, the subject will likely undergo either introjection and mourning or may potentially incorporate racial objects.

If introjection is the process by which the self is created, are student teachers allowed and encouraged to "mourn" the loss of old desires and identifications around their racial objects, or are these losses minimized and silenced?

Would the introjective efforts of an African-American struggling to adapt to teaching in an all-white school be encouraged? Are student teachers "encouraged" to desire and identify as "white" in order to teach, and how might incorporative effects manifest themselves as a result? Would the introjective process be discouraged or silenced if a white student-teacher were to discuss and mourn the loss of desired white classes of students because of working in a school of nonwhite children? Case studies of student-teachers adapting to new school and community cultures would be important testing grounds for a theory of introjection and may indeed reveal incorporative effects of the self if such culturally and personally traumatic border crossings are not articulated. Such case study research could lead to important new theories of cultural adaptation, trauma, and coping mechanisms for student-teachers. Perhaps more important such research might reveal the limited amount of professional and social support offered student-teachers in their process of learning to teach, a lack that exaggerates the private, while impoverishing the public practices of mourning and adaptation.[44]

READING *INSIDE* AND *OUTSIDE* PEDAGOGY

Through Abraham and Torok's clinical cases, desire seemingly reveals itself to be a force that interrupts processes of introjection, the metaphorical replacement of words for lost objects. Desire as antimetaphor seems to refuse any "safe" practices of reading, and questions the more traditional reading practices learned in "detective school." I have offered here one alternative reading practice, that of Abraham and Torok's anasemic reading (reading as anasemia) as a differing approach in order to articulate the sometimes complex relationships between desire and identity. No doubt, such a practice of reading may unsettle many conceptualizations of agency and identity in current curricular and pedagogical theorizing.

Anasemic reading is offered, however, in the hope of extending to the field of pedagogy not simply "another" method (perhaps more consonant with poststructural conceptions of curriculum and pedagogy) but also a larger project of anasemically reading the field of education itself, a "translation into itself outside itself." Anasemic reading provides not just a means by which pedagogical or curricular *scenes* can be read but also a means by which the methods that construct the "objects of study" for the fields of pedagogy and curriculum *themselves* can be read. In this sense, anasemic reading (reading as anasemia) offers both method for, and immanent study of, educational practices.

NOTES

1. Gilles Deleuze, "What is Desire?" in *The Deleuze Reader*, ed. Constantin Boundas (New York: Columbia University Press, 1993), 136.

2. Ibid., 137–38.

3. Robin Usher and Richard Edwards, *Postmodernism and Education* (New York: Routledge, 1994), 11.

4. See Peter Brooks, "Fictions of the Wolf Man: Freud and Narrative Understanding," *diacritics* 9, no.1 (1979), 74. See also Carlo Ginzburg, "Morelli, Freud, and Sherlock Holmes: Clues and Scientific Method," in *The Sign of Three: Dupin, Holmes, Peirce*, ed. Umberto Eco and Thomas A. Sebeok (Bloomington: Indiana University Press, 1983), 87.

5. For several examples of how educational documentary films, for instance, construct a "safe" reading of themselves as texts, see Elizabeth Ellsworth, "I Pledge Allegiance: The Politics of Reading and Using Educational Films," in *Race, Identity, and Representation in Education*, ed. Cameron McCarthy and Warren Crichlow (New York: Routledge, 1993), 201–19.

6. In a well-known passage in *Beyond the Pleasure Principle*, Freud discusses the behavior of his grandson, little Ernst, who plays a game of throwing a reel-and-thread out of his bed and then repetitively drawing it back in, each time with pleasure and relief. Freud interpreted the little boy's mutterings during the game as "fort . . . da" ("gone . . . there"), and linked it to a reenactment trauma of his mother's absences, as if the little boy were reassuring himself that in the end she would always return. See Sigmund Freud, "Beyond the Pleasure Principle," in *The Freud Reader*, ed. Peter Gay (New York: W. W. Norton & Company, 1989), 594–626, especially 599–602. Jacques Derrida reads Freud himself as involved in the same risk-safety game and shows how Freudian texts allow a temporary loss of mastery only on the condition that theoretical and textual command can be regained in a concluding show of mastery. See Derrida's reading of "fort . . . da" in "Coming into One's Own," in *Psychoanalysis and the Question of the Text*, ed. Geoffrey Hartman (Baltimore: Johns Hopkins University Press, 1978), 114–18.

7. In his distinction between "reading" and "writing," Roland Barthes seems to imply the former is a "passive response" to a pregiven, authorized work and the latter the "active creation" of a work. I use the term "production" or "producing" to indicate a reading/writing of identity-texts that is neither "passive" nor "active" because it cannot be completely controlled by an autonomous, conscious, intending subject. In this sense, the subject is both determined by and determining of the social forces surrounding it.

8. As Michael Apple notes, "The sphere of symbolic production is a contested terrain just as other spheres or social life are." See Apple, "Constructing the Other: Rightist Reconstructions of Common Sense," in McCarthy and Crichlow, *Race, Identity, and Representation in Education*, 34.

9. Barbara Johnson, *The Wake of Deconstruction* (Cambridge: Blackwell, 1994), 72.

10. Peggy Kamuf, "Abraham's Wake," *diacritics* 9:1 (1979), 34–35.

11. See also Maria Torok's discussion of this passage in "The Story of Fear: The Symptoms of Phobia—the Return of the Repressed or the Return of the Phantom?" in Nicolas Abraham and Maria Torok, *The Shell and the Kernel: Renewals of Psychoanalysis*, ed. and trans. Nicholas Rand vol. 1 (Chicago: University of Chicago Press, 1994), 179. The passage itself is from Lou Andreas Salome's *The Freud Journal*, trans. Stanley Leavy (London: Quartet Books, 1987), 169–70.

12. Jacques Derrida, foreword *"Fors:* The Anglish Words of Nicolas Abraham and Maria Torok," trans. Barbara Johnson, in Nicolas Abraham and Maria Torok, *The Wolf Man's Magic Word: A Cryptonomy,* trans. Nicholas Rand (Minneapolis: University of Minnesota Press, 1986), xxxiii.

13. The descriptors "definite, possessive, personal" are from Gilles Deleuze's critique of psychoanalysis found in Deleuze, "Psychoanalysis and Desire," in *The Deleuze Reader,* 105–6.

14. Derrida, *"Fors,"* xvii.

15. "Introjection" was first conceptualized in 1909 by Séndor Ferenczi; it was later taken up by Freud, Karl Abraham, Melanie Klein, and others (Karl Abraham is of no relation to Nicolas Abraham.) Torok distinguishes clearly that incorporation is a process very distinct from and not a subset of the latter, as Freud and others have utilized it. She suggests Ferenczi's original concept of "introjection" has undergone an impoverishing reduction in meaning. Torok summarizes Ferenczi's concept of intro-jection as "the extension of autoerotic interests, the broadening of the ego through the removal of repression, and . . . an extension to the external world of the [ego's] original autoerotic interests." She suggests that this definition has been reduced in the writing of Ferenczi's contemporaries to "taking possession of the object through *incorporation,* that is, by putting it into the body or the psyche." See Torok, "The Illness of Mourning," in Abraham and Torok, *The Shell and the Kernel,* 110–13, 116.

16. Ibid., 113.

17. Torok makes it quite clear that it is a misconception to suggest that the object itself is introjected. See ibid., 112–13, 116. See also Nicolas Abraham and Maria Torok, "Mourning *or* Melancholia: Introjection versus Incorporation," in *The Shell and the Kernel,* 130.

18. Ibid., 130.

19. Ibid., 128.

20. Nicholas Rand, "Introduction: Renewals of Psychoanalysis," in Abraham and Torok, *The Shell and the Kernel,* 12–13. Guy de Maupassant's short story can be found in *Contes de la Becasse* (Paris: Ollendorff, 1901).

21. I utilize the phrase "touching-touched" in a somewhat similar way to Maurice Merleau-Ponty's work in *The Visible and the Invisible* (Evanston, IL: Northwestern University Press, 1968).

22. Abraham and Torok, "The Lost Object—Me: Notes on Endocryptic Identification," in *The Shell and the Kernel,* 141–42. (See also "'L'objet perdu—moi': Notations sur l' identification endocryptique," *Revue Française de Psychanalyse* 39, no. 3 (1975), 411–26); see also Abraham and Torok, "Mourning *or* Melancholia," 125–38.

23. Both cases are described in Abraham and Torok, "The Lost Object—Me."

24. Derrida, *"Fors,"* xv.

25. Deleuze, "Psychoanalysis and Desire," 112–13.

26. Judith Butler, *Gender Trouble* (New York: Routledge, 1990), 71.

27. Paralleling the argument that reading and pedagogy are analogous, if not even related metaphorically (reading as pedagogy, pedagogy as reading), see Deborah Britzman's argument that "the problem of curriculum is a problem of identity," in "Structures of Feeling in Curriculum and Teaching," *Theory into Practice* 31, no. 3 (summer 1992), 253–54.

28. Derrida, *The Ear of the Other: Otobiography, Transference, Translation,* ed. Christie McDonald, trans. Avital Ronell and Peggy Kamuf (New York: Schocken Books, 1985), 87.

29. Derrida, "*Fors*," xxxii.

30. Ibid.

31. Jacques Derrida, "Me—Psychoanalysis: An Introduction to the Translation of 'The Shell and the Kernel' by Nicolas Abraham," *diacritics* 9, no. 1 (1979): 6.

32. Ibid., 8.

33. Nicolas Abraham, "The Shell and the Kernel: The Scope and Originality of Freudian Psychoanalysis," in Abarham and Torok, *The Shell and the Kernel*, 80.

34. Ibid.

35. Derrida, "Me—Psychoanalysis," 11.

36. Abraham states: "[We must not] . . . give to *somatic* and *psychic* the meanings of naive empiricism. [Neither should we] . . . constitute them phenomenologically as the body proper and the habitudes of the Ego, respectively. . . . The somatic must be something quite different from the body proper." In Abraham and Torok, *The Shell and the Kernel*, 87.

37. Ibid.

38. Abraham, "The Phantom of Hamlet, or the Sixth Act *Preceded by* the Intermission of 'Truth'," in Abraham and Torok, *The Shell and the Kernel*, 187–205. Note that Abraham refers to the ghost of the dead king as "King Hamlet" to differentiate from "Hamlet," the son who returns to Denmark.

39. Nicholas Rand, "Secrets and Posterity: The Theory of the Transgenerational Phantom," in Abraham and Torok, *The Shell and the Kernel*, 189.

40. Toni Morrison, *Playing in the Dark: Whiteness and the Literary Imagination* (New York: Vintage Books, 1992).

41. Ibid., 66.

42. See the work of Ken Zeichner, "Educating Teachers for Cultural Diversity," NCRTL Special Report (East Lansing, MI: National Center for Research on Teacher Learning, 1993).

43. See Leslie Roman, "White Is a Color! White Defensiveness, Postmodernism, and Anti-Racist Pedagogy," in McCarthy and Crichlow, *Race, Identity, and Representation in Education*, 71–88; and Ruth Frankenberg, *White Women, Race Matters: The Social Construction of Whiteness* (Minneapolis: University of Minnesota Press, 1993).

44. See the stories of "Jamie Owl" in Deborah Britzman, *Practice Makes Practice* (Albany: SUNY Press, 1991), 61–115.

8

Integrative Feminist Pedagogy, C.G. Jung, and the Politics of Visualization

KAARINA KAILO

> I lived in a glass house into which my mother could look at any time. In a glass house, however, you cannot conceal anything without giving yourself away, except by hiding it under the ground. And then you cannot see it yourself either.
>
> —Alice Miller, *The Drama of the Gifted Child*

The above quotation from Alice Miller's study on blocked creativity aptly expresses what happens when desire cannot articulate itself, even as something elusive, unfathomable, and inexhaustible. The Swiss psychoanalyst Miller notes that to be a creative individual, a healthy "narcissist," an individual must be in touch with his or her authentic feelings of anger, jealousy, rage, and so on and must trust the parents' love in order to remain untouched by "bad" behavior. Although universities do not claim to have as their mission the formation of "healthy narcissists," it is important to understand better how they contribute to blocking rather than releasing women's creativity. Together with other institutions, the mainstream educational system replicates the male-as-self and woman-as-"other" attitudes that characterize patriarchal gender relations. Hence, the male-centeredness (masked as "neutrality") of the dominant educational model privileges the formation of healthy male "narcissists" while further alienating women from their Self and "desires." Many women are b/locked inside "glass houses" and under physical and psychological "glass ceilings" because of narrowly defined sex roles that are reinforced by the political, educational, and religious institutions as well as by the media. An educational system at large based on a politically naive myth of objectivity is, like science, in the words of Jacques Lacan, "the ideology of the suppression of the subject."[1]

What then can be done through pedagogical reform to transform this bias and lack of equilibrium implicit in the dominant, exclusionary learning desire? If it is necessary to expose and act on the harmful representations of gender through education, it is also important to consider the assumptions and desires that dominate in women's studies circles where alternative transformational practices are allegedly being applied.

I discuss in this paper how a new modality of learning and teaching—the politics of visualization—may help integrative feminists meet a challenge of the 1990s; to release the blocked energies, imaginations, and intellects of women from a myriad of cultural backgrounds. By showing how the enlightenment models of teaching and learning are being revamped in the wake of the debates on inclusivity and pedagogy, I describe the emergence of "visionwork" as central to pedagogical renewal. "Visionwork"—a term referring to the politics of visualization—is an umbrella concept for all strategies of creative self-knowledge that women in different communities across time and space have relied on to gain wisdom, knowledge and to train their imaginative powers, and to release the creative energies so necessary for all intellectual and spiritual expression. It comprises a variety of techniques such as guided imagery, dream interpretation, active imagination, and individual and group meditation. However, in this context, I focus on a form of guided imagery exercise that is most appropriate for women's studies, modeled on the Jungian practice of "active imagination." My own integrative practices are rooted in both feminist and Jungian theories and practices, although I am also acutely aware of the differences between the two. Despite the Jungians' general lack of political sensibility, the Jungian technique of visualization, "active imagination," and some of Jung's views on educational philosophy can be adapted for the purposes of a feminist transformative practice. In my view, it is important for "integrative" feminism to adopt any ideas and practices that help it reach its goal: the creation of a "third space" between all polarized realms of knowledge, with the aim of increasing educational equity, diversity, and justice.

I begin by discussing the links between the "unsaid" in educational practice, theory, and gender relations. The so-called banking-model of education has links with Freudocentric epistemic assumptions, and it impacts differently on male and female students. To understand the importance of the "midwife" model for women requires understanding how the male-as-the-norm biases of educational theory reinforce negative gender stereotypes. It is the "unsaid" of Freudocentric and banking-model education that allows androcentric desire to dominate throughout Western-inspired educational practices. I then expose what the dominant desire marginalizes by discussing the "unsaid" in non-Freudocentric and women's studies' pedagogical thought.

The section on Jungian theory begins with Jung's pedagogical views, his notion of "desire" (the Self) as linked with individuation, the ego/self axis, and his concept of "active imagination." Finally, I outline in more detail the politics of visualization as a transformative antihegemonic practice of relevance to all pedagogical reformers.

"THE UNSAID" AND DOMINANT LEARNING DESIRE:
FROM BANKING MODEL TO MIDWIFE

In this section, I wish to briefly consider the banking and midwife models of learning in their gendered aspects in preparation for discussion of the Jungian and feminist perspectives on creativity and pedagogy. Despite the recent "paradigm shifts" and debates on diversity, the dominant North American educational model still grounds its epistemological premises on merely one of the senses, promoting a patriarchal knowledge and learning base along a linear, disembodied, and cognitively narrow semantic path. According to Mary Belenky et al. in *Women's Ways of Knowing* "the tendency for women to ground their epistemological premises in metaphors suggesting that speaking and listening are at odds with the visual metaphors (such as equating knowledge with illumination, knowing with seeing, and truth with light) that scientists and philosophers most often use to express their sense of mind."[2] The dominant learning desire can, at its worst, be criticized for controlling and policing, rather than promoting and fostering, thought and human creativity. In reference to the dominant educational model, Paulo Freire writes that "[the banking model of education] attempts to maintain the *submersion* of consciousness."[3] Instead, "midwife-teachers" assist in the emergence of students' own tacit knowledge, not that of authorities and experts. Establishment education is, like Freudocentric desire, erected on an implicit avoidance or distrust of m/others, on keeping the Law of the Father safe from other desires, and on ensuring control over the "polymorphously perverse" (Freud), the diverse, the multicultural, the feminine.[4] In psychoanalytic parlance, the "unsaid" evokes psychoanalytic concepts referring to traces of unconscious desire, for Lacan "the desire of the other." His view of desire is intimately connected to the notion of a "lack" or irreversible incompleteness at the heart of being and knowing, of which erotic appeal is merely a symptom. The relevance of Lacanian and post-Freudian discussions of "desire" and of unconscious fantasies for contemporary debates resides in their recognition that complete rationality and objectivity are impossible, unachievable goals. Hence, "scientific" endeavors are greatly improved when scholars begin to admit to the inevitable subjectivity of priorities, choices, and sociopolitical issues that surround all research, teaching and learning. The "unsaid"—whichever way it is defined in different discourses—is tied in with unconscious desires leading to the necessity for serious, disciplined, ethical scholars to be self-reflexive about the impact of their values. In my interpretation of the term, the "unsaid" refers to whatever the dominant pedagogical desire in North American universities has excluded in its mission statements and practice—and it consists particularly of all the suppressed "foreground" and "background" knowledge that is possessed and valued (and partially suppressed or lost) by women and marginalized groups.[5]

On the surface, the dominant educational model, grounded in privileging sight, the enlightenment "Gaze," as the vehicle of, and metaphor, for knowledge, also epitomizes the epistemological limits of Freudocentric desire.[6] The dominant androcentric Gaze is caught up in the "hallucinatory," affect-laden memory-traces of its own signs and traces of desire, whose particular linguistic configurations it often mistakes for nongendered, shared structures of perception. Although recognizing the role of both the imaginary and fantasy, educators rooted in the Freudian or post-Freudian traditions still fail to recognize their complicity in marginalizing alternative structures of reality. The banking model is a telling example of how educational practices can help reinforce sex roles while remaining blind to their engendered, rather than "neutral," nature.

The banking model of teaching of course, need not be quite as sharply opposed to the midwife model as is assumed by the most political strategists of pedagogical transformation; both models have their pedagogical virtues, and the ideal is, no doubt, to teach students both to appreciate competent "experts" and to defend their own truths and processes of knowledge construction. However, promoting the midwife model helps integrative feminist pedagogy to formulate what it does not wish to replicate in its own practice and to focus on agentic learning. Any one-sidedly authoritarian lecturing format of teaching implies training women to accept the modes of passive receptivity that would further alienate them from becoming agentic experts of their own values and knowledge acquisition. Although the authoritarian model may be harmful for all, in some respects it is particularly so for the groups whose conditioning is already rooted in modes of passivity. The banking model of teaching would further reinforce women's conditioning in objecthood, accentuating for them the harmful impact of sex-role prescriptions. Not playing an active role in the learning process is all the more disempowering for women if most of their role-model teachers are men; that reinforces the way many other fields represent women as "patients" or "clients" to whom men sell their definitions, products, values, and "expertise"—even regarding woman-specific experiences. Psychology, history, science, biology, and any number of other disciplines not only focus on the white man as the self and the norm, but also the worst representations of femininity and of woman associate her with deviation from the (male) norm, as a sort of deficient or aborted, imperfect man (Freud, Schopenhauer, Aristotle).

The banking model, then, is anything but nongendered; it is an example of the very biases that some feminists see operating behind the entire dominant scientific model. Its "unsaid" is precisely that its ideological, androcentric desire is not recognized. The banking model aligns itself with Enlightenment ideals of objectivity that are premised on a sharp demarcation of boundaries between self and world. By placing trust in "experts" without concern for their unconscious desires (possibly of control, mastery) and libidinal investments, the promoters of this model express their own "unsaid" under the veil of "objectivity," masking a male object relation.

C. G. Jung's educational views and the basic tenets of analytical psychology offer an alternative visioning of the "unsaid" from within androcentric theorizing. Jungian psychology promotes the midwife model of interaction and is hence compatible, in my view, with aspects of feminist thought. Jungian psychology and integrative feminism share a suspicion over any socially sanctioned, but uncritically adopted and enforced, norms. It is not the role of education or therapy to instill universal values and lifestyles, but rather to help individuals become aware of, create, and defend their own worldviews, in addition to many other educational aims. The Jungian version of "desire," or the "unsaid," implicit in the perspective of the Self is expressed in opposition to the "deficit-orientation" of Freudocentric formulations that label the psychic "underground" in reductive terms, equating femininity, the unconscious, and the ineffable as something to be penetrated and mastered. Jung did not use the term "desire," for in his rivalry with Freudian formulations, he did not wish to make a sharp linguistic split between the spiritual and the erotic. For him, they are aspects of the same "numinosity" of the psyche, irreducible to either. In trying to help his analysands articulate their psychic "unsaid"—whatever one's dreams and waking fantasies might seek to express—he referred to terms such as the "shadow," the contrasexual "anima" and "animus," and, finally, the perspective of the Self, the total-psyche-in-potentia.[7] The shadow and the contrasexual manifestations of the psyche are aspects of the Self. Anima and animus are the results of sex-role prescriptions and the limitations they impose, whereas the shadow includes aspects of oneself that are incompatible with a positive self-concept. Instead of treating the unconscious and the feminine and the whole configuration of meanings in which they are enmeshed as something to be penetrated and mastered, Jung looked upon them as the raw material with which to build our psychic home ground. The unconscious does not harbor dragons that a hero needs to kill, even though the Self, unheeded, can exert a destructive power on us. A more typical image for Jung is that *The Self* is like a spider in its web, pulling us toward its creative activity. For Jung, the "unsaid" does not result from the rift that separates need and demand (Lacan), enhanced by a missing anatomical "complement," but from the nonexpression of any psychic contents whose conscious and dynamic articulation would help create psychic wholeness, balance, and a felt increase of vitality and creativity. Jung stresses the role imagination and the psyche play in playfully reuniting the symbolic sexual partners, instead of focusing on the gap and the whole arsenal of missing links.[8]

C. G. JUNG AND INDIVIDUATION

Feminists are often accused of overdrawing the differences between male and female roles, reproducing the very polarizations that they critique themselves. For marginalized groups to use two-category systems as heuristic tools to expose injustices does not have the same impact as that of the polarizations they seek to displace. However, it is true that many feminists are guilty of representing all male scientists and educators as a monolithic, homogeneous group. Jung's theories are a case in point. From the Freudocentric perspective, Jung is the "hysterical, mother-identified male" in the patriarchal body politic, dismissed by numerous Freudians and "phallic" thinkers as too mystical, "feminine" and "unscientific." Although the dismissal of Jung as being too "feminine" in his values has earned him the same disrespect as woman-defined women, this does not, of course, mean he is free of sexism. However, aspects of Jungian theory are, in my view, of relevance and value to integrative feminist practice.

Jung's writings on education, the midwife model, and the therapeutic process all converge on the following: the importance of helping children and clients in therapy give form to and defend their own unique values, existential purpose, and psychic itinerary. The perspective of the Self is Jung's version of "the desire of the other" and is best understood in connection with the process he calls "individuation." Active imagination, based on Jungian analytical psychology, is a praxis of the inward Gaze and considered to be one of the core processes of analytical psychology. It is of relevance also for education, for it allows knowledge to come to us via channels other than the idolized Gaze, or rational ways of knowing. It is a practice that puts authoritative, expert-based, ego-oriented knowledge in its place.

Individuation refers to the conscious realization and fulfillment of one's unique being. For Jung, it is the "writing" of that fiction that is our truth, an open-ended and nondogmatic practice of personal and cultural "storytelling" in the broader and narrower senses of the term. The achievement of unique personality is nothing less than the optimum development of everything an individual is capable of becoming and being. The individuation process can also be interpreted as that state of life dynamism in which consciousness realizes and expresses itself as a separated personality that yearns and strives toward union with its unknown and unknowable partner, the Self. Although this in itself echoes the Lacanian "lack" and the impossible search for the "missing anatomical complement," Jung is not reductive and focuses more on the possibility of numinous, and life-enhancing, if fleeting, encounters with the "Other" than do Freudians. Individuation has less to do with merely recognizing the lack at the heart of being and focuses more on the techniques of "becoming," following the Self as the "goal" of the individuation process. The Self has been likened to the pole star: one may plot one's course by it, but one does not expect to reach it. For Edward Whitmont: "The many symbolic representations of the Self, of which we can give only a few examples, are images that point to totality or wholeness—of either a psychological or a transcendental (infinite or eternal) character—as well as to a central entity of order and direction."[9]

Active imagination is the method used to access the Self's vantage point. The Self can also be defined as the organizing force of the personality, and it differs from the ego in that it transcends conscious and unconscious strata, dwelling at the midpoint between ego and shadow. Ego, in contrast, refers to the center of consciousness and is the seat of the individual's experience of subjective identity. The Self is not only the center but also the whole circumference that embraces both conscious and unconscious; it is the center of this totality, just as the ego is the center of the conscious mind.[10] To quote Jung in *Psychology and Education*:

By virtue of its indefinite extension, the unconscious might be compared to the sea, while consciousness is like an island rising out of its midst. This comparison, however, must not be pushed too far; for the relation of conscious to unconscious is essentially different from that of an island to the sea. It is not, in any sense, a stable relationship, but a ceaseless welling-up, a constant shifting of content; for like the conscious, the unconscious is never at rest, never stagnant. It lives and works in a state of perpetual interaction with the conscious. Conscious contents that have lost their intensity, or their actuality, sink into the unconscious, and this we call forgetting. Conversely, out of the unconscious, there rise up new ideas and tendencies which, as they emerge into consciousness, are known to us as fantasies and impulses. The unconscious is the matrix out of which consciousness grows; for consciousness does not enter the world as a finished product, but is the end result of small beginnings.[11]

Since the ego is only the center of one's field of consciousness, it is not identical to the totality of our psychic life. For Jung, the Self is the subject of our urge toward wholeness. In this sense, the Self would be an (ideal) factor that embraces and includes the ego. In unconscious fantasy, the Self often appears as an "ideal" personality. The more conscious and norm-bound ego strives to preserve the *status quo* of the personality and its value systems; the Self instead is more intent on change and readjustment, a seeming threat or challenge to the established ego perspective. Whitmont compares the ego to the mayor of the city (of the psyche), with the Self representing all the inhabitants that the "mayor" represents but cannot know.[12] To use another metaphor, the Self contains all the "actors" and factors in our inner theater, which act on us when we don't pay heed to them: ". . . The ego stands to the self as the moved to the mover, or as object to subject, because the determining factors which radiate out from the self surround the ego on all sides and are therefore supraordinate to it. . . . It is not I who create myself, rather I happen to myself."[13]

In his writings about the Self, active imagination, and individuation, Jung is not only interested in outlining the practice of analytical psychology; rather, his concerns overflow into the realm of general human psychological and spiritual unfolding and the education of children. For Jung, the Age of Enlightenment emphasized the rational attitude of a conscious mind, overrating intellectual enlightenment as the highest form of insight, thereby seriously endangering psychic wholeness: "An inflated consciousness is always egocentric and conscious of nothing but its own existence."[14] Jung created "active imagination" as a method for suspending the primacy of ego-knowledge, for he criticized Western metaphysics for ignoring the validity of the psyche in its totality.

As a method of introspection, the use of imagery aims at bringing out, and allowing one to observe, the stream of interior images as they come alive in one's innerworld. One begins the process by focussing one's attention on some soul-provoking, mind-boggling dream-image, or on a spontaneous visual picture, and one then observes the changes taking place in the imagery. It is necessary to suspend all judgment and criticism, and to observe the happenings with maximal "objectivity;" i.e., suspension of judgement and mental analysis. We are to "go with the flow," yield to the movement of the fantasies, perspectives, colors, and shapes that come to animate the imagery. As a state of mind, active imagination is distinct from the process of making up a story and from the immediate dream experience, for it is an in-between state of consciousness. As a means of activating the Self, it is linked with the effort to highlight the core psyche from all possible perspectives. The core is not an essentialist transcendent referent that one day we might "grasp" although some of Jung's formulations (read in isolation) give that impression. Through active imagination, Jung also advocates "claiming" and acknowledging previously unknown parts of ourselves—our individual and collective "unsaid." Individuation thus consists of two itineraries—both a claiming of the unconscious perspective and becoming distinct and separate from it, so that we are not at its mercy. Through conscious reliance on, and analysis of, imagery, we can achieve distance from compulsive inner voices. In Jung's view, "a psychoneurosis must be understood, ultimately, as the suffering of a soul which has not discovered its meaning."[15] Active imagination helps in the discovery, or rather, the invention of this meaning. It is not possible to incorporate more than a fragment of the vast totality circumscribed as the Self within the limited range of human consciousness, but active imagination facilitates contact with it.

Individuation has to do with the lifelong interaction and ongoing process of ego/Self negotiation. According to Jung, we circle around this "core" all our lives, or alternatively, this "Self" pulls us as a magnet toward its field.[16] In other words the Self prompts us to realign ourselves with its "desire," guiding us toward psychic integrity and balance, if we are willing to let go of stifling and one-sided tendencies and let the Self guide us.

The Self, linked with active imagination, is, above all, a heuristic device for discussing a perspective other than the conscious one, whose impact we can measure, even if it is impossible to prove its sources except as a cluster of multidirectional social and psychological forces. As the psychic organ of meaning that functions as the central integrating principle of the conscious and unconscious, the Self has affinities with the contemporary focus on transitional spaces and processes, the "third space."[17] It echoes the notion of a space where mutually conflicting aspects of our identities are negotiated, whether the part-selves are spiritual, metaphysical, national, ethnic, or other. By heeding the voices and manifestations of both Self and ego, Jungians enter the *temenos,* the space of transformation among the collective and individual self's "desires."

Practicing active imagination is actively seeking this midpoint, entering a third space at the interface of ego and Self through our imaginations. Jung defines the third perspective also as the "transcendent function." The idea of a *temenos* as the site where soul desire and self-knowledge are negotiated has, of course, associations with a creative, even religious mythopoetic space that more empirically oriented psychologists tend to shun as too "unscientific" or even too "mystical." The term *temenos* refers to a psychic and physical area that has been ritually set aside, "cut off," so to speak, from the mundane, so that one may focus on the "unsaid." Andrew Samuels provides a useful summary of Jung's concept:

> A word used by the early Greeks to define a sacred precinct (i.e. a temple) within which a god's presence can be felt . . . is the psychically charged area surrounding a complex, unapproachable by consciousness and well-guarded by defences of the ego; [also] an analytic precinct, i.e., of the transference within which analyst and patient feel themselves to be in the presence of a potentially overwhelming unconscious and daemonic force; the area of the psyche most foreign to the ego and characterised by the numinosity of the self . . . and the psychological container shaped by analyst and patient during analysis and distinguished by mutual respect for unconscious processes, confidentiality, a commitment to symbolic enactment and trust in one another's ethical judgment. . . . [18]

Active imagination attempts to broaden our conscious attitudes toward the process of individuation; it can also help us overcome our "splitting tendencies," for it seeks to bring about a more fluid interaction between the conscious and the unconscious so that we can find a balance between creative chaos and the sterility of the overly rational mind.[19]

The Self as a concept has an unsuspected pedagogical potential; although it is used by Jungians to refer primarily to individual self-realization, its impact reaches to welcome all types of "otherness." Critical of dualistic models, Jung proposed a polycentric model of the psyche, and he wrote of a multiplicity of partial consciousness like stars or divine sparks, "luminosities."[20] To train ourselves to perceive through paradox and multilayered symbols, in fluid rather than phallic/dualistic ways, reinforces our ability to accept and welcome diversity and difference on all levels. Of course, the Jungian language of conscious/unconscious and so forth *is* heuristically dualistic, but the goal of his use of guided imagery is precisely to undo the hold of the dualistic imagination. This is the aspect of active imagination that I find useful for creating a gynocentric practice of visionwork. It has the potential to help us face our stereotypes and internal scenarios more tangibly and to withdraw our most self-centered projections from the external world. Through the activated imagination, we enter into contact with the representations that populate our psychic theater. As Robert Bosnak notes:

> In doing active imagination it is important first to alter our state of awareness into an image consciousness. We can accomplish this through the very

detailed recall of a dream image. Through this, the sense of reality of the image world intensifies and the I-figure can begin to move *through* the space of the image.

If you do not begin active imagination in such a state of consciousness, there is a chance that you will just fabricate stories, which produces a sense of unreality. In active imagination, you don't have the feeling of unreality; it is rather as if you participate in two equally true realities simultaneously; the world that is actively imagined *and* the world in which you know that you are involved in active imagination.[21]

The relevance of active imagination for educational transformation resides in its potential for affecting changes in one's perceptual habits. Perceptual open-mindedness may well pave the way for a more radical generosity regarding diverse mental models.

One of the meanings of "objectivity" as stated over and over again by Jung and Jungians is, of course, the capacity not to project the contents of one's own mind onto the external object. Belenky et al. refer to this in its most simple form as the difference between separate and connected knowing. Those who fail to act on their prejudices and who refuse to consider alternative desires as valid can be aligned with the separate knowers who "weed" out of others what they fear or deny in themselves. As Belenky and her colleagues note, separate knowers are intent on suppressing the self, taking as impersonal a stance as possible toward the object. They try to "weed out the self" so that "the flowers of pure reason may flourish."[22] *Women's Ways of Knowing* notes that as a consequence of "connected knowing" and teaching, students may move from an interest in the factual details of other people's lives to a focus on other ways of thinking. Whereas separate knowers learn how to use the lens of a discipline, connected knowers use the lens of another person.[23] By trying to put themselves in the shoes of another, they open themselves to visions other than their own. Active imagination serves, implicitly, the same goal, but it allows one to go even further; we open up, also, to alternative "lenses of knowledge."

JUNG'S VIEWS ON EDUCATION AND INDIVIDUATION

In *Psychology and Education*, Jung promotes his version of the midwife model of teaching, implicitly condemning the authoritative banking model of teaching as contrary to the mission of education. Jung's model counteracts the androcentric dogmatism that lurks underneath the most "enlightened" and supposedly self-reflexive Freudocentric learning models. Jung notes that both

parents and teachers, who are unconscious of their projections and unenlight-
ened about their faults, risk passing on to children or students what they have
themselves failed to develop or make conscious in themselves. By implication,
to be "good enough" and creative role models of individuation, educators
should enhance the individuation process by both introducing alternative
teaching methods to expand the Self and by embodying in themselves the
principles of diversity and openness to otherness. For Jung, a midwife
teacher's role is to free the child/student to individuate, not to have a transference on the teacher as an expert-authority to imitate uncritically (what Lacan
would call a "*sujet supposé savoir*"). For Jung, we reinforce the process of the integration of consciousness in children by education and culture; school is in
fact a means of strengthening in a purposeful way the integration of consciousness.[24] Throughout the *Collected Works*, Jung makes it clear how much
he values the role of imagination for personal, social, educational, psychological, and spiritual growth. In "Psychic Conflicts in a Child," he notes that great
harm is done to children if we deny them the world of imagination and fantasies and force them to adopt an overly scientific, concretistic outlook.[25] He
asks why children and "primitive" people, as he calls them, cling to mythological accounts of birth, even though they have knowledge of the facts of life.
He then proceeds to explain this as evidence for human beings' need for parallel, nonscientific mythopoetic narratives:

> The fact that the fantasy activity simply ignored the right explanation
> seems, in my view, to be an important indication that all freely developing
> thought has an irresistible need to emancipate itself from the realism of fact
> and to create a world of its own. . . . The freedom of the mind's develop-
> ment would merely be suppressed through such rigid consistency, and the
> child forced into a concretism of outlook that would preclude further de-
> velopment. Side by side with the biological, the spiritual, too, has its invio-
> lable rights.[26]

For Jung, children prefer a mythological explanation, itself freed from the
trammels of concretism:

> It is not hard to see that in these facts, so frequently observed among prim-
> itives, [sic] there lie the beginnings of abstraction, which is so very impor-
> tant for culture. We have every reason to suppose that this is also true of the
> psychology of the child. If certain South American Indians really and truly
> call themselves red cockatoos and expressly repudiate a figurative interpre-
> tation of this fact, this has absolutely nothing to do with any sexual repres-

sion on "moral" grounds, but is due to the law of independence inherent in the thinking function and to its emancipation from the concretism of sensuous perceptions.[27]

For Jung, "to reduce the origins of thinking to mere sexuality is an undertaking that runs counter to the basic facts of human psychology."[28] Jung's articles on education and on gifted children offer an important alternative to Freudocentric attitudes toward fantasy, which not only deny the validity for psychic wholeness of "daydreaming" and of the conscious use of imagery but also associate such psychic phenomena with neurotic behavior. Freud writes: "A happy person never phantasies, only an unsatisfied one. The motive forces of phantasies are unsatisfied wishes, and every single phantasy is the fulfilment of a wish, a correction of unsatisfying reality."[29] Jungians and many holistic feminists share the belief that a clear distinction needs to be made between pathological, unhealthy psychic phenomena and creative activity in its life-enhancing positive functions, as they are modes of spiritual expression that cannot be reduced to instinctual sublimations. Jung offers the following description of the nature of fantasies:

> In the gifted child inattentiveness, absent-mindedness, and day-dreaming may prove to be a secondary defence against outside influences, in order that the interior fantasy processes may be pursued undisturbed. . . .What does reveal the gift, however, is the nature of these fantasies. For this one must be able to distinguish an intelligent fantasy from a stupid one. A good criterion of judgment is the originality, consistency, intensity, and subtlety of the fantasy structure, as well as the latent possibility of its realization. [30]

With this said, Jung raises important questions—also relevant to the pedagogical mission of integrative feminism—as to what, ultimately, is an educational mission. Jung's theories on education stress learning for life, not for skills or the ability merely to become economically independent. As Jung suggests, the role of parents and teachers alike is to refrain from personal value projections and, instead, train the young for a life rooted in their own visions. For Jung, active imagination and the subsequent processes of seeing the relation of the material to one's life gives the patient/(student) the "inestimable advantage of assisting the analyst(/teacher) with his [sic] own resources and of breaking a dependence which is often felt as humiliating. It is a way of attaining liberation by one's own efforts and of finding courage to be oneself."[31] Jung came to believe that turning willfully to the unconscious while awake, "purposive introversion," was the "basic condition for the act of creation and the integration of the personality."[32] Guiding students to find the sources of their creativity was then his way of dealing with "transference," which he looked upon as breaking, not creating, dependency on educational experts (cf. the midwife model). For Jung, it is important to get rid of the separation between the conscious and unconscious by recognizing the significance of contents of the unconscious in compensating for the one-sidedness of consciousness. Analytical treatment or educational role-modeling can be described likewise as a readjustment of psychological attitude achieved with the help of the doctor or the teacher. Jung's learning desire converges at several points with comments made by Alice Miller, in her book on creative children, about how parents' or analysts' projections prevent such children from developing into "healthy narcissists."[33] Jung's pedagogical ideals are grounded in respect for the other's desire—or Self—even though his personal "shadow" imbues the comments with a dated sexist and racist language. For Jung, "an educator must not be satisfied with merely pounding the curriculum into the child; he [sic] must also influence him through his [sic] personality. This latter function is at least as important as the actual teaching, if not more so in certain cases."[34] Educators out of touch with their Self risk not only projecting and possibly imposing their unconscious life on the students, but they also leak ambiguous, confusing psychic energies that may endanger the "safety" also of a women's studies "holding environment." For Jung:

> An understanding heart is everything in a teacher. The curriculum is so much necessary raw material, but warmth is the vital element for the growing plant and for the soul of the child... For ... the highly strung and gifted natures, school curriculum should not wander too far from the humanities into over-specialized fields. For the gifted child, in particular, a balanced education is essential as a measure of psychic hygiene.[35]

Jung was remarkably postmodern in some, if not all, of his educational and epistemological views. He saw meaning in general as being paradoxical in nature; each attempt to posit meaning is a conjecture, a human interpretation, since there is no means of establishing "objective" meanings. Meaning is dependent on subjective verification—not allegiance to Freudian or Jungian dogma—as our ultimate measure. The politics of visualization also rests on this premise; as students get in touch with their own tacit learning desire, they can be further encouraged to invent and create their own meanings—"write" those fictions that are their truths. These truths need not, of course, be couched in Jungian terms. By definition, one could only be "Jungian" by not being a Jungian. Jung understood that naming our own discourses itself partakes of Self-creation. He would agree, I think, with the idea often expressed in postmodern thought that the world is experienced according to the manner in which it is named, that any alteration in the meaning of the name alters our experience of the world, and that no narrative is value-free:

> Any honest thinker has to admit the insecurity of all metaphysical positions, and in particular of all creeds. He [sic] has also to admit the unwarrantable nature of all metaphysical assertions and face the fact that there is no evidence whatever for the ability of the human mind to pull itself up by its own bootstrings, that is, to establish anything transcendental. Psychology therefore holds that the mind cannot establish or assert anything beyond itself.[36]

The Jungian method of listening to psychic manifestations through the "third ear" and its' insistence that students be grounded in their own values through a midwife model show Jung's partial affinities with the feminist search for alternative approaches. Contrary to his reputation as an "essentialist" archetypalist, the comments noted earlier also link him with postmodern attitudes that shy away from any unchanging, immutable truths. As for many feminist teachers, for Jung, the role of instructors is to be mind stretchers, not mind stuffers. My own practice of visualization emerges from this theoretical background and hence is not, strictly speaking, either Jungian or "feminist" but rather my own combination and selection of many discourses of "desire." I will now describe the applicability of active imagination for feminist pedagogical visionwork.

THE "UNSAID" AND INTEGRATIVE FEMINIST PEDAGOGY

I employ the term "integrative feminism" to circumscribe the ideological orientation of my own teaching practice, philosophy, and research. It is a practice and long-term vision through which I am trying to orient my pedagogical approach and "raise my own and others' Nature" within women's studies pedagogical circles.[37] It is a response to what I see as dominating the "ideal learning desire" of women's studies: an antiracist, interdisciplinary, holistic, cross-cultural, multicultural pedagogy that favors the "midwife model" over the "banking model" of learning/teaching.

Many women's studies teachers see themselves as facilitators of the others' learning desire, not as dogmatic preachers of their own truths. I have participated in and organized inclusivity workshops myself where we attempted to challenge feminists' own blind spots, to articulate our own "unsaid." As Catharine R. Stimpson puts it, "a consensus now exists about feminist theory; it is a contested zone, or, more accurately, a cluster of contested zones."[38]

It needs to be stressed that, contrary to media distortions and representations, the most recent dominant trends in women's studies (what many refer to as "integrative feminism") encompass transforming society to be more equitable to all underrepresented and neglected groups—not just to the most vocal women. The efforts to implement "inclusivity" throughout North American women's studies departments have aimed at curriculum transformation in terms of ethnically and philosophically diverse teachings and beliefs. Despite the reality of mere lip service, many women's studies programs seek to represent the full range and spectrum of women's experiences, not merely to exchange the male as the norm for the white middle-class female "norm." The very assumption that all women suffer from passive versus active conditioning can be shown to apply more to white, mainstream women than to all women at large. Being Black, Native, and/or working-class certainly impacts on whether women can "afford" to remain in the glass bastions of passivity. In the very process of writing this paper, I am becoming aware of the "unsaid" in my own writing. I recognize then that a pragmatic response to the feminist "unsaid" is missing in mainstream feminist transformative theories. What is more, when it comes to curriculum changes, attitudes toward academic structuring, and organization of syllabi, the predominant voice we still hear is what Audre Lorde has called the "white man methodology."[39] The mainstream feminists' focus on the multicultural, diverse curriculum has prevented them from focusing on the mode of expression of the "unsaid," not just on its culturally varied contents—the contested zones. As Barbara Christian expresses it:

> For people of color have always theorized—but in forms quite different from the Western form of abstract logic. And I am inclined to say that our theorizing (and I intentionally use the verb rather than the noun) is often in narrative forms, in the stories we create, in riddles and proverbs, in the play with language, since dynamic rather than fixed ideas seem more to our liking. . . My folk, in other words, have always been a race for theory— though more in the form of the hieroglyph, a written figure which is both sensual and abstract, both beautiful and communicative.[40]

Christian refers implicitly also to the formats of learning and "theorizing" that have been relegated as "other," to the realm of mere "poetry" even within white mainstream feminist pedagogical circles. Lorde, too, refers to the epistemic importance of modes of thought that are not seen as "rational" and are thus disqualified as modes of teaching:

> As they become known to and accepted by us, our feelings and the honest exploration of them become sanctuaries and spawning grounds for the most radical and daring of ideas. They become a safe-house for that difference so necessary to change and the conceptualization of any meaningful action. Right now, I could name at least ten ideas I would have found intolerable or incomprehensible and frightening, except as they came after dreams and poems. This is not idle fantasy, but a disciplined attention to the true meaning of "it feels right to me." We can train ourselves to respect our feelings and to transpose them into a language so that they can be shared. And where that language does not yet exist, it is our poetry which helps to fashion it. Poetry is not only dream and vision; it is the skeleton architecture of our lives. It lays the foundations for a future of change, a bridge across our fears of what has never been.[41]

It is on this and many other inspiring examples of differently, "poetically" radical thought that I base my notion of transformative feminist visionwork. Implicitly or explicitly, many feminists reject the Freudian reductive view of visions and fantasies, raising them to the status of much-sought-after and appreciated raw materials for imaging new realities. As I intend to demonstrate, the goal of diversity through diverse contents *and* approaches can be reached through reliance on visionwork.

THE POLITICS OF VISUALIZATION AND WOMEN'S STUDIES

Integrative feminism and Jungian educational theories share the belief in the value of the midwife model of learning, to the extent that it facilitates an individual's access to her self-defined worldview and to her full creative potential. In the broadest sense, the politics of visualization condenses all those forms and discourses of desire excluded from dominant pedagogical practices. Paradoxically, in line with androcentric tendencies, most white, mainstream feminists equate "knowledge" with the foreground of consciousness, treating promptings from our psychic background (the m/others) as unreliable, trivial, or "mystically" irrelevant. This fact in itself bears the seeds of ethnocentrism and the suppression of the "other's" desire, as minority women have already pointed out,[42] hence the need to politicize the pedagogical imaginary also in women's studies.

Women's studies cannot facilitate the unfolding of learning desire in its broadest spectrum if feminists practice merely the "add-and-stir" type of diversity training, tagging on a "bit of color" to an unchallenged, disembodied body of theory. I propose the politics of visualization as an approach that allows us a better way than dominant pedagogical approaches to creating a "holding environment" for the expression of alternative ways of knowing.[43]

Visionwork is political, for it is a means of tapping *or* constructing knowledge through all the senses, not just through the illuminating, penetrating Gaze. Of course, the very term "visionwork" still aligns itself with associations of "seeing," the very sense that dominates Western cognition and theories about cognition. Still, there is a major difference between "the third eye" and inner vision, and the Male Gaze, which has resulted in unsightly envisionings of femininity. Throughout time, psychic and soul knowledge have been circumscribed with various terms having to do with inner visions, but without the domination of Sight and without excluding the role of the other senses.[44] Paradoxically, of course, visualization is practiced mostly with the eyes closed and with all of the senses (touching, hearing, smelling, seeing, tasting) open to contact.[45] Visionwork greatly expands the spectrum of visionary options for women committed to sociopolitical transformation because it shakes itself loose from enlightenment models of "seeing" and is receptive to all of the channels through which knowledge can be received/constructed. I will, however, describe in more detail how to use guided imagery, based on Jungian theory, in the classroom.

Active imagination has inspired me to bring into the women's studies classroom a set of practices that likewise challenge the dominant learning desire of mainstream feminism. As I have had a chance to observe, women's studies students are increasingly impatient not just with lecture-style classes but even with interactional, participatory class structures that are based on Western educational models of group work, discussions, debates, and writing. Although students of all backgrounds have expressed a wish for meditative visionwork rituals and practices, it is particularly Native American students and black students who, in my experience, have criticized the ethnocentricity of excluding such teaching techniques as meditation, imagery, role playing, and storytelling. Some have accused the feminist mainstream of privileging writing over orality and auracy, speaking and listening. As long as the majority of women's studies instructors are not from cultures more rooted in storytelling and other neglected modes of learning, it is not simple for them suddenly to invent or become competent in alternative pedagogical practices. However, it is not impossible to integrate into the classes holistic, differently rational methods, such as active imagination.

As I have discussed here earlier, the participatory midwife model of teaching is appropriate in women's studies because many students continue to struggle with gender-role conflicts. Many need to shake passive tendencies and develop their agentic, autonomous Self, learning to be more assertive and not to fear success or competence, even though such behavior is often punished and tends to scare off the stereotypical male. In constrast, in women's studies there are also many outraged women who limit the safety of the classroom by projecting their frustrations and angry feelings on anyone, indiscriminately or with very poor judgment. Both the overly compliant and passive and the indiscriminately aggressive female students need to become more conscious of their psychic mechanisms and their self-maiming tendencies. Although it may not be possible or even appropriate for the instructors to provide psychological counseling and insights in women's studies classrooms, the use of imagery can put students in touch with modes of self-knowledge that have the potential of releasing the hold of fixations and one-dimensional modes of self-expression. Using imagery expands on the range of options available to students with different cognitive styles. The use of traditional debates privileges the self-expression of anger of some of the more vocal students intent on hearing their own voice and ideology, whereas the use of imagery and artistic expression may draw out the best in the verbally silenced. Rage is an issue that must be tackled seriously in women's studies. When women come to see how their conditioning has led them to block their creative thought and being, disproportionate anger often flows where lack or awareness (or unthinking) once reigned. Rage is not self-expression; it needs rechanneling and transformation to become the fuel behind creativity and action. [46]

One might, of course, question how teachers without Jungian training could begin practicing active imagination or related visionwork rituals. First of all, I believe that women's studies programs would, in general, do well to incorporate a basic understanding of psychological mechanisms into the core offerings. Teaching students the central concepts of interpsychic and intrapsychic communication (or lack thereof) would help greatly in making the class a safe place. I see no problem in introducing the Freudian or Jungian concepts of Self/other, projection, psychic reality, displacement, repression, denial, and so on to students (critically, of course). I feel that a great disservice is done to students if they are not introduced to some of these most influential psychoanalytic concepts in Western culture, whether or not they adopt them for use.

However, it is possible to include guided imagery exercises without lengthy psychoanalytic discussions. There are simple, commonsensical alternatives with which to supplement, rather than replace, the typical educational focus on "clear and orderly writing."

As a practical example, I sometimes use a simple exercise: I show the students a picture drawn by my former student, Leslie Quinton, of the "pickled woman," a girl stuffed inside a glass container.[47] I encourage the students (as an option) to enter into an imaginary dialogue with her through guided imagery. No in-depth lectures on Jungian psychology are needed. I provide a handout on the basics of "active imagination" but have found that little explanation is necessary. Students have welcomed this learning strategy with enthusiasm and creativity, suggesting to me that "simultaneous" multiple images arose spontaneously, without any lengthy lecturing on postmodern paradox. During the midterm examination, my students could choose to discuss selected assigned feminist articles through the image and to relate the theories to their own lived experiences. They have produced highly creative and insightful interpretations of our readings by grounding them in their "gut reactions" to the image. The picture made the dry academic theories come alive and affected the students' style, zeal, and communicative skills. It seems that the picture put them in touch with the ways in which women's desire is bottled up, the free movement of their spiritbodies, bodyminds b/locked. Obviously, students who did not feel any "s/existential bottled-up emotions" could choose other, including more traditional, assignments and could, as we often did, debate the pertinence of the exercise and focus on, through the picture, women's alleged victimization. Far from encouraging victim thinking, I used guided imagery exercises to trigger increasingly more complex and nuanced debates on female status. The release of dualistic cognitive patterns is particularly urgent when it comes to women's studies theories about women's victimization. By meditating on the image of the "pickled" woman, students can both assess and experience their own experience of being "pickled" and b/locked in the glass house. What follows may be a more balanced assessment of the relationship between the Self's shifting position on the scale of Self/other victimization and Self/other victimizing, provided active imagination is practiced in a theoretical feminist framework, also giving students the intellectual tools for understanding, say, a postmodern explanation of how an identity is negotiated. The politics of visualization is an ongoing dynamic process of Self-reflection, Self-alignment, Self-invention and Self-discovery, a creative process that is never complete and that constantly negotiates political expediency and goals *and* individual, spiritual needs.

Jung believed that the acts of allowing the images to arise while being conscious and aware and of participating with them invest "the bare fantasy with an element of reality, which lends it greater weight and greater driving power."[48] In my view, because visionwork relies on different states of consciousness, it results in the stimulation of imagination and creativity, which in turn stimulate new and innovative ideas, images, plans, and solutions to problems, useful to both personal healing and group work. The writings on the pickled woman also brought out and channeled the undercurrent of free-floating rage that was starting to gather momentum during class discussions about the failures of the "shared sisterhood." White "mainstream" students had the luxury of focusing on being limited by hetero/sexism, whereas black and Native American students expressed the impact of the image of the white girl's "pickledness" on their more multilayered obstacles to self-expression. As we contemplated the imagery through journals and drawings, it began to take on a life of its own. Some saw the glass break from the pressure of Western alienation, with the bottled-up frustration of the individual Self encouraged to focus on Self-actualization in his or her ivory tower/glass castle. Others told me the image was totally inappropriate; it is whole peoples who are surrounded by and imprisoned by colonial, racist, supremacist, capitalistic glass bastions. Why focus on an individual white woman's s/existential anguish? The challenge, now, was to channel rage into articulating, inventing full-bodied "lost" desire. The students expressed, in a variety of styles and ways, how they all suffered from some form of s/existential anguish, enhanced by additional experiences of oppression to do with issues of ethnicity, dis/ability, age, and social location.[49] Among other assignments I give students is to rewrite a fairy tale or story that has stuck in their psyches, that somehow represents the core complex of their relatedness to the world and the Self. Also very popular, this exercise has allowed the students to "overwrite the phallus," to use their imaginations to break the hold of negative acculturation scripts and to repossess their own desire.[50]

Explicitly addressing the importance of nonrational, neglected forms of wisdom can lead to important further dislocations of the traditional phallic knowledge base. The banking model of thinking, learning, and teaching may in part be rooted in an unconscious desire to control and ward off the fear of m/others. It is premised on an object relation that seeks to establish clear, unequivocal boundaries between self and other, which in the case of the male psyche guarantees the superiority of the male, patriarchal, androcentric role and form of relatedness. In the phallic economy of One, consensus and the recognition of diverse structures of Self and desire threaten power relations and male domination, hence the suspicion also over paradoxical truths, the possibility that nonrational forms of knowledge might be equal to the position of linear, logical, positivistic ego-knowledge. Trinh T. Minh-ha draws attention to a form of "unsaid" when she engages in her "disrespectful" mixing of theoretical, militant, and poetical modes of writing, expressing a postmodern politics of form and exposing the limitations of mere writing for clarity:

> *Clear* expression, often equated with *correct* expression, has long been the
> criterion set forth in treatises on *rhetoric*, whose aim was to order discourse
> so as to *persuade*. The language of Taoism and Zen, for example, which is
> perfectly accessible but rife with paradox does not qualify as "clear" (para-
> dox is "illogical" and "nonsensical" to many Westerners), for its intent lies
> outside the realm of persuasion.[51]

Visionwork complements writing aimed at persuasive "clarity," learnt so
often at the expense of other modes of writing and self-expression. I am not
advocating that we stop teaching clear expression but rather that we also recognize the importance of training students in creative expression as an integral part of all learning. Why should we only train the mind, and not also
discipline the imagination? This goal is recognized also by Dorothy I. Riddle
who writes: "'Conquest revolution' duplicates male domination modalities in
women's groups, while 'consensus revolution' shifts the view of 'might being
right' to the recognition that paradoxical, conflicting versions of reality and
political/spiritual visions can co-exist."[52] Visionwork, modeled on active
imagination and its derivatives, can be shown, explicitly, to lead from the
rejection of merely dualistic learning modes to a rejection of all modalities
based on one truth, one Self, one mode of Self-expression. Active imagination can be shown to consist in the tolerance of paradox, simultaneous or
parallel truths and visions, and, ultimately, the tolerance for double or multiple perspectives on reality. Thanks to active imagination, students may find
themselves face to face with the paradoxes of psychic reality; the angry can
learn to see and feel their rage as being simultaneously the dam against, and
the release of, their creativity. The silenced and the overly vocal can succeed
in integrating insights beyond any perceptual and interpretative extremes by
observing and becoming aware of fluidity and complexity in their imagery.

For me, the challenge of the politics of visualization resides in this: teach-
ing/learning about the ways in which women are prevented from participating
in life fully, benefiting in a fairer proportion with regard to their greater work-
load, yet teaching/learning them/us also to take responsibility for improving
our situations and inner lives without falling into Self-destructive, other-blam-
ing habits. In other words, we cannot give up the politics, but it is necessary to
ensure that we do not drain our spiritual Self through nonconstructive rage.
Through visionwork, we can also replenish our Self, heal the anger, breathe in
vital energies, relax, seek broader perspectives, reevaluate our goals and habits
on a permanent basis. This can happen when we pay attention to the emergence of the elusive third, what Jung calls the "transcendent function."[53] The
use of imagery is, in a way, postmodernism in action; it seeks to make the "third

space" available in pragmatic, not just abstract, intellectual ways. In the transcendent function, meaning arises out of the interaction of "rational" and "irrational" perspectives, both of which thereby modify each other.[54]

Practices of "Self-befriending" such as active imagination may be all the more appealing to women in that they already relate to the world through a dual or plural lens. Many theorists believe that women, by virtue of their social status, are not only better at "hemispheric cross-talk"[55] but are better in opening themselves up to all alternative modes of knowing. According to Hélène Cixous, "Because illusion of self-presence and fullness of meaning has not historically been part of woman's experience, woman's voice has always been several, multiple, hysterical. Because woman has never really been the subject of discourses, she has intimate knowledge of 'the other bisexuality.'"[56] Cixous celebrates women's privileged access to "writing as ambiguity" for "woman" has a privileged understanding of the "not-me," which she in a way embodies. Visionwork brings the "not-me" to the level of the "other bisexuality" in pedagogical techniques. Perhaps women's studies is a fertile ground for meditation and other visionwork practices precisely because women are more at ease with modes of knowing based on receptivity to psychic multiplicity. Political correctness and multicultural curricula are not just about increased justice; they are also about releasing massive blocks in the Western body politic; integrative feminism is about releasing movement and motion in the collective glass house of Western academe. The neglect or fear of visionwork attests to the fact that we still have far to go to integrate all desires in our politics of difference. Without creative revisionings, our creativity remains blocked in the glass case of mental functioning, and we are trapped in bodies that function as brains, under a glass bell, in a bell jar.

CONCLUSION

The academy is a glass house where feminists continue to have to hide their desire, to exist as an oppositional, much-maligned underground. Jungians and feminist theorists, however, have helped to create a set of pedagogical concepts that promise to foreground the underground's neglected knowledge and to realign all those marginalized with their specific individual and cultural desire. Through visionwork, we can continue articulating new generative visions to precede the formation of new theories. The imagistic power of visionwork is endless, for such a constant shifting of perspectives would allow us to cultivate that much-needed paradoxical, yet political, "third space." What holistic practices offer is the opportunity for women to recover their own sources of wisdom and to establish new expanses of being and living. The political implication of self-healing includes not only the empowerment of the Self, but also the creation of new definitions of our potential as members of human society. To heal is to become whole. The woman in the glass house is no longer an oppressed, objectified victim if she has Self-knowledge and, hence, options. She can choose to play the patriarchal game, to compromise or to assert an alternative way of going about life and everything it entails. Being creative is learning to tolerate ambiguity and paradox and to negotiate one's individual and social desires. I will end with Jung, "the sexist" who, paradoxically, led me to "raise my own being" and to rename the Self through the "spirit language" of my own culture:

> Every educator . . . should constantly ask himself [sic] whether he is actually fulfilling his teachings in his own person and in his own life, to the best of his knowledge . . . Psychotherapy has taught us that in the final reckoning, it is not knowledge, not technical skill, that has a curative effect, but the personality of the doctor. And it is the same with education: it presupposes self-education.[57]

NOTES

1. Quoted in Denise Fréchet, "Toward a Post-Phallic Science," in *(En)gendering Knowledge. Feminists in Academe,* ed. Joan E. Martman and Ellen Messer-Davidow (Knoxville: University of Tennessee Press, 1991), 205.
2. Mary Belenky, B. M. Clinchy, N. R. Goldberger, and J. M. Tarule, *Women's Ways of Knowing: The Development of Self, Voice, and Mind* (New York: Basic Books, 1986), 18.
3. Paulo Freire, *Pedagogy of the Oppressed* (New York: Seabury Press, 1971), 68.
4. According to Fréchet: "Modern scientific ideals of objectivity, based on a clear delineation of the boundaries between self and world, on detachment and renunciation of a libidinal investment in the object of study, and on control and mastery of nature, can be identified with masculine modes of thinking. Nancy Chodorow and Evelyn Fox Keller trace the origin of these pervasive associations to the sexual division of labor within the family and its consequences for early childhood development" ("Toward a Post-Phallic Science," 208). All of the above clearly applies to education at large in North American universities.
5. For Freud, fantasies, playing, and creativity represent the overcoming of symbiotic needs and express the child's capacity to sublimate the instinctual needs directed at the mother. But fantasies are still derivatives of forbidden erotic needs and impulses. The "unsaid," when linked to fantasies in the Freudocentric tradition, thus resides in premises that are very different from those governing Jungian thought. For Jung, fantasies are the essential raw materials for creative living and cannot be reduced to narrowly defined sexual impulses or the sublimating drives.
6. For Lacan, the gaze—the dominant model also for educational "scopophilia"—is

always in excess over mere seeing: as in the case of all drives, the gaze is fundamentally oriented toward a lack (*The Four Fundamental Concepts of Psychoanalysis*, trans. Alan Sheridan [London: Hogarth Press, 1977]).

7. Jung, *Psychology and the East*, "Foreword to Suzuki's 'Introduction to Zen Buddhism,'" in *Collected Works*, ed. Herbert Read, M. Fordham, G. Adler, W. McGuire, trans. R. F. C. Hull, *Bollingen Series* 20 (Princeton: Princeton University Press, 1978), par. 897, 151. (All future references to Jung's writings are to the collected works in this series and will be identified merely by title of the volume, volume number, year, paragraph, and page numbers, if applicable). Jung links fantasies with our deepest creative, spiritual/sexual desires (he does not separate sex and spirit) and when analyzing the dreams of children, concludes that children need to be encouraged in their creative play as much as they need to be taught about "reality": "All freely developing thought has an irresistible need to emancipate itself from the realism of fact and to create a world of its own." "The Gifted Child," *Psychology and Education* (1974 [1954]), *CW* 17, par. 79, 34. In this article, Jung also anticipates Winnicott's theories of the child learning to play in the "transitional space."

8. Lucie Jadot calls Jungian approaches an "instaurative" rather than "reductive," hermeneutics and relates Jung to many other philosophers and thinkers who likewise do not treat spiritual and creative impulses as merely compensatory, derivative, sublimated erotic phenomena; see Lucie Jadot, "From the Symbol in Psychoanalysis to the Anthropology of the Imaginary," in *Jung in Modern Perspective*, ed. R. K. Papadopoulos et al. (Hounslow, Middlesex: Wildwood, 1984), 109–119.

9. Edward C. Whitmont, *The Symbolic Quest: Basic Concepts of Analytical Psychology* (Princeton, NJ: Princeton University Press, 1969), 221–22.

10. Andrew Samuels, *Jung and the Jungians* (London: Routledge, 1985), 91.

11. Jung, *Psychology and Education*, par. 102, 41–42.

12. Whitmont, *Symbolic* Quest, 217.

13. Ibid., 217–18.

14. Jung, *Psychology and Religion: West and East* (1958 [1978]) *CW* 11, par. 269.

15. Jung, *Psychology and Religion. East and West (*1978), *CW* 11, par. 497.

16. In *Dreams* (1974) CW 16, Jung refers to this process through the image of the spider in its web; "We can hardly escape the feeling that the unconscious process moves spiral-wise round a centre, gradually getting closer, while the characteristics of the centre grow more and more distinct. Or perhaps we could put it the other way round and say that the centre—itself virtually unknowable—acts like a magnet on the disparate materials and processes of the unconscious and gradually captures them as in a crystal lattice. For this reason the centre is (in other cases) often pictured as a spider in its web, especially when the conscious attitude is still contaminated by fear of unconscious processes" (par. 325).

17. See Homi Bhabha, "Interview: The Third Space," in *Identity: Community, Culture, Difference*, ed. J. Rutherford (London: Lawrence and Wishart, 1990), 207–21. Also, Norman Holland quotes André Green, who has remarked that "the real analytic object is neither on the patient's side nor on the analyst's, but in the meeting of these two communications in the potential space which lies between them, limited by the setting which is broken at each separation and reconstituted at each new meeting . . . the analyst does not only unveil a hidden meaning. He constructs a meaning which has never been created before the analytic relationship began" (quoted in "Freud,

Physics, and Literature," *Journal of the American Academy of Psychoanalysis* 12, no. 2 (1984), 317). This view of analysis—by one of the most distinguished French analysts—is quite the opposite of Freud's.

18. Andrew Samuels, *A Critical Dictionary of Jungian Analysis* (London: Routledge, 1986), 148–49.

19. It can, of course, be argued that the very dualism of ego/Self duplicates dichotomous thinking; however, we must distinguish between dichotomous models created as heuristic tools and those that serve to create hierarchies of "superior/inferior." Freud's devalorizing attitude toward the unconscious contrasts sharply with Jung's view that the ego and the Self are two equally valid vantage points; he would not agree with the Freudian dictum that "where the id was, there ego shall be." Despite postmodern rereadings of Freudian ambivalence, Freud does make it clear in many instances that he views the stirrings in the id, the unconscious, as psychic elements to be made conscious and transformed, if not "exhausted."

20. Samuels, *A Critical Dictionary*, 107.

21. Robert Bosnak, *A Little Course in Dreams: A Basic Handbook of Jungian Dreamwork* (London: Shambala, 1988), 44–45.

22. Belenky et al., *Women's Ways of Knowing*, 109.

23. Ibid., 115.

24. Jung, *Psychology and Education*, par. 103, 42.

25. Jung, *Psychology and Education*, par. 79, 34.

26. Ibid. Donald Winnicott's writings on children and creativity echo many key elements in Jung's views expressed in this and other articles. The concept of "good enough" parenting is ascribed to Winnicott, but in this article, Jung stresses this same view, as well as defending a broader view of creativity than the Freudian one allows for, anticipating Winnicott's departure from "orthodox" Freudian formulations.

27. Ibid.

28. Ibid., par. 79, 35.

29. Sigmund Freud, "Creative Writers and Day-Dreaming" (1908 [1907]), in vol. 14 of *The Standard Edition of the Complete Psychological Works of Sigmund Freud*, ed. and trans. James Strachey (London: Hogarth Press, 1953–1974), 134.

30. Jung, *Psychology and Education*, par. 235, 127.

31. Quoted by Mary Watkins, *Waking Dreams*, 3d ed. (Dallas: Spring Publications, 1984), 49.

32. Ibid., 48.

33. Of course, Jung resorts to his own language of individuation, not the Freudian language of "narcissism," when discussing the ways in which parents and teachers can halt or block a student's or child's development. Despite differences in discourse, both Miller and Jung, however, focus on how the parents' or teachers' psychic life impacts those around them.

34. Jung, *Psychology and Education*, par. 107a, 45.

35. Jung, "The Gifted Child," in *Psychology and Education*, par. 250, 134.

36. Jung, *Psychology and Religion*, par. 82, 56.

37. "Raising one's nature" is the ancient Finnish technique for going "to one's own being," i.e., listening to one's inner visions and expressing the desire of one's self *and* of one's extended family (including ancestors), as interpreted within the world view of shamanism.

38. Catharine R. Stimpson, "How Did Feminist Theory Get This Way?" in *Politics*,

Theory, and Contemporary Culture, ed. Mark Porter (New York: Columbia University Press, 1993), 23.

39. According to *Webster's First Intergalactic Wickedary of the English Language*, conjured in cahoots by Mary Daly and Jane Caputi (Boston: Beacon Press, 1985), methodology is "a common form of academic idolatry: glorification of the God Method; boxing of knowledge into prefabricated fields, thereby hiding threads of connectedness, hindering New Discoveries, preventing the raising of New Questions, erasing ideas that do not fit into Respectable Categories of Questions and Answers" (82).

40. Barbara Christian, "The Race for Theory," in *Making Face, Making Soul*, ed. Gloria Anzaldúa (San Francisco: Aunt Lute, 1990), 336.

41. Audre Lorde, *Sister Outsider* (New York: Crossing Press, 1984), 37.

42. See, for example, Paula Gunn Allen, *The Sacred Hoop: Recovering the Feminine in American Indian Traditions* (Boston: Beacon Press, 1986), 284.

43. Donald Winnicott's term "holding environment" refers to the psychological climate of good-enough "mothering" that allows a child to emerge from mother/child symbiosis with his or her sense of individual self and creative capacity for symbolization and "play" intact. See his *Playing and Reality* (New York: Basic Books, 1971).

44. See, for example, Constance Classen, *Worlds of Sense: Exploring the Senses in History and Across Cultures* (London: Routledge, 1993) for a discussion of the "hierarchy of the senses" and their relevance to the Western ordering of the channels through which we receive knowledge.

45. As a boundary-crossing psychic event, visualization by feminists can be related to the "gynaesthesia" that Mary Daly describes as "the vivid, complex interplay and expansion of senses . . . experienced by Muses and Mediums who are overcoming the State of Amnesia, regaining our Sense of Direction, Unforgetting our Psychic Sensory Powers," in *Webster's First Intergalactic Wickedary*, 136.

46. For a thorough analysis of the rage that prevails in women's studies, see Bernice Resnick Sandler, "Women Faculty at Work in the Classroom, or, Why It Still Hurts to Be a Woman in Labor," *Center for Women Policy Studies*, Washington, D.C. (May 1993): 1–16.

47. My student Leslie Quinton had drawn the picture for an issue I edited on "Women and Folklore/femmes et contes" in the *Simone de Beauvoir Institute Bulletin/Bulletin de l'Institut Simone de Beauvoir* no. 12, 2 (1993), 104–33. This image was all the more appropriate in that it has already expressed women's blocked creativity in the writings of Anaïs Nin and Sylvia Plath. The former explored it in *Under a Glass Bell*, the latter in the famous *Bell Jar*. For a discussion of this motif, see Kaarina Kailo, "Refusing to Hold Our Tongues: Women's Folklore, Women's Orality as Self-Recovery," *A Room of One's Own* 17, no. 1 (March 1994), 86–94.

48. Jung, *The Practice of Psychotherapy*, CW 16 (1954b), par. 106.

49. A student with a disability seized the image to express how able-bodied people further imprison her in her half-paralyzed body. Unable to speak, she wrote about the image passionately, detailing the ways in which our society's focus on "health" and "wholeness" and fear of aging, bodily disintegration, and death makes people withdraw their attention from her, avoiding her as if she were Medusa's Gaze of impending disability for all. Her comments were to me a striking revelation of my own classroom "unsaid"—all the ways in which students with disabilities have their learning desire neglected.

50. I published the best rewritings of my students' fairy tales in *Simone de Beauvoir Insti-*

tute Bulletin/Bulletin de l'Institut Simone de Beauvoir 13 (1993), in a special issue on folk tales, "Beyond Pickled and Phallic Women."

51. Trinh T. Minh-ha, as quoted in Cough, *Feminist Thought* (Oxford: Blackwell, 1994), 121.

52. Dorothy I. Riddle, "Politics, Spirituality, and Models of Change," *The Politics of Women's Spirituality. Essays on the Rise of Spiritual Power Within the Feminist Movement*, ed. Charlene Spretnak (New York: Doubleday, 1982): 372–81.

53. The "transcendent function" has been described in terms of an intercommunication between the brain's hemispheres—physiologically, the *corpus callosum;* see Samuels, *A Critical Dictionary*, 46 for references to neurological support for this Jungian concept.

54. Jung's notions of the purposive and creative aspects of the unconscious, as well as its objective status, required a different attitude toward, and way of working with, the unconscious than had previously been created by modern psychology. An attitude was needed through which the unconscious and conscious could work together, "a combined function of conscious and unconscious elements, or, as in mathematics, a common function of real and imaginary quantities." Jung, *Psychological Types* (1971), *CW* 6, par. 184.

55. The scientific discourse dealing with gender-related physiological differences has used the term and theory of *hemispheric asymmetry* or *cerebral lateralization*. Susan Leigh Star, in her article "The Politics of Right and Left: Sex Differences in Hemispheric Brain Asymmetry," in *A Reader in Feminist Knowledge*, ed. Sneja Gunew (London: Routledge, 1991), discusses the dangers of gender-biased brain research. She refers to a study on brain differences between girls and boys that generated findings such as this: "When asked to think about something without emotion, males were less able to do so than females . . . Females have better control over the direction of their EEG asymmetry than do males—i.e., they can utilize *either* hemisphere more precisely depending on appropriateness" (245). Whatever the scientific "truth" about gender and hemispheric asymmetry, I retain the value of "hemispheric cross-talk" as the ideal mental/psychological functioning for both sexes.

56. Hélène Cixous and Cathérine Clément, *The Newly Born Woman* (Minneapolis: University of Minnesota Press, 1986), 5.

57. Jung, *Psychology and Education*, par. 240, 30.

Part 5

Desire and Bodies

9

Beyond the Missionary Position

Teacher Desire and Radical Pedagogy

ERICA MCWILLIAM

There is an old joke about teaching that tries hard to be off-color. It concerns a brothel in which teachers are the most successful prostitutes. When a potential client listens in at the keyhole to discover the secret of their allure, he hears a very no-nonsense instruction: "I don't care how often we have to do this. You're going to stay here until you get it right!" For many, the joke is offensive at a time when teaching is increasingly feminized, and in the context of heightened tension about abusive pedagogy, when it is assumed that the relationship between teacher and student needs to be more regulated and disciplined. Nevertheless, I want to insist on what the joke offers as a transgressive entrée into viewing all pedagogical work, including radical pedagogy, as a desiring production.[1] In the classroom-as-brothel, no one is disembodied, innocent, or safe from infection.

I seek to inform a radical pedagogical project in a number of ways. The most important preliminary task is to point to the exhaustion of much self-declared "radical" pedagogy as a social production in the field of education. I refuse psychoanalytic pedagogical models as *the* alternative, given that such models tend to conflate the social relationship of teacher-to-student with that of analyst and analysand. Instead, I work toward the reconfiguration of a radical model of pedagogical instruction that invites and anticipates those *uncertainties* and *irregularities* that are necessary to any dramatic enactment of social transformation and yet remain the Unsaid of radical pedagogical discourse. In particular, I consider the radical possibilities of understanding pedagogy as a troublesome field of bodies, utterances, spaces, and texts, a field in which eros *matters*[2] as a necessary and ambiguous element in the sort of "deindividualizing" and "denormalizing" social process that radical pedagogy is.

The discussion that follows explores "radical" pedagogy in the 1980s and 1990s as a process of social production, that is, as a set of imperatives to social action within and outside educational institutions. I then move on to examine some performances of this version of radical pedagogy as teaching practices in the academy, drawing on the work of Gilles Deleuze and Felix Guattari to critique problematic rituals in its enactment. My point is to argue that a radical pedagogical politics demands attention to *substantive* conceptions of *desire* and *eroticism* working in the service of a communication of contagion. By substantive notions, I mean notions that allow the pursuit of thoroughly material questions about the "essence" and circulation of desire as revolutionary counterinvestment, questions that rework normalizing representations of the pedagogical body politic in that they reconfigure it as corporeal and relational, yet undetermined and ambiguous.

It is easy to abandon an ideological ship that appears to be overly weighed down with the burden of its own idealism and the heavy responsibility it places on a dwindling crew of radical teachers. It is also easy to write, as I do, from a position of privilege as a university lecturer in a department of sociology with a strong record of social justice initiatives in pedagogical work. However, it is also naive to insist that a radical pedagogical project of earlier times is adequate for the late 1990s. There is a need to redefine radical pedagogy in terms of modern territorialities (i.e., a multiplicity of changed social arrangements, including the "real" social production of virtual sexual and transmuted cyborgian identities). I begin with a genealogy of critical pedagogy as an avant-garde literature of the 1980s, before I attempt to continue the work being done to prevent its congealment as an academic orthodoxy.

WHAT "RADICAL" PEDAGOGY?

Getting radical, or getting at the roots of pedagogical work as a set of social practices, is always a project in the making. In the decades that have passed since M. F. D. Young's *Knowledge and Control,*[3] there have been many elaborations on the theme of what constitutes the "essential" nature of educational objectives and processes. These analyses have been informed by a range of perspectives—neo-Marxist and other politically and economically oriented scholarship, feminism, psychoanalysis, phenomenology, hermeneutics, structuralism, post-structuralism, and historical discussions of the field of curriculum.[4] In the 1980s, such work produced pedagogical analyses that were variously described as "reconceptualist curriculum theory,"[5] a "knowledge base reform movement,"[6] "reflective,"[7] "avant-garde,"[8] "critically reflective,"[9] or even a *postmodernist* vision of pedagogical re/form.[10] In the 1990s, the work that has come collectively to represent the most fundamental attack on orthodox models of pedagogical work still draws on the theoretical framework provided by the *new sociology* of the 1970s and subsequent socially critical work. It is usually referred to by its advocates as the *literature of critical pedagogy*[11] and is now more likely to be characterised *by/within/against* interrogations of postmodernism, post-structuralism and postcolonialism.[12]

Broadly speaking, critical pedagogy has pitted itself against both an old order based on behaviorist models of teaching, and a new order that further refines such "scientific" models in terms of industrial effectiveness or fast capitalist logic. The notion of "critical" here is aligned with conceptions of critical thinking that derive from the Frankfurt school (Herbert Marcuse, Max Horkheimer, Jürgen Habermas) rather than with John Dewey's understanding of the term. Although Dewey's call was certainly for a transformative pedagogy, it did not draw on a neo-Marxist discourse of liberation as radical political action. Critical pedagogy insists that education is always a moral and political endeavor. Its social reconstructionist agenda works against any technicization of the process of production and exchange that takes place in the interaction of teacher, learner, and the knowledge jointly produced.[13] Advocates write and speak to draw attention to the conditions-necessary to maximize opportunities for effecting social reform. In particular, they focus on the *power relations* within which knowledge is produced.

Theorizing the pedagogical relation as a power relation[14] has been a very important aspect of this work. In the 1980s, calls to *critical pedagogy* blamed positivistic, ahistorical, and depoliticized analyses of liberal and conservative educational critics for the failure of education to engage or "transform" teachers and students. Drawing on its radical sociological roots,[15] critical pedagogy opposed mainstream discourse communities in education, in particular those versions of cognitive science and humanistic psychology that abet the values of competitive individualism in educational institutions. For the critical pedagogue, these models constituted a depoliticizing of the educational project, reworking cultural difference into a social pathology.

Thus, critical pedagogical writing in the 1980s confronted many mythologies and generated many possibilities for pedagogical work as a "deindividualizing" and "denormalizing" social process.[16] Claims to value-free knowledge or neutral methodology were made decidedly problematic. Critical educational research began to interrogate Eurocentric and androcentric knowledges and cultural practices in terms of their capacity to delegitimate the claims of those disadvantaged by their identity position in terms of race, class, culture, gender, and ecology. Phenomenological and ethnographic work increasingly focused on the *language* through which human beings give meaning to their educational experiences, the linguistic context in which this occurs, and the social relations of the research act itself. This helped educators to address the genuine problem of sociolinguistic estrangement and the impoverished theory and method through which such estrangement is generated and maintained.

The work of Paulo Freire[17] was taken up as making an important contribution toward this project. Freire attended to the processes by which it becomes possible to reflect on educational tasks in an "empowering" way by bringing forth the contradictions or "limit-situations" that characterize the reality of the participants. In seeking to end education's "complicity" in reproducing gendered inequality, feminists drew on Freire's emancipatory agenda,[18] but they also warned against "Freirean idolatry" taking the place of the development of critical consciousness in the project of a liberatory education.

Overall, actual technique in pedagogical instruction merited less attention than the development of a radical political language. "Good" (i.e., politicizing) teachers were heralded as *transformative intellectuals* who *empower* and *emancipate* themselves and others, while refusing the role of passive recipient of top-down reforms. Henry Giroux and Peter McLaren's clarion call was typical:

> The concept of teacher as intellectual must carry with it the political and ethical imperative to judge, critique and reject those approaches to authority that reinforce a technical and social division of labour and thus silences and disempowers teachers and students. In other words, emancipatory authority is a concept that demands that teachers and others critically confront the ideological and practical conditions which enable or constrain them in their capacity as transformative intellectuals.[19]

Classroom performance could not be ignored, however, inasmuch as the call to critical pedagogy was also a call to "liberatory" interventions on the part of the radical teacher. Feminist sociologists analyzed pedagogy as a lived experience for girls and women in particular. They called for more rigorous scrutiny of the daily pedagogical practices used in tertiary institutions by those who train future teachers.[20] The overwhelming impetus from critical feminism in the 1980s was to an adversarial stance against patriarchal social relations in all their manifestations, including their eroticization.

It is hardly an overstatement to claim that by the end of the decade, critical pedagogy had come to adopt "the missionary position" by supplying a redemptive social vision for pedagogical work in universities and schools. Although not a monolithic or coherent enterprise, critical pedagogy served to decry the false gods of instrumentalism and technocratic rationality, bringing the good news of transformative pedagogical possibility to those who have been either oppressors or the oppressed in transmissive and reproductionist pedagogical cultures.

In the 1990s, there has been increasing discomfort with the self-congratulatory and somewhat evangelical tone that characterized critical pedagogy as a system of rhetoric. The work of Elizabeth Ellsworth[21] is significant in any genealogy of critical pedagogical writing, inasmuch as Ellsworth expressed not simply a concern to address the politics of identity in her own classroom but also her dis/ease about what were apparently the repressive effects of so-called emancipatory discourses in general. Her analysis marked, in effect, a reconfiguration of critical pedagogy as a form of rhetoric. This work has been built upon subsequently by many writers seeking to ensure a greater fit between pedagogical intentions and educational outcomes, writers who trouble over any inclination critical pedagogy might have to be unreflective about its own agenda. Thus, the 1990s have witnessed a retreat by some from the evangelical tone that has characterized much of the "alternative" or avant-garde writing in the 1980s. With post-structuralism's insistence that "all Holy Wars require casualties and infidels, all utopias come wrapped in barbed wire,"[22] calls to liberation in the classroom have been themselves made problematic. A more skeptical *postcritical* turn in critical pedagogy became evident in a new generation of feminist analyses.[23]

Within/against positions have since been opened up by writers like Madeleine Grumet[24] and Roger Simon,[25] to allow writers to "perform" their critiques in ways that point to their own lack of innocence. Simon does so by exploring *"the difference that difference makes for the complex dynamics of pedagogy."*[26] He considers the way in which "teaching as a Jew" focuses his attention on how the performative invocation of his own identity is both a valuable and troubling enactment as a politics of difference. Patrick Palmer's "Queer Theory, Homosexual Teaching Bodies, and an Infecting Pedagogy" does similar work in considering how the framing of the homosexual teaching body as a viral transmitter can open up spaces of radical pedagogical possibility.[27] It is in this newly emerging body of postcritical pedagogical writing that I would situate the critique and reconfiguration I attempt here. By *postcritical*, I mean a text that refuses the final vocabulary of ideological critique while insisting on the importance of the struggle against real material conditions of oppression and marginalization.

CRITICAL PEDAGOGUES PERFORM "GROUP FANTASY"

Using Deleuze and Guattari's conception of radical action, critical pedagogy may be read as an enactment of a "group fantasy" or "social utopia," a counter-investment of revolutionary desire "plugged into an existing social field as a source of energy."[28] Deleuze and Guattari's notion of "group fantasy" is useful in that it refuses the idea of the *fantasy* as constituted merely in the Symbolic or "dream" that is generated out of the lack of the *real* object of desire. This permits discussion of the social vision of critical pedagogy as the real presence of "desiring production," not as a free-floating wish that exists in the ether, separate and distinguishable from technical or social machines/productions. For Deleuze and Guattari: "There is no such thing as the social production of reality on the one hand and a desiring production that is mere fantasy on the other. . . *There is only desire and the social and nothing else"* [their emphasis].[29] Thus "fantasy," they go on to argue, can never be "individual." It is always "group fantasy" and, as such, its utopias are always "agents of the real productivity of desire," allowing the possibility of disinvesting the current social field.[30]

   This makes it possible to speak of critical pedagogy as productive in ways that can be literally observed and lived out, not simply experienced as a "lack" on the part of the "sad militant"[31] or individuals on the margins. It invites and anticipates substantive exploration of the "group fantasy" of critical pedagogy as a "lived relation of power and knowledge"[32] in which the "good" teacher embodies, and performs within, a broader social process of knowledge production. In their interrogation of radical politics as a social production, Deleuze and Guattari make it clear that it is the connection of desire to reality (and not its retreat into the forms of representation) that possesses revolutionary force.[33] In doing so, they invite exploration of some of the strengths and also the weaknesses of critical pedagogy when enacted as a radical educational politics in university teaching. It has to engage with actual people, who, under local conditions in late capitalist societies, may fight for their servitude "as stubbornly as though it were their salvation."[34] These individuals, including our own students and colleagues, are not "innocent dupes" but are enacting most powerfully the perversion of desire—they may genuinely *want* the fascism and fast food of fast capitalism. This is a painful and difficult message for those teachers in the academy whose analysis of late capitalism is played out with the intention of exposing "the truth" to undergraduates made ignorant or deceived by galloping consumption. An invitation to *deconstruct* the global consumerism has all the allure of a dose of castor oil for those about to consume food from McDonald's.

Thus, critical pedagogy is always at risk as a radical educational project, because it is not lived abstractly but is embodied in the continuous production of real desiring identities in institutions of learning. It can quickly and easily become a somewhat jaded set of ritualized performances if it is not performed as both fluid and disconnected from uniform and totalizing systems of representation, including its own. Achieving fluidity and disconnection demands more attention to the ways critical pedagogy is *materialized* as a social production, that is, to "how a multiplicity of new collective arrangements against power"[35] come to be generated through the forms of cultural exchange being enacted or performed in the teaching and learning space.

My own lived experience of critical pedagogy as teaching performances in the academy suggests that some versions may have come to look less like counterinvestment in the social field and more like an investment in some of the more repressive forms of orthodoxy that critical pedagogues challenge. I refer here to the vocabularies, utterances, and performances of teachers "doing" critical pedagogy, the sorts of ritualized gestures and forms of representation that constitute its rhetoric. The "equity lecture" (always a problematic oxymoron) can come to share much of the rhetoric of Christianity as a totalizing system—romantic martyrdom, moral prudery, evangelical calls to redemption, the repetition of creeds, and heightened surveillance of/for the socially and spiritually vulnerable. Although the appeal of victory through redemption is undeniable, given the popularity of televangelism in recent years, salvation may be framed as an "out-of-body" experience, a higher order ethics of self-denial that is the antithesis of engagement with the "low, hidden, earthly, dark, material, immanent, visceral" dimensions of existence.[36]

One of the risks that critical pedagogy continues to run as a redemptive project is its propensity to frame the critical pedagogue as heroic, even martyred—and certainly disembodied—teacher. Staying "on top" in matters of pedagogical ethics can mean adopting some quite awkward postures for re/lating in the classroom. It is a notion of empowerment that insists that teacher authority derives from a self-declared "ethical" stance, not from a position of power conferred by an educational institution. Pedagogical authority here would be argued as legitimate only where the pedagogue allows students to perceive their own growing role in altering oppressive social conditions.

It is appropriate that, in the context of First World university privilege, those lecturers who perform as advocates for the Freirean model of pedagogy as the epitome of student-centered teaching have come in for criticism in the *postcritical* literature. Chris Amirault, for example, argues that such a model becomes a "fantasy of good teaching" in the university context, with "fantasy" to be read as "lack" in this case.[37] For Amirault, a Freirean pedagogical relationship allows an academic, paradoxically, "a more viable authority" as a teacher because s/he gives us "the hierarchically institutionized authority bestowed . . . by the university."[38] He argues:

> I find myself increasingly filled with doubts about this pedagogy that dismantles and reinvents its own authority . . . a pedagogy that disparages hierarchical, institutionalized authority and dreams of eradicating and celebrating local, intersubjective authority democratically shared with students is only fooling itself. What's more, only by and through such hierarchical institutional authority are teachers allowed such dreams.[39]

Likewise, critical feminism in universities demands constant reconfiguration to prevent collapse into "totalising paranoia."[40] Nullifying pedagogical oppression raises important matters around ethical behavior and classroom vulnerabilities. The important task of naming abusive pedagogy must not disallow exploration of the lack of innocence of feminist "vulnerability" discourse, including the question of the ethics of seeming to *require* vulnerabilities from particular social groups. In the daily challenge of enacting an ethical pedagogical process, we may give the impression of a feminism that "refuses to acknowledge its own will to power"[41] in order to "defend . . . [its] imagined virginity against the corruption of phallocentric infection."[42] Women's "passion for power in learning, our delight in the flirtatiousness of intellectual debate, in the game of competing . . . in the sexiness of winning"[43] may be obscured. Moreover, radical feminism can be made to look trivial and mean-spirited as a set of ritualized and repetitive incantations around a Holy Trinity of "gender-class-ethnicity" and thus become a target of parody by undergraduates in "gender equity" lectures. It also can and does take the form of some of the most exciting pedagogical action, as evidenced in much recent work on erotics, technology, sexuality, corporeality, and pedagogy.[44]

As this new feminist work makes evident, it is not only through the specificities of gender, class, and ethnicity—and even sexuality—that a new body politic gets produced as social "being." Other inscriptions on the body—"illness, aging, reproduction, nonreproduction, secretions, lumps, bloating, wigs, scars, make-up and prostheses"[45] demand attention. So, too, does the matter of the transmuted body or cyborg body let out to play in the riot of the World Wide Web, where identities are as *volatile*,[46] as freakish, and as uncanny as the bodies that these are lived in and through. Representations of a predetermined identity become stumbling blocks rather than pedagogical tools for transformation. We need reminding that identity formation is the social production of a desiring body that *matters*, not a troublesome excess baggage in pedagogical work.

FLESHING OUT TEACHER DESIRE

The challenges I have alluded to for the reconfiguring of critical pedagogy have largely focused on what is distinctive about it as a set of pedagogical rituals or postures. In his work *Geometry in the Boudoir: Configurations of a French Erotic Narrative*, Peter Cryle provides the pedagogical metaphor of the premodern instructor in the erotic arts "display(ing) the bodily discipline at work in an erotic culture"[47] by generally "rehears[ing], and thereby enact[ing], the teaching and learning of erotic 'attitudes' as a set of venereal positions."[48] He cites the work of Nicolas Chorier who, writing in 1655 about ancient representations of the figures of Venus, depicted erotic art as a set of tableaux, setting out a range of venereal positions in such a way as to allow them to be taught by a female elite to women of lower class. Cryle elaborates:

> They set out all they knew, and conceivably all there was to know, so that it could be understood and followed by others . . . the nature and number of those skills appeared quite finite . . . the set of postures is likely to be numerically precise—as is the space of effort available to the learner.[49]

> [T]he examples . . . to be imitated . . . continue[d] to be made present by the on-going practice of postural modeling as erotic learning. Later when the originals [were] lost, this procedure . . . continue[d] of itself.[50]

In classrooms, all pedagogues display their disciplines at work in the culture by rehearsing and enacting a finite number of "positions" in relation to knowledge. As teachers, we model knowing by striking a range of scholastic poses through which the learner is mobilized to desire to learn, to reject the seductive power of ignorance. This posture is maintained in pedagogical processes as an imprint of the "original" pedagogical body after the latter has been removed. For example, where critical teachers might have replaced rigid content, examinations, and lectures with electives, seminars, and journals, arguing that the former are the tools of authoritarian, transmissive pedagogical cultures, the traces of this shift may linger beyond any one generation of professors. There may be a residual mawkishness or timidity around new forms of pedagogical practice, despite the conviction that there is no ideological purity in any pedagogical process *of itself*. In the rush to name the impossibility of the "equity lecture," the tyrannical possibilities of "group discussion" present themselves, perhaps to be addressed, in turn, by the reconfiguration of both these pedagogical events .

Whatever form the pedagogy takes, however, a teacher who takes part in pedagogical events is forced to confront the limits of his or her own anatomical body as well as her disciplinary "bodies" of knowledge. Roland Barthes points to this as a difficulty for many academics:

> I can do everything with my language but not with my body. What I hide by my language, my body utters. I can deliberately mould my message, not my voice. It is by my voice, whatever it says, that another will recognize that "something is wrong with me" . . . My body is a stubborn child, my language is a very civilized adult.[51]

This is a stark reminder that pedagogical work demands material engagement. This is true for the "volatile" teaching body (e.g., as the printed text that constitutes an e-mail address) as well as for an anatomical body (a fleshly presence in a lecture theater). Barthes's insistence on the troublesome presence of the teacher's own *dys-appearing*[52] body protruding awkwardly and immaturely into the pedagogical space "gauges the intensive activity of substances rather than [merely] focussing on postural distinctions."[53] Just as in eighteenth-century French fiction, in which classical forms of desire displaying the "proper attitudes of pleasure"[54] became displaced by a physiology of animation that discerned the "visible effects" of desire, so, too, radical pedagogy has options beyond postural containment. When reliably contained by moral certainty, the enactment of radical pedagogy can be stiff and mawkish as a set of postural distinctions. But it can also be performed as the fluid circulation of desire that "move[s] readily from the physiology of inner pressure to the drama of communication as contagion."[55] Such a movement around and through a physiology of the inner world must engage with *dys-appearing* or grotesque bodies in pedagogical spaces. Mary Russo indicates the importance of this engagement for critical pedagogues: "The grotesque body is open, protruding, irregular, secreting, multiple, and changing; it is identified with non-official 'low culture' or the carnivalesque, *and with social transformation*" [emphasis mine].[56]

To probe radical pedagogy as the grotesque and freakish enactment of an uncertain drama of transformation requires fresh understandings of the pedagogical events being enacted in the academy. In *Sex and Violence, or Nature and Art*, Camille Paglia flags a number of these. She writes of modern criticism as "project[ing] a Victorian and . . . Protestant high seriousness upon pagan culture that still blankets teaching in the humanities."[57] Against modernist techniques of demystification leading to the imposition of social models and forms of identity, she asserts the murky, contradictory, and ambivalent world in which the erotic is always the "disorderly companion of love and art," never to be "'fixed' by codes of social or moral convenience."[58] It is in the erotic, she argues, that our strivings for virtue and order will continue to be subverted. While she acknowledges that "a perfectly humane eroticism may be impossible,"[59] Paglia endorses the idea of human limitation by nature or by fate. She turns away from the clear clarion call of Marx to catch the sound of Sade's strange laughter. "Nature," she says, "is always pulling the rug out from under our pompous ideals."[60] This is not to endorse Paglia's broad agenda but to insist on opening up a space for imagining radical pedagogy when confronted by the possibility that every road from Rousseau might just lead to Sade.[61]

Calls to ethical practice always run the risk of sounding like "pompous ideals." The difficulty here, of course, is how to enact the call to ethical practice in such a way as to ensure that a "good" teacher does not require the erotic nerve to be extracted. As I have argued elsewhere, teachers have become the no/bodies of education precisely because of an insistence on the un/materiality of the teacher on the part of both the progressivist and the technicist.[62] Psychoanalytic theorists would perhaps express this in transcendental terms— teachers are increasingly unable to "occupy the symbolic position of subject supposed to know."[63] Moreover, as a result of effective anti-abuse lobbying, homophobia, and the desiccated vocabularies of official discourses about teacher "quality," teachers are denied the possibility of any claim to seductive power or their own embodied pleasure in the pedagogical act. In insisting on the importance of seductive power to critical pedagogy, I draw on Ross Chambers's definition of seductive power as "the power to achieve authority and to produce involvement . . . within a situation from which power is itself absent . . . the instrument available to the situationally weak against the situationally strong."[64] Critical pedagogues are *situationally weak*, in a social systemic world in which neither the logic of fast capitalism nor that of the enclave is likely to serve marginal identities well.

I want to "flesh out" teacher desire and desirability more fully by suggesting that a teacher's desire to teach is ambiguous and duplicitous in pedagogical events. It is eros that dwells and moves in the *matter* of her students and her self. It is a (corporeality that is experienced and rehearsed as student and teacher relate (with) each other. This idea both incorporates and transcends the notion of the erotic as "our imaginative lives in sexual space."[65] As a phenomenon of physiological *in*/tensity,[66] it pervades bodies and circulates through bodies in pedagogical events. According to Stephen Ungar, in the "privileged [seminar] space where eros and knowledge converge," eros circulates ambiguously as a "troublesome presence of subtle desires, mobile desires."[67] The ambiguity of eros continues to render it troublesome as an intimate and disturbing physical and psychic pleasure experienced in pedagogical events, not simply for those educators who work out of mind/body distinctions. Claiming the desire to instruct as their own may push critical pedagogues beyond a redemptive project in which a teacher can claim more pleasure than the pinched satisfaction of the reforming zealot. Yet it must at the same time present a different set of dilemmas for the performing identities in the classroom. I am aware that much of what follows focuses on the teaching body. Thus, it could be legitimately argued that I seem to have lost sight of the other (Othered) pedagogical body necessary to the teaching act. I do however want to "transgress" in this way partly because so much of the recent literature in education as a cognitive science ignores the teaching body altogether, speaking of it, if at all, as "facilitating," one undifferentiated resource in the project of "lifelong learning."[68]

Powerful teaching is erotically stimulating. Critical pedagogues' disciplining of their own and other bodies in pedagogical events is, of course, no less a form of policing than many of the authoritarian practices they seek to overturn. If policing is "the dominant mode of eroticism in our culture,"[69] then more disciplining of bodies can only mean, ironically, an intensification of the eroticism in pedagogical work, whatever the intention of that program of surveillance. Thus, there will be moments of ambivalence and duplicity in any pedagogical event, including those in which there was an expressed commitment to overturning racist, sexist, and classist practices. This does not mean stepping away from the radical pedagogue's insistence on moral responsibility. Rather, in Cryle's terms, we need to reconceive of an erotics of pedagogy "without being overwhelmed by the thematics of desire in its radically subjective forms."[70] Teachers need to be better placed to claim the desire to teach through understanding the discursive authority at work in transmitting the notion of a desire to learn. Desire as teacher-centeredness, or embodied self-interest, should not therefore be dismissed as the antithesis of progressivism in educational work, nor as the first symptom of potentially abusive pedagogy. The desiring body of the teacher need not continue to be misconstrued as mere maleficence, to be eradicated in the service of pedagogical purity. Indeed, its earthly materiality and vulgarity might well sustain the teacher who might otherwise join the swelling ranks of burned-out educational radicals. What a radical political project does not need are models of the good teacher as Virgin Mother or as clinician with a charisma bypass.

Fortunately, literary and artistic traditions have been less prone than the social sciences to elevate abstract ideals and the mind above "lower-order" issues around desire/sexuality/the body. Enough "transgressive" literature exists to inform the reconfiguring of critical pedagogy as a radical pedagogy.[71] Unlike much of the literature of critical pedagogy, this work does not confine itself to recent educational history, exploring the teaching and learning in the last two centuries of European practices, but looks outside and beyond familiar traditions and theoretical frameworks in order to allow alternative interrogations of present practices.

The notion of pedagogy as knowledge production remains useful. So, too, is the "transgressive" feminist and queer literature that still works out of a recognizable identity politics, such as that of Elizabeth Grosz or Judith Butler. What this new literature brings is a focus on the embodiment of the pedagogical act. It insists on knowledge and capability as carnal, visceral, inextricably linked with more than the ir/rationality of the "mind." The mind/body dualisms of mainstream "learning" literature are refused as a starting point for discussions of "good" pedagogy, whether as "effectiveness" or "emancipation." Out of this refusal, facilitation transgresses and slips into seduction, motivation slips into desire, effect into eros; and all those metaphors about pedagogical bodies (bodies of knowledge or thought, the student body) become pregnant with meaning in ways that protrude and thereby disturb orthodox representations of the teacher-student relationship. Teachers teach some body, not just any body. Pedagogical work becomes more than "the marriage of (two) true minds."

As key players in this literature, psychoanalytic feminists have drawn much attention to the importance of desire in pedagogical events. They have drawn on the work of Lacan and Freud in particular to argue that teaching is not purely a cognitive, informative experience but also an emotional, erotic experience, indistinguishable in many ways from love. Teachers are understood to be symbolic fathers to whom the respect and expectations attached to the omniscient father of childhood are transferred. Transference as the acting out of the reality of the unconscious is therefore central to the pedagogical act: "The person in whom I presume knowledge to exist thereby acquires my love ... The question of love is thus linked to the question of knowledge.... Transference is love.... I insist: it is love directed toward, addressed to, knowledge. Inasmuch as knowledge is itself a structure of address, cognition is always both motivated and obscured by love."[72] Jane Gallop's transgressive work has achieved a certain notoriety in this field.[73] She has argued that the position of a teacher "implies a mastery over knowledge, a mastery only possible by mastering desire."[74] Gallop draws a parallel between the relationship of academic examination as a probe of the mind and the medical examination's probe of the body.[75] Teachers are held to be "knowing subjects": pedagogy is an economy in which the student is prey, with teaching a form of student-capture that is also, simultaneously, self-capture.[76] This work insists that teachers engage in an "ethics of interruption"[77] of their own position to work against the inherently patriarchal relations of the pedagogical act.

Against this, Meaghan Morris questions the limits of any model of feminist pedagogy "which metonymically centralizes 'sex' as *the* feminist issue, as *the* explanatory key to a feminist understanding of the world."[78] Morris challenges psychoanalytic feminists for working out of a limited model of nuclear familial sex, according a universal and explanatory power to "that culturally specific and historically limited genre."[79] I want to add to Morris's critique my own concern that despite the importance of feminist work that insists on naming desire in pedagogical events, examples of pedagogical practice that appear in these texts are almost always drawn from teaching in higher education. Many teachers in secondary and primary schools experience little of the kudos or the "love of teaching self" that characterizes authoritative teaching.

I have witnessed at first hand the results of this in a project that involved bringing certain courses of the university in which I teach to a cohort of teachers in a disadvantaged community in my home city. These teachers are under constant pressure from government bureaucrats and radical reformers alike to solve the problems of the community through their "transformative" pedagogical work. They are tired and overworked in a place where socioeconomic need is a black hole that, try as they might, they cannot fill. Although their grim humor sustains them in part and though they do have psychic rewards from some fleeting successes, they have no sense of their right to claim pleasure from their work or to experience their own seductive power. Their brief is to provide equity for others, not to pleasure themselves. Yet there is much evidence to suggest that those teachers who have established reputations for teaching powerfully to overcome disadvantage do so with a strong sense of their own right to give pleasure and to be pleasured.[80]

"In touch with the erotic," says Audre Lorde, "I become less willing to accept powerlessness."[81] What then might be possible for teachers who claim all pedagogical space, including the virtual, as an erotic field where 'volatile' bodies can and do engage intimately and productively with each other in a giddy and fumbling embrace? What uncanny, irregular, and powerful productions of knowledge might a radical pedagogy then be able to generate? How contagious might we be?

I have begun elsewhere to explore some of these questions in relation to power and the female/feminist teacher.[82] This includes the importance of sexed and gendered bodies in the construction of the great teacher as a cultural phenomenon. For example, I have been moved to ask whether a man's utterance (male diction) *necessarily* becomes *malediction* (seduction) when produced out of a female pedagogical body. This question can, of course, be answered within the predictable theoretical terrain of critical feminism. But it can also generate a narrative that troubles critical feminist pedagogy as much as it troubles orthodoxies about teaching as a cultural identity.

There is also something to be gained for female/feminist teachers in the academy by naming the gendered rules about what constitutes an authoritative posturing of academic scholarship.[83] This, of course, flies in the face of the myth that eccentricity and academic genius operate outside rules. How teachers successfully learn and enact "the rules for breaking the rules" is important, because a performance that *matters* is more than cheap theatrics. (Some of my own theatrics have been very expensive indeed, both for me and for my students!)

As a feminist I am interested in how female pedagogues can transcend the choice of being Sir or simply staying Mum. In theoretical terms, this means "extend[ing] [pedagogical] thought to the point of madness and [pedagogical] action to the point of revolution,"[84] to understand radical pedagogy as "a point of departure as well as a point of destination."[85] I continue to ask how the teacher's body is *material* to a radical pedagogy. The exploration of the pedagogue as a "body of knowledge," one that is facialized as a political surface/body subject, invites examination of pedagogical bodies as both the *site* and *sight* of pedagogical display.[86] It has also led me to reconsider the possibilities presented by the notion of the "stunt," as taken up by Mary Russo in her reading of Amelia Earhart's flying practice, a project that for me now exists only in embryo. If the stunt is to be understood as "any manoeuver not necessary for normal flight,"[87] then it may indeed offer much to a "de-normalizing" pedagogy as radical action. What deliciously transgressive possibilities it seems to afford!

NOTES

1. This term draws on the work of Gilles Deleuze and Felix Guattari, *Anti-Oedipus: Capitalism and Schizophrenia* (London: Athlone, 1983). Their theorizing of *desire* is a departure from, and a critique of, "psychic" readings of desire as the production of the unreal or fantasy, induced by the fear of lacking some thing or object.

2. Judith Butler's work *Bodies That Matter: On the Discursive Limits of "Sex"* (New York: Routledge, 1993) makes use of this double play to insist on opening up spaces to talk about sexuality in terms of its discursive limits, refusing the distinction of *either* the corporeal *or* the textual.

3. Michael F. D. Young, ed., *Knowledge and Control* (London: Collier Macmillan, 1971).

4. See Madeleine Grumet, "Generations: Reconceptualist Curriculum Theory and Teacher Education," *Journal of Teacher Education* 40, no. 1, (1989), 13–17; also Paul Shaker and Craig Kridel, "The Return to Experience: A Reconceptualist Call," *Journal of Teacher Education* 40, no. 1 (1989), 2–8.

5. See William Schubert, "Reconceptualising and the Matter of Paradigms," *Journal of Teacher Education* 40, no. 1 (1989), 27–32.
6. See James A. Henderson, "Curriculum Response to the Knowledge Base Reform Movement," *Journal of Teacher Education* 39, no. 5 (1988), 13–17.
7. See Jennifer Gore, "Reflecting on Reflective Teaching," *Journal of Teacher Education* 38, no. 2 (1987), 33–39.
8. See Richard Smith and Anna Zantiotis, "Practical Teacher Education and the Avant Garde," *Journal of Curriculum Theorizing* 8, no. 2 (1988), 77–106.
9. See Freema Elbaz, "Critical Reflection on Teaching: Insights from Freire," *Journal of Education for Teaching* 40, no. 2 (1988), 171–81.
10. See William Doll, "Foundations for a Post-Modern Curriculum," *Journal of Curriculum Studies* 21, no. 3 (1989), 243–53.
11. See the recent collection *Thirteen Questions: Re-framing Education's Conversation*, ed. Joe Kincheloe and Shirley Steinberg (New York: Peter Lang, 1995) for an enactment of this tradition as a response to a series of "pragmatic" questions.
12. Peter McLaren's edited volume *Postmodernism, Postcolonialism, and Pedagogy* (Albert Park, Australia: James Nicholas, 1995) is an exemplar here.
13. David Lusted, "Why Pedagogy?" *Screen* 27 no. 5 (1986), 3.
14. See, for example, Basil Bernstein, "On Pedagogic Discourse," in *Handbook of Theory and Research in the Sociology of Education*, ed. J. Richardson (Westport, Conn.: Greenwood Press, 1986), 205–40. See also Pierre Bourdieu and Jean-Claude Passeron, *Reproduction in Education, Society, and Culture* (London and Beverley Hills, Ca.: Sage Publications, 1977).
15. See Michael Apple, *Ideology and Curriculum* (New York: Routledge and Kegan Paul, 1979); Bob Connell, *Teachers' Work* (Sydney: George Allen and Unwin, 1985); Andy Hargreaves, "The Significance of Classroom Coping Strategies," In *Sociological Interpretations of Schooling and Classrooms: A Reappraisal*, ed. L. Barton and R. Meighan (Driffield, UK: Nafferton, 1978), 73–100.
16. See David Seem's introduction in Deleuze and Guattari's *Anti-Oedipus*, xxi.
17. These include Paulo Freire's *The Politics of Education: Culture, Power, and Liberation* (South Hadley, Mass.: Bergen and Garvey, 1985) and *Pedagogy of the Oppressed* (New York: Seabury Press, 1973).
18. Some examples include Frances Maher, "Toward a Richer Theory of Feminist Pedagogy: A Comparison of 'Liberation' and 'Gender' Models for Teaching and Learning," *Journal of Education* 169, no. 3 (1985), 91–100; Ira Shor, *Freire for the Classroom* (New Hampshire: Boynton and Cook, 1987).
19. Henry Giroux and Peter McLaren, "Teacher Education and the Politics of Engagement: The Case for Democratic Schooling," *Harvard Educational Review* 56 (1986), 226.
20. See Jennifer Gore, "Reflecting on Reflective Teaching;" and Margo Culley and Catherine Portuges, ed. *Gendered Subjects* (Boston: Routledge and Kegan Paul, 1985).
21. Elizabeth Ellsworth, "Why Doesn't This Feel Empowering? Working Through the Repressive Myths of Critical Pedagogy," *Harvard Educational Review* 59, no. 3 (1989), 297–324.
22. Dick Hebdige, *Hiding in the Light: On Images and Things* (New York: Routledge and Kegan Paul, 1988), 196.
23. See Elizabeth Ellsworth, "Why Doesn't This Feel Empowering?"; Patty Lather, *Feminist Research in Education: Within/Against the Postmodern* (Geelong, Australia: Deakin University Press, 1991); Jennifer Gore, "On Silent Regulation: Emancipatory

Action Research in Preservice Teacher Education," *Curriculum Perspectives* 11, no. 4 (1991), 47–51; Jennifer Gore, *The Struggle for Pedagogies: Critical and Feminist Discourses as Regimes of Truth* (New York: Routledge, 1993); and Erica McWilliam, *In Broken Images: Feminist Tales for a Different Teacher Education* (New York: Teacher College Press, 1994).

24. Madeleine Grumet, "Scholae Personae: Masks for Meaning," in *Pedagogy: The Question of Impersonation*, ed. J. Gallop (Bloomington and Indianapolis: Indiana University Press, 1995), 36–45.
25. Roger Simon, "Face to Face with Alterity: Postmodern Jewish Identity and the Eros of Pedagogy," in Gallop, *Pedagogy*, 90–105.
26. Ibid., 92.
27. Patrick Palmer, "Queer Theory, Homosexual Teaching Bodies, and an Infecting Pedagogy," in *Pedagogy, Technology, and the Body*, ed. Erica McWilliam and P. Taylor (New York: Peter Lang, 1996), 79–88.
28. Deleuze and Guattari, *Anti-Oedipus*, 30.
29. Ibid., 28–29.
30. Ibid., 30–31.
31. Michel Foucault, preface to Deleuze and Guattari, *Anti-Oedipus*, xii.
32. Stephen Ungar, "The Professor of Desire," *Yale French Studies* 63 (1982), 85.
33. Foucault, preface to *Anti-Oedipus*, xiii–xiv.
34. Deleuze and Guattari, preface to *Anti-Oedipus*, 29.
35. Seem, introduction to *Anti-Oedipus*, xxi.
36. Mary Russo, *The Female Grotesque: Risk, Excess, and Modernity* (New York: Routledge, 1994), 1.
37. Chris Amirault, "The Good Teacher, the Good Student: Identifications of a Student Teacher," in Gallop, *Pedagogy*, 67.
38. Ibid.
39. Ibid., 69, 71–72.
40. Foucault, preface to *Anti-Oedipus*, xiii.
41. Vicki Kirby, "Response to Jane Gallop's 'The Teacher's Breasts,'" in *Jane Gallop Seminar Papers, Proceedings of the Jane Gallop Seminar and Public Lecture "The Teacher's Breasts," June 1993*, ed. J. J. Matthews (Canberra: Humanities Research Centre, 1994), 17.
42. Ibid., 20.
43. Ibid., 19.
44. See, for example, Judith Butler's *Gender Trouble: Feminism and the Subversion of Identity* (New York: Routledge, 1990) and her more recent *Bodies That Matter*. See also Elizabeth Grosz, *Volatile Bodies: Towards a Corporeal Feminism* (New York: Routledge, 1994); Mary Russo, *The Female Grotesque;* and Zoe Sofia, *Whose Second Self?: Gender and (Ir)rationality in Computer Culture* (Geelong, Australia: Deakin University, 1993).
45. Russo, *The Female Grotesque*, 14.
46. This is from the title of Elizabeth Grosz's provocative feminist text, *Volatile Bodies.*
47. Peter Cryle, *Geometry in the Boudoir: Configurations of a French Erotic Narrative* (Ithaca and London: Cornell University Press, 1994), 3.
48. Ibid., viii.
49. Ibid., 12–13.
50. Ibid., 18.
51. Roland Barthes, "The Death of the Author," *Image-Music-Text*, trans. Stephen Heath (London: Fontana, 1977), 45.

52. Drew Leder makes use of this term in *The Absent Body* (Chicago: University of Chicago Press, 1990), a phenomenological study of corporeality and identity.
53. Peter Cryle, "Marble and Fire: The Thematic Metamorphosis of Sculpture in French Erotic Literature," invited lecture, School of Language and Linguistics, University of Melbourne, 1995, 10.
54. Ibid., 3–6.
55. Ibid., 13.
56. Russo, *The Female Grotesque*, 8, (my emphasis).
57. Camille Paglia, *Sex and Violence, or Nature and Art* (London: Penguin Books, 1995), 9.
58. Ibid., 19.
59. Ibid., 5.
60. Ibid., 9.
61. Ibid., 20.
62. See Erica McWilliam, "Gender (Im)material: Teaching Bodies and Gender Education," *Australian Journal of Education* 41, no. 3 (1997) 48–58; and Erica McWilliam, "(S)education: A Risky Inquiry into Pleasurable Teaching," *Education and Society*, 14, no. 1 (1995), 15–24.
63. Penelope Deutscher, "Eating the Words of the Other—Ethics, Erotics, and Cannibalism in Pedagogy," in *Jane Gallop Seminar Papers*, 40.
64. Ross Chambers, *Story and Situation: Narrative Seduction and the Power of Fiction* (Minneapolis: Manchester University Press, 1984), 211–12.
65. Paglia, *Sex and Violence*, 13.
66. Cryle, "Marble and Fire," 8.
67. Ungar, "The Professor of Desire," 81.
68. See C. Jennings, "Organisational and Management Issues in Telematics-based Distance Education," *Open Learning* (June 1995), 29–35, as an exemplar of this sort of writing.
69. Joseph Litvak, "Discipline, Spectacle and Melancholia in and Around the Gay Studies Classroom," in Gallop, *Pedagogy*, 26.
70. Cryle, *Geometry in the Boudoir*, viii.
71. See Chris Shilling's *The Body and Social Theory* (London: Sage Publications, 1993), for an account of some of this literature.
72. Lacan, cited in Shoshana Felman, "Psychoanalysis and Education: Teaching Terminable and Interminable," chapter 1, this volume, 31–32.
73. See Jane Gallop's edited collection *Pedagogy: The Question of Impersonation* (Bloomington and Indianapolis: Indiana University Press, 1995) which includes her paper "The Teacher's Breasts." See also her work *Reading Lacan* (Ithaca and London: Cornell University Press, 1985) and "The Immoral Teachers," *Yale French Studies* 63 (1982), 117–28. For a journalist's view of Gallop's own pedagogy, read Margaret Talbot's "A Most Dangerous Method," *Lingua Franca* 1 (January–February, 1994), 23–40.
74. Gallop, "The Immoral Teachers," 122.
75. Ibid., 125–126.
76. See Deutscher, "Eating the Words of the Other" and Luce Irigaray, *J'aime à toi* (Paris: Grasset, 1992).
77. Michele Le Doeuff, "Women and Philosophy," *Radical Philosophy* 17 (summer 1977), 2–12.

78. Meaghan Morris, "Discussion: Jane Gallop, 'The Teacher's Breasts'," in *Jane Gallop Seminar Papers*, 26.

79. Ibid.

80. See bell hooks, "Eros, Eroticism, and the Pedagogical Process," *Journal of Cultural Studies* 7, no. 1 (1993), 58–63; and George Noblit, "Power and Caring," *American Education Research Journal* 30, no. 1 (1993), 23–38.

81. Audre Lorde, *Sister Outsider* (New York: Crossing Press, 1984), 58.

82. I explore these issues more fully in "Seductress or Schoolmarm: On the Improbability of the Great Female Teacher," *Interchange: A Quarterly Review of Education*, forthcoming.

83. See my chapter, "Performing Between the Posts: Authority, Posture and Contemporary Feminist Scholarship," in *Representation and the Text*, ed. William Tierney and Yvonna Lincoln (Albany: SUNY Press, forthcoming).

84. Seem, introduction to *Anti-Oedipus*, xx.

85. Ibid., xix.

86. See Maria Angel, "Pedagogies of the Obscene: The Specular Body and Demonstration," in *Jane Gallop Seminar Papers*, 61–72. Angel draws on the work of Deleuze and Guattari in her analysis of the pedagogical corpus/corpse.

87. Amelia Earhart, cited in Russo, *The Female Grotesque*, 19.

10

Looking at Pedagogy in 3-D

Rethinking Difference, Disparity, and Desire

SHARON TODD

The postmodern appeal to a politics of difference in radical pedagogy has been a much-needed response to neoconservative assaults on multiculturalism. It has insisted upon addressing existing social constructions of disparity rooted in perceptions of difference and identity.[1] This appeal makes the hybrid subject, as a fusion of often conflicting racial, ethnic, class, gender, and sexual identities, an important element in transformative education and refuses the commonplace assumption that all differences are "equal." In addition, the explicit emphasis on difference in radical pedagogy is an attempt to disturb the security of identity politics and to recognize the fragmentary nature of subjectivity. Difference among, between, and within individuals disrupts a "unified concept of identity."[2]

Moreover, drawing on the work of such cultural critics as Stuart Hall, Homi Bhabha, and Gayatri Spivak (to name a few), transformative educators have highlighted the shifting nature of social and cultural differences themselves.[3] In this sense, difference lies within a set of particular configurations that undermines any universalizing of, for instance, *a* working-class, lesbian, Black, or feminine identity. The focus of transformative pedagogy has been to challenge the disparities that structure social differences differently by encouraging students and teachers alike to uncover the ways in which culture (e.g., popular film, books, music, advertising, and language) sets the conditional limits and possibilities for their own identities. Radical pedagogy thus concentrates on developing links between cultural forms of representation, on the one hand, and, on the other, individual and collective attitudes, behaviors, and affects. In this sense, working across, through, and with difference means seeing that shifting social articulations (representations) of difference (along various axes of race, gender, class, ethnicity, and sexuality) constitute numerous identity *positions*, rather than a singular, fixed identity.

However, unless difference is also seen in relation to specifically embodied subjectivities, where the interplay of such factors as desire also shapes how social difference is *mediated*, the radical commitment to a "politics of difference" may fail to break what it wanted to in the first place: the stranglehold of the identity politics copula, where social location *is* one's identity and the ground of one's activism.[4] In this view, identity, as Lawrence Grossberg points out, can be subsumed under the logic of difference with the assumption that "such structures of identity belong to certain subject groups."[5] Ironically, then, a "politics of difference" can end up (in practice, at least, if not always in theory) assuring a causal connection between difference and identity and may, in Grossberg's words, "too quickly assume a necessary relation between identity (ethnicity) and culture."[6] And this can be the case despite the assertion that cultural differences are never stable. Bhabha warns us that "the representation of difference must not be hastily read as the reflection of *pre-given* ethnic or cultural traits set in the fixed tablet of tradition."[7] Even in underlining the radical democratic potential of working across, through, and with difference, examples of tokenism, hierarchies of oppression, and the burdens of minority teachers are often raised.[8] Moreover, difference is not questioned at the moment of being produced in radical pedagogical practices themselves. Thus, theorizing and practicing a politics of difference raises complex issues about how subjects are formed—but not overdetermined—through an ever-changing field of representation of difference.

In my view, it is helpful to rethink the relation between identity and difference by considering what Bhabha calls the space "in-between." He writes: "It is in the emergence of the interstices—the overlap and displacement of domains of difference—that the intersubjective and collective experiences of *nationness*, community interest, or cultural value are negotiated. How are subjects formed 'in-between,' or in excess of the sum of the 'parts' of difference (usually intoned as race/class/gender, etc.)?"[9] In peering beyond a seemingly *causal* relation between difference and identity and into the *interval* between identity and difference, Bhabha opens up a new terrain of questioning, a new horizon of possibility for discussions of difference in pedagogy. He creates a space for a psychoanalytic inquiry into the ways in which difference is never fully secured or solidified into *an* identity position, and beckons us to look closely at what factors intervene in the process.

The way I have chosen to approach this rethinking, and it is by no means the sole way of approaching it, is through the metaphor of 3-D. This essay not only invokes an alliterative play on difference, disparity, and desire, but it is also concerned with "fleshing out," as it were, the scene of learning, where difference is not only "handled" or "dealt with" but is also produced and constituted in the pedagogical encounter itself between embodied subjects. Moreover, it argues for the need to develop an awareness of desire as a mediating factor in the recognition and enunciation of difference. It regards desire as that which ceaselessly circulates through the *unsaid* of classroom life (manifesting itself in expectations, hopes, visions, and fears), even as it intersects with the *symbolic and spoken* discourses uttered by teacher and student alike. Desire is, therefore, not only produced through the spoken discourse between teacher and student; nor is it only an "impulse" projected onto the pedagogical scene. It is occasioned by (and made apparent through) another kind of textuality as well: a body discourse where gesture informs any teaching and learning experience. Here, desire signals an unconscious want or longing produced and born out of intersubjective contact (both said and unsaid); and insofar as intersubjective interaction always takes place within specific settings and at specific historical junctures, desire is not a neutral term but rather a dynamic saturated in the patriarchal, neocolonialist, capitalist, and homophobic contexts from which it emerges.[10] Naturally, this does not mean that all desires are sexist, racist, classist, or heterosexist—indeed, they are often otherwise—but it does mean that they cannot simply be extracted from the social and cultural parameters in which they are forged.

Clearly, then, I do not subscribe to the Lacanian view of desire as *ontological* lack—insofar as this looks at all forms of social organization and symbolization as alienating devices—preferring instead to heed the social transformative potential of Luce Irigaray's dialectical thinking, which emphasizes that changes in the symbolic can reshape desire, can serve one's desires (in a community) more fully, and are themselves impelled by desires of excess.[11] After all, if we think that desires are not alterable or cannot find alternative forms of expression, then we would have little reason or hope in struggling for social transformation. By placing desire at the heart of the excess, of Bhabha's "in-between," it is my intention to show the importance of the specificity of desire for engaging a politics of difference in the university or adult-education classroom.

The first part of this essay draws, in part, on Homi Bhabha's work in order to discuss how pedagogy in its advocacy of a politics of difference is involved in the process of "articulating Otherness" and uses a reading of Roger Simon's articulatory practice of "teaching as a Jew" to illustrate the significance of desire in the scene of pedagogy. Following this, I focus more on the unsaid aspects of "articulating Otherness," demonstrating the significance of gesture for theorizing desire and difference in pedagogy. Here, I draw upon Luce Iri-garay's work on gesture and psychoanalytic practice to explore bodily arrange-ments in the class and what they signify about difference. The chapter then concludes with practical implications for working across, through, and with difference. I turn now to situate the overall premise of disparity underlying the essay.

DIFFERENCE, DISPARITY, AND PEDAGOGICAL AMBIVALENCE

A major assumption underlying this chapter is the distinction made between "difference," meaning "non-same," and "disparity," meaning "unequal in dif-ference." It is a distinction that suggests that difference and disparity go hand in hand as conceptual tools, for without maintaining a notion of disparity in the material conditions that structure differences *differently*, difference can—and often does—collapse into an individualized and psychologistic rendering of what is often labeled "diversity." This is obviously something I wish to avoid in claiming that desire is an important category of analysis. Keeping an eye on disparity brings into question conventional, liberal notions of differ-ence that essentially claim that all differences are created equally. In this view, everyone's identity, while unique and different, is also paradoxically represen-tative of ethnic and racial differences that are only "skin deep" and that are of-ten measured against some imaginary, yet powerful, standard (middle-class, white, Christian, and English-speaking). It is, therefore, important to main-tain at the fore of our analyses the material conditions that unfortunately con-tinue to support social and economic disparity, in order to avoid the problems associated with leveling all kinds of difference. Building bridges across differ-ences means understanding the ways in which discrimination, poverty, and stereotypes function—along with privilege, wealth, and imaginary stan-dards—to sustain difference. What I am suggesting here is an engagement of difference that does not fail to understand the oppressive conditions that shape people's lives differently, and that simultaneously work toward relieving these conditions. In other words, an engagement of difference that fully rec-ognizes the play of difference within identity.[12]

However, this essay specifically emphasizes desire as a psycho-social prod-uct and discusses how in struggling against disparities of injustice, desires are produced, mobilized, and frustrated in the pedagogical encounter with differ-ence. If pedagogy is a site of negotiation involving subjects of difference and subjects of desire, then teaching through, with, and across difference has a bearing upon the kinds of desires that are allowed to circulate. The specific quandary we face as transformative educators is that, inevitably and unavoidably, we reproduce categories of difference while seeking to undermine the ways in which these differences are treated in society. For instance, whereas radical pedagogy calls into question racialized, classed, and sexed readings of popular media, canonical literature, and institutionalized practices of power, it reinscribes the "popular," the "canonical," and the "institutional" in terms of "race," "class," and "gender," iterating specific markers of difference.[13] In this sense, difference is not only something that is inscribed "outside" the classroom, but it is part of the discursivity that organizes what we learn, teach, and read "inside" the class as well. It is not that race, class, and gender are invalid categories of analysis. Quite the contrary. The point is that in order to "talk" about race, class, and gender, teachers continually re-present social and cultural difference to their classes. Thus, there is a "doubling effect" in transformative pedagogy: a tension between *transforming* disparity in relation to difference, and *forming* conceptions of difference in the process.[14] Viewing pedagogy as a "doubling effect" suggests that we should examine how difference is *articulated* through words, images, and actions in the scene of pedagogy and how this process of articulation acts like a Freirean "limit-situation," producing, mobilizing, and frustrating both learning and desire. Transformative pedagogy, it seems, might learn to live with its ambivalence if it can begin to view itself as a site of articulation and performativity, as well as one of transformation and radicality.

THE SCENE OF PEDAGOGY AS THE SCENE OF "ARTICULATING OTHERNESS"

As discussed briefly earlier, the appeal to a politics of difference brings with it two pressing issues. On the one hand, there is the danger of installing a causal connection between difference and identity in such a way that invites an overdetermined view of the subject. On the other hand, radical teachers are faced with the ambivalence of naming, performing, and re-presenting difference in their classrooms, even as they seek to dismantle the disparity that supports specific differences. Both of these issues can be addressed more fully, I believe, if we begin to look beyond difference as "being an Other" to difference as "articulating Otherness," making a shift, therefore, from an ontological to a symbolic question of difference.[15]

Difference conceived as "being an Other" often equates the social meanings of race, ethnicity, sexuality, and gender with an originary notion of identity. Here, the assumption of a "unified concept of identity"[16] remains intact, despite the recognition of the constructedness—and, therefore, the mutability—of difference. According to Joan Scott, this view occupies a central place in the rhetoric of "diversity," which "refers to a plurality of identities and . . . is seen as a *condition of human existence* rather than as the *effect of an enunciation of difference* that constitutes hierarchies and asymmetries of power" [my emphasis].[17] This notion of "being an Other," risks viewing difference as lying in an immediate relation to identity and, often, experience.[18]

With respect to pedagogy, difference as "being an Other" is thus often seen as having been constituted prior to the pedagogical encounter. The specific identities produced in relation to difference, through the matrix of class, race, or gender, are simply "brought" to school, along with books, pencils, and paper. Of course, not all difference is forged in schools, to be sure, but even in interrogating how schools produce or encourage certain roles, identity positions, and sets of expectations, the question of how difference *becomes* identity is rarely asked. That is, the very conception of difference as "being an Other" is not often seen as a problem. Difference constituted as "being an Other" carries with it the dangers of establishing a logic of identitarianism, a rigid identity politics in the university classroom contributes little to working across, through, and with difference as a form of social intervention. As a result, people may be viewed (simply!) as "being" working class, Black, Jewish, or gay, and there is not sufficient attention directed to how the processes of naming ourselves or being named, are also points of articulation, points open to *symbolic* identification, and a plurality of meaning. As Spivak notes, "identitarianism can be as dangerous as it is powerful, and the radical teacher in the university can hope to work, however indirectly, toward controlling the dangers by making them visible."[19] "Controlling the dangers by making them visible" suggests to me that pedagogy may need to see itself as implicated in the articulatory practices that make difference a lived phenomenon.

Difference as "articulating Otherness" places the emphasis on the symbolic practice of demarcating difference and, to my mind, largely avoids the debilitating reduction of difference to secure identity positions.[20] As Bhabha writes, "What is theoretically innovative and politically crucial, is the need to think beyond narratives of originary and initial subjectivities and to focus on those moments or processes that are produced in the *articulation* of cultural differences [my emphasis]."[21] Focusing on these moments of articulation enables a close examination of the specific ways "articulating Otherness" offers up the textual, discursive, and visual material with which subjects identify, with which subjects constitute their identities. In other words, as Bhabha suggests, a re-presentation of difference does not lead to any single identity position but is open to the play of the "ambivalent, psychical process of identification."[22] For example, whether difference is articulated as a stereotypical representation of the colonial Other or as a radical appeal to a subaltern, marginalized Other, the language and images through which these differences are articulated do not produce the same identifications for all.[23] Witness the images of *hijab*-wearing women, in whom the mobilization of desire and identification, although tied to complex patterns of history, geography, gender, ideology, personal history, and religion, nevertheless precludes any homogenization of identity positions based on any single one of these factors. What prevents an image, a textual reference, an uttered statement, or a lyric from ever securing a stable identity position—and, therefore, a stable meaning—is at once the changing historical, cultural landscape of its circulation and the unforeseeable influence of identification and desire.

I say both identification and desire, for insofar as identification is an assimilation of an image or an ideal into the subject and desire is an unconscious want produced through said and unsaid practices, the "chicken-and-egg question on the temporal sequence" of both is unanswerable.[24] Being *like* an Other cannot be easily separated from *wanting* to be like an Other or, perhaps, *wanting* that Other. However, this does not mean that the conscious wanting to be like an Other is *the* desire in and of itself but rather that the identification may be an expression of (and give rise to) another unconscious desire. In other words, an identification with a celebrity such as Michael Jordan may not be read simply as revealing *the* desire "to be like Mike," to borrow Michael Eric Dyson's phrase, but rather that the identification can be alloyed with a *host* of desires that may involve issues of sexuality and recognition which have been formed through previous identifications and that take place in a society where Michael Jordan is a culturally overdetermined signifier.[25] It seems to me, then, that what lies "in-between or in excess of the sum of the parts of difference" is the not-so-easily-read identification-desire dynamic.[26] This suggests that the outcome of any identification with an ideal, a celebrity, or an image cannot be fully determined or controlled by cultural signification; nor can the desires be easily named. Indeed, as Bhabha notes, "It is only by understanding the ambivalence and the antagonism of the desire of the Other that we can avoid the increasingly facile adoption of the notion of a homogenized Other, for a celebratory, oppositional politics of the margins of the minorities."[27] However, this is not to say that in "articulating Otherness" the words, actions, and images (re)presented do not carry stains of meaning, as if each articulation is heard anew in a decontextualized space. Certainly meanings are not entirely "free-floating," and the iconographic history of an image or text or individual will certainly predispose it to certain meanings.[28] Yet, what must be remembered is that symbolic material is constantly undergoing changes of context that, when coupled with the indeterminacy of desire, may become both the nemesis and ally of transformative pedagogical practices.

Pedagogically speaking, difference as "articulating Otherness" necessitates having to confront the limits and possibilities of pedagogy in a way that does not foreclose on attempts to transform people's evaluation of difference at a social level. If we are to view the site of pedagogy as a site of articulation, then we need to acknowledge that what we say about difference and how we demarcate it offers the symbolic material through which individuals in the class identify and desire. Teachers who wish to work across, through, and with difference are always offering up categories of race, gender, sexuality, ethnicity, and class. Whether championing Native American educational aims, bringing gender issues to bear on philosophical inquiry, or looking at the racist subtext of a popular film, teachers are engaged in cultural activity, *producing* difference rather than reinterpreting or relating difference in an aloof manner. "Articulating Otherness" means that difference is performative, constantly (re)iterated, (re)presented, (re)enacted, and (re)defined. Viewing difference as an articulation, as performativity, can have a number of effects on our conceptions of classroom interaction. For instance, thinking about pedagogy as a site of articulation allows us to question how our words, actions, and images produce differences in such a way as to open up or close down certain kinds of desires in the pedagogical encounter. It also compels teachers to be self-reflexive about their own invocations of difference, to see more as iterative practices, and less as mimetic practices that merely repeat the mantra of race, class, and gender.[29] Furthermore, this approach gives students and teachers an opportunity to examine the symbolic dimensions of difference, since by focusing attention more on "articulating Otherness" and less on "being an Other," critical distance is developed. Finally, it opens up the possibility for educators to begin to think about how they might intervene in the "in-between" space of identification and desire.

However, viewing pedagogy as a site of articulation also raises questions concerning what is possible for pedagogy. For example, with respect to the indeterminacy of desire, where does this leave educators committed to social transformation? If teachers do not control the dynamic of desire, then how do we know when we are fueling, installing, or frustrating the kinds of desires that may, for instance, secure rather than dislocate stereotypes and discriminatory practices? Since our articulations occur within what Spivak would call particular "teaching machines" that are far from equitable, to what degree do desires "reflect" such disparity? There are no easy answers to these questions. Perhaps it may be helpful in considering these questions to reflect on an example, a case study of "articulating Otherness," and to probe into some of the implications of desire in engaging a "politics of difference."

"ARTICULATING OTHERNESS:" A CASE STUDY

Roger Simon's "Face-to-Face with Alterity: Postmodern Jewish Identity and the Eros of Pedagogy" focuses on the problems of re-presenting difference in teaching practices. Simon discusses the importance of eros and desire within the specific context of doctoral studies and explores how his own transgressional practice of "teaching as a Jew" is implicated in the dynamic of desire between teacher and student.[30] I wish to dwell on this essay, for Simon's sensitive discussion of difference and desire offers some important insights into the way teaching can enact difference (consciously and unconsciously) through "articulating Otherness." Simon's view of his teaching practice is concerned with *the exploration of the difference that difference makes for the complex dynamics of pedagogy*" (92). In a postmodern move, Simon cites *his* (not *a* or *the*) Jewish identity as part of his teaching; it is an identity that is neither reducible to "one's Jewishness nor . . . [to] a rendering of one's self within another's version of what constitutes Jewish characteristics" (94). In teaching as a Jew, he brings to the fore that which is usually suppressed in the pedagogical exchange, drawing into the field of pedagogy his ethnic identity as a re-presentation of difference. In "articulating Otherness," Simon's teaching is a political gesture, both in challenging the effacement of identity in teaching and in attempting to elaborate upon "what it might mean to live and work ethically within the embrace of heteronomy" (92). Simon's teaching is profoundly *connected* to his identity but is not *directly* determined by it. Instead, he *cites* his identity, articulating Otherness in order to politicize the pedagogical encounter. In so doing, Simon questions the effect this has on doctoral students who are, like him, simultaneously caught up in the "play of desire" between teacher and student (95).

According to Simon, desire in doctoral education is marked by a "distinctive intimacy" and "a dynamic wherein the acts of each party in the pedagogical relation are structured by how each 'reads' and 'invests in' the other as the locus of ambitions, aspirations, fears, and anxieties" (95).[31] This dynamic comprises specific desires that Simon experiences as a teacher and that students experience as students. For instance, some of his professional desires involve the desire "to arouse and instruct desire of others," a narcissistic desire to see himself in his students; a desire for an "intellectual partner," and a desire for "solidarity" for collectivity (96–97). Students' desires, he notes, are connected to power relations inherent in traditional university settings, where students' lives are structured by dependent relationships to faculty. Moreover, students often experience a "conflictual and uncomfortable process of unlearning that involves abandoning a safe position" (97). These situations can lead to an eroticization of faculty based on desires for a professor as a subject presumed to know, a teacher who knows how to know, a teacher who provides hope, and an intellectual home (97–100). When students are confronted with Simon's articulation of Otherness, the interplay of these desires conditions the receptivity of difference in the doctoral exchange. In this way, then, difference as "articulating Otherness" is set within the context of these ongoing student-teacher dynamics.

However, the issue I am interested in pursuing is slightly different from Simon's and has more to do with the specific investments forged through a practice of "articulating Otherness." Thus, my comments here are not meant as a critique of his position so much as an attempt to raise questions about the nature of desire in the actual pedagogical exchange. In articulating difference, what kind of desires are set in motion between individuals, and how does this affect the transformative impetus of the articulation itself? Although Simon's "teaching as a Jew" may certainly alter or coincide with the *general* expectations that structure the institutional lives of teachers and students, how does the *particular* encounter challenge (or not challenge) anti-Semitism on a larger scale? One way to begin a response is to acknowledge how the articulation itself provokes, reassembles, and produces desires. Re-presenting difference does not *only* "occur" or "take place" within the dynamic of the institutional desires mentioned above, nor does it *only* disrupt or support these "background" desires. It also re-presents to students the teacher's own desire to teach through his identity; his desire to articulate Otherness, his desire to define himself as a Jew. Students come face-to-face not only with a citational practice but also with the desire that structures that practice, that makes the citation possible. In other words, students encounter the desire, on the one hand, as it is *produced* in the performativity of the teaching—that is, through the articulation of difference itself. On the other hand, they may also conceive of it as *underlying* the citational practice—that is, see it as the desire to engage in such a practice in the first place. And it is these double desires (the manifest and latent, for lack of better terms) whose meanings always leave themselves open to student interpretation, identification, and desire.[32]

The flip side, then, of the teacher's "articulating Otherness" is the range of student responses. Students may question, identify with, or even deny the importance of Simon's articulation of his own identity in the pedagogical exchange, and in so doing, they may risk securing or alienating more than symbolic difference in the process. They risk the relationship with the teacher as well. This is because they are also responding to the teacher's desire in its symbolic form: an unconscious want played out through the articulatory practice. Therefore, the stakes are high for students confronting alterity, for the teacher's assertion of that alterity is highly invested. Moreover, the stakes are high for the teacher since student response may challenge or reinforce that initial investment.[33] As well as being highly varied, student response appears to achieve two things. First, it sets into motion a dialectical interaction with the teacher that will continue to define the dynamics of a particular class. In this sense, Simon's citational practice is never played out the same way twice, even though the conscious "hope . . . that the pedagogical encounter with difference, on different terms, will reveal the inadequacy of the categories used to understand another" may remain the same for all his classes (102–103). In this way, coming "face-to-face with alterity" produces different group dynamics. Second, student responses to this particular manifestation of difference are set into motion by their own desires. How they interpret "teacher's desire" and how they articulate their own identification, disavowal, or indifference through words, textual practices, and "body language" installs their own desires—both conscious and unconscious—in the scene of pedagogy. It seems that students, in the act of confronting alterity, are not only confronting a symbolic Other of someone else's creation but also a psychical aspect of themselves—a symbolic Other of their own creation forged in the encounter with difference. Engaging a politics of difference, then, suggests that students need to learn how to confront these desires and that teachers need to learn to understand how pedagogy as performativity produces and manifests at some level, in varying degrees, teachers' own desires as well.

It is this dual form of learning that might be used in making meaningful connections among the many levels of difference, disparity, and desire at work here. As we have seen, on one level, difference is institutionally and socially framed. That is, Simon's practice of "teaching as a Jew" is already marked by systems of disparity that mark Jewishness as Otherness in the university context. Further, desires are socially and institutionally located insofar as they partake of both the *general* climate and history of a North American urban center (replete with social roles and both past and present anti-Semitic practices) and the *specific* environment of student-teacher relations in doctoral education at OISE, where Simon teaches. On yet another level, desires are profoundly idiosyncratic within these contexts, revealing complex personal histories that factor into (but do not determine) the perception and reception of alterity. Together, these three levels interact symbolically in the pedagogical encounter, as Simon's discussion has shown. My own point is that unless the individual desires that structure the pedagogical scene are acknowledged as an integral part of the politics of difference, the personal transformation necessary to envision social relations anew cannot be fully addressed. Thus, the specific encounter must not only be "interpreted" or "predicted" by theoretical commitments to a "politics of difference" but, as we shall see, must also reinform the discourse of pedagogy itself.

My suggestion to "acknowledge," "learn," and "understand" teacher-student desires needs to move from generalities to specific. However, in order to offer more practical approaches to engaging a politics of difference and to "flesh out" this difficult terrain of desire, it is necessary first to delve a little deeper into the unsaid dimensions of "articulating Otherness." I believe this will help us to rethink what concrete action is appropriate and to consider how pedagogy is not only about verbalized discourse but also about the ways students and teachers interrelate through their embodied presence. So far, my discussion has parenthetically alluded to the body and gesture in suggesting that "articulating Otherness" is performativity. This discussion must now explicitly take into account the often silent workings of the classroom through which this performativity is enacted, difference articulated, and desires forged. It seems to me that we need to understand more fully how desire operates in its specificity to sustain as well as challenge existing forms of disparity in terms of both the symbolic *and* the embodied nature of the pedagogical encounter. Therefore, I now turn to a broad view of "articulating"—a view that considers gesture and desire as part of the discursivity of the class—explored through a reading of Luce Irigaray's work on the importance of specificity in psychoanalytic practice.

ARTICULATION AND GESTURE: IRIGARAY'S *PRATICABLE*

Discussions on the relation between difference and the body often focus on "visible difference," on how the body is "read" through ideological constructions of race, ethnicity, and gender, or on the way the body is interpreted as being "resistant" or "docile," engaged in subversive or acquiescent behavior.[34] However, in focusing on gesture, I am inquiring into how it actively constructs the discursive limits of the class through which desires are negotiated and difference is articulated. As part of the scene of articulation, gesture here denotes bodily positioning through a spectrum that includes movement and stillness, posture and comportment.

Luce Irigaray makes some compelling remarks about what is in French is called the *praticable* of psychoanalytic practice, that is, those conventions and gestures that make up the encounter between analyst and analysand. Irigaray proposes that gesture in the analytic scene is fundamentally part of the "discourse" produced in the encounter and suggests that psychoanalytic discourse as a whole needs to pay closer attention to what actually occurs in the analytic situation itself. Indeed, as I have intimated above, it is my contention that our conceptions and discourses on the politics of difference also need to pay closer attention to the specificity of the pedagogical scene and to the desires that circulate through the said and unsaid practices of "articulating Otherness" in that scene. I hope to draw an analogy here between Irigaray's thoughts on the analytic *praticable* and the pedagogical scene of articulation, drawing attention to the geography and transferential relations that develop in conjunction with the unsaid dimensions of "discourse."[35]

Critiquing the way psychoanalysis neglects gesture "in favour of what is verbally expressed," Irigaray places gesture at the heart of the *praticable*.[36] In the sections that follow, I examine two dimensions of Irigaray's rendering of gesture in the *praticable*: first, in terms of the "geography of the analysis," that is, the placement and movement of bodies in the analytic scene; and second, in relation to the ongoing transference (i.e., the part of the therapeutic relationship in which analyst and analysand project their desires onto one another), which Irigaray sees as connected to this geography.[37]

1. *Geography of the Analysis.* The traditional gesture marking the analytic geography has now been infamously stereotyped: the analysand lies down on a couch, with the analyst seated behind it. "The analyst's body is lacking to the analysand's gaze. And the landmarks reverse themselves: from being face-to-face, right corresponding to left and left to right, there they are, one behind the other: left corresponding to left, right to right. As if the analyst and the analysand were looking at themselves in the same mirror?"[38] For Irigaray these *gestural* positions produce the conditions out of which arise the potential for *speaking* positions. The scene is set up for the analysand to remember (lying down)[39] and for the analyst to help the analysand build "his or her house of language."[40] But by positing the possibility that analyst and analysand look into the same mirror, Irigaray suggests that the geography of the analysis involves them both, encapsulates them both within the same gaze, the gaze of psychoanalytic discourse. In this "primal" analytic scene, however, the enacting of smaller gestures cannot be divorced from the discourse—the utterances—that occur during the analysis, nor from the discourse of psychoanalysis that governs the *praticable*. For instance, the analysand's twisting of rings and shuffling of feet are

> far from irrelevant to what he or she is talking about. All of this forms a
> whole which must be perceived and treated as such. Furthermore, all of this
> combines with the psychoanalyst's gestures to constitute a whole where the
> gestures of the one give the lead to the gestures of the other—and of course
> this dynamic includes instances in which the analysand's gestures deter-

mine the analyst's. Often it may be necessary for the psychoanalyst to invent gestures which prevent the economies of the two subjects becoming intricated.[41]

This give-and-take between the analyst and analysand, or what Irigaray calls a "seesawing back and forth,"[42] characterizes the nonspeaking exchange that makes or breaks discursive communication. Moreover, Irigaray recognizes that gesture and the way it is taken up by the participants in the analytic scene enacts difference: "Psychoanalytic practice is gesturally quite distinctive, in terms of discursive and communicative practice, in a way which is not neutral."[43] Gesture is not neutral in that, for Irigaray, it exists along an embodied, therefore sexuate, axis where the difference between the sexes makes itself felt. For instance, "the sexual connotations of lying down are different, depending on whether one is a man or woman."[44] Irigaray is neither claiming woman's "natural" attitude or posture nor valorizing the missionary position but is demonstrating that the meaning of asking someone to "lie down" is contingent upon the connotations associated with lying down for each of the sexes in a patriarchal economy (economy here signaling an exchange between the sexes). It is the *articulation* of the material sexed bodies *through culture* which determine this sexed difference, not a biological predisposition. In this way, the body is a marker of difference, and the gesture it enacts cannot be wrested from its relation to disparity, for the gesture performs that disparity, reenacts that inequality. Thus, for Irigaray, the gestures in the analytic scene are encoded gestures that do not have to be spoken about in order to have signifying power. Although bodies do not speak for themselves since they are always already encoded, they nevertheless do not rely upon a verbal enunciation in order to have meaning for another. According to Irigaray, the analytic scene must incorporate—literally speaking—the body's gestures into its discursive structure, rather than seeing these gestures as incidental to the analytic process.

2. *Transference.* In Freudian and Lacanian terms, transference generally alludes to the projection of the analysand's unconscious desire onto the analyst and to the resulting "acting out" of past problems and fantasies in the analytic encounter. The analyst as recipient of these projections may enact a *counter-transference* in response. However, Irigaray proposes an alternative in suggesting that transference is also something beyond this action-reaction constellation. For her, the drama of the transference is produced in relation to the gestures (the sexed gestures) of the protagonists and not only as a result of a prior psychical state initiated by the analysand. Irigaray privileges not only the past, but also the present as the condition for the transference.[45] Given

that Irigaray believes that the gesture of the one affects the gesture of the other, the transference is from the beginning located in the dynamic between the two (*entre deux*). The starting point of transference is not in the presumption of a subject who knows, which provokes love and desire, as Lacan elaborates, but in the way gesture between the two participants functions as its source. Paradoxically, Irigaray writes that "within the transference, a certain limit, a certain threshold is never crossed and always transgressed—the porosity of the mucous membranes."[46] I read this as indicating that the transference is the form of space-time that is indeterminate—it is not entirely a flowing from the analysand (the traditional view of transference), nor is it a flowing into her (the countertransference). Rather, it is a "third space" (to borrow again from Bhabha) a mucous space, a shared space where each is involved in an exchange with the other. Irigaray uses the mucous here to symbolize what psychoanalytic discourse has largely—because of its phallocentrism, according to Irigaray—failed to symbolize.[47] In this sense, then, I do not interpret her as claiming that the analytic scene has no boundaries or that it exists in a state outside of signification and symbolization. Rather, Irigaray's mobilization of the mucous metaphor suggests the need to think the analytic scene differently, through its difference, through the way difference emerges in the dynamic of desire that marks the transference. Irigaray is challenging the way the analytic scene has been constructed through the language of psychoanalysis, from Freud onward. Moreover, she challenges the way transference has been taken up in this discourse and insists, unlike Freud and Lacan, that the analyst must constantly reinterpret her/his transference (not *counter*transference), as it provides the basis on which the analyst gives space-time to the analytic situation, the space-time in which s/he listens.[48]

In drawing an analogy between analysis and pedagogy, I do not wish to suggest that one can easily and without qualification graft onto the pedagogical scene the structure of an analytic situation, that one can simply substitute teacher for analyst and student for analysand. To do so would be to ignore the many differences between them. First, the situation in a classroom is not one-on-one, as in an analytic setting (although the situation between thesis supervisor and student can at times approximate this setting). Indeed, part of what makes the classroom so stimulating is the dynamics among all its participants. Second, the purposes of the two encounters are inherently different insofar as the social aim of education is quite distinct from the therapeutic aim of psychoanalysis. Third, transference and desire circulate in very different institutional arrangements, where their acceptance as objects of interpretation and analysis in the institution of psychoanalysis is quite different from the often rigorous denial of their presence in educational institutions. Nevertheless, the analytic and the pedagogical are both about scenes of production: of meaning, of knowledge, and of desire. Moreover, both entail arrangements where inter-subjective dynamics play an important role in this production. Further, both rely heavily upon entrenched expectations of speaking and nonspeaking posi-tions: who speaks when to whom, why, and how. More specifically, I see Iri-garay's rendering of the geography of the analysis, along with her views on transference, as especially helpful for exploring the unsaid dimensions of "ar-ticulating Otherness" and for thinking through the pedagogical encounter an-alytically. Her views lead to what I see as a number of important issues for a pedagogy committed to a politics of difference.

First, in recognizing that gesture is not neutral but tied to cultural articula-tions of sexual difference, Irigaray opens up the possibility for questioning how gesture is also affected by other articulations of difference. In pedagogical terms, teachers and students need to be sensitive to how the geography of the classroom (e.g., seating arrangements and rules of comportment for students and teachers) signifies differently for different members of the class and to how this signification is related to the encoding of particular articulations of difference in our society.

Second, by reconceiving transference through metaphors of mucous, fluid, and interchange, Irigaray highlights the interactional, dialectical character of the analyst-analysand relationship in a way that compels both to examine the gestural relations out of which the transference arose. Pedagogically, teachers need to become aware of how their own practices are not only infused with their own desires but how these operate along with student desires in an am-niotic-like setting (to push Irigaray's metaphor to its limit), creating a "third space" where it is not so easy to tell whose desires are whose any longer.

Third, Irigaray emphasizes that gesture is part of the discourse of analytic theory and practice and is not an incidental matter. For pedagogy, this re-quires that critical attention be directed toward the way gesture operates as a defining feature of classroom experience and not merely as an epiphenome-non of what is said explicitly in the class. In this way, desire can be thought of in terms of how it is produced in the unsaid, in the seesawing back and forth between students, as well as between teacher and student.

Fourth, taken together, I view these issues as necessitating a reconsideration of our interpretive stance vis-à-vis gesture. Too often, gesture is read as being *either* resistant *or* acquiescent in dominant relations of power. Irigaray's views create a mode of analyzing the specificity of the class that cannot always be so easily read, for if gesture is not neutral, if it gives rise to desires in transfer-ence, and if it is the unsaid dimension of pedagogical articulation (including the articulation of difference), then our gestures may indeed be contradictory, ambivalent, or at least ambiguous. In this sense, then, gesture must be read simultaneously from these three levels: difference, disparity, and desire.

CONCLUSION: SOME PRACTICAL CONSIDERATIONS
FOR A POLITICS OF DIFFERENCE

So far, I have suggested here that (1) a pedagogy committed to transforming social disparity through a politics of difference needs to examine that "in-between" space where identity resists being determined by social difference, that space of desire (and identification); (2) in order to examine this space, transformative educators need to look beyond difference as "being an Other" and view difference as "articulating Otherness," something that occurs in the performativity of teaching itself; and (3) this scene of articulation involves paying attention to the specificity of the class, focusing on how gesture is part of the discursivity that arouses desire and articulates difference. In this conclusion, I attempt to offer some practical considerations for looking at pedagogy in 3-D: through difference, disparity, and desire simultaneously.

Perhaps the best way to address these considerations is to return to this question: Where does the indeterminacy of desire leave transformative educators? For me, this is perhaps *the* crucial question facing those of us who continue to work across, through, and with difference. The indeterminate dimension of desire means that educators can never expect what they say about difference to "produce" predictable outcomes. Desire, is not, therefore, something we can control. We cannot make others take on the desires we want them to have, no matter how socially just and morally sensitive we might think those desires are. However, we can assume neither that desires are immutable, totally abstracted from the contexts out of which they arise nor that they are unaffected by systems of representation. Indeed, this essay has attempted to demonstrate how desires are intimately connected to articulatory practices that recognize language, images, and gesture as part of the pedagogical scene. Thus, in order to transform desires, we must create the kind of pedagogical space that paradoxically acknowledges their unpredictability, their indeterminacy. Given this ambivalent state of affairs, in what way is viewing pedagogy in 3-D, that is, seeing the interconnections among difference, disparity, and desire, helpful to educators attempting to negotiate these very murky waters?

Practically speaking, I am suggesting that teachers and students participate in an environment where each assumes responsibility for self-questioning, for recognizing the play of desire in their acceptance, rejection, or indifference to difference. However, this is no easy task. For students are, practically speaking, incapable of creating such an environment without the teacher's full support, and teachers go out on an institutional limb to make the pedagogical dynamic itself part of the "subject matter" under study. Incorporating desire into the "discourse" of the class would require introducing students to the vocabulary of desire, discussing how desires often conflict with one's public identity and political commitments, how they may be more entrenched in stereotypical modes of expression than perhaps otherwise thought, and how their ambivalence can structure the way we receive, hear, and respond to articulations of difference. In other words, students and teachers alike would need to constantly ask themselves the question: How might my conscious response to articulations of difference be conditioned by unconscious desires that are at once private and eminently connected to public attitudes, representations, and norms? Furthermore, this type of class might emphasize how the intersubjective dynamic of desire *takes place within* social and cultural demarcations of difference along the trajectories of race, class, gender, ethnicity, and sexuality and that desire *arises out* of the said and unsaid classroom articulations of Otherness. In short, it would encourage both teachers and students alike to "read" their desire as, simultaneously, an idiosyncratic, intersubjective, and sociocultural dynamic.

This does not mean that pedagogy becomes another form of talking cure, in which teaching is another therapy fad. Instead, I am suggesting that teaching and learning be talked about in the classroom in ways that underscore both the general role of desire in our understanding of difference and the particular ways in which unconscious desire may be informing the pedagogical discourse. Perhaps beginning with a text or situation not so close to students' lives might be helpful. Examples from literature, psychoanalytic case studies, memoirs, news reports, or ethnographies may offer opportunities to interpret how desire functions in relation to specific articulations of difference (for instance, in the support of stereotypes or in the celebration of marginality) from a "safe distance." These interpretative strategies can then become the initial bases for *pedagogical* interpretation. I stress *pedagogical* here, for teachers *do* need to retain professional limits regarding what is under discussion, always returning desire to the specificities of the class and sociocultural context and not focusing, for instance on, an individual's sexual fantasies and personal history.

I suspect the danger for abuse in this approach is no greater than that which currently exists, for desire already circulates through our articulatory practices whether we acknowledge it or not. Pedagogy is always a risky business in this respect. Nevertheless, it may be wise to acknowledge that the risks might be different when desire itself becomes the subject of our articulations; that is, we might iatrogenically produce the symptom of desire through our interventions (e.g., obsessively seeing desire everywhere), and we need to be ever vigilant about this. Perhaps it would be helpful to remember that in discussing the dynamic of pedagogical desire and in consciously articulating the presence of desire along with Otherness, the point is not to put students or teachers on "hot seats," where the goal is to "name another's desire." Rather, the point for a politics of difference is to allow the space for self-interpretation in a way that makes evident that the "self" is profoundly connected to social roles, representational systems, and intersubjective relations, as well as being psychically constructed. This means encouraging students—and teachers—to talk about how desires may be produced and manifested in relation to (1) what is being said in the class, (2) what remains unsaid in the class (i.e., the pedagogical transference and the geography of the class), (3) cultural systems of representation that "articulate Otherness" (i.e., film, advertising, and media), and (4) social disparities that structure differences differently. For instance, in showing the class examples of stereotypical representations of women, we might consider: What makes these images stereotypical? What do they tell us about desire? Whose desire are we talking about? Are there other ways in which desire can be reconfigured here? How does the history of misogynistic representation factor into how we identify with the images put before us? As women and men, as gays, bisexuals, and straights, how do we deal with desires that may conflict with our public personas? And how does the fact that the teacher presents this image to the class affect the way the class as whole speaks about these desires?

Looking at pedagogy in 3-D, then, through the interconnections of difference, disparity, and desire, challenges us to be constantly critical of the way our actions are implicated in the complexity of other people's lives. This means that a different kind of understanding is required to interpret and reinterpret the desirous interchange between teachers and students. In other words, teachers, in "articulating Otherness," in discussing the significance of race, class, gender, ethnicity, or sexuality in a number of contexts, need not only have an understanding of subject matter but also a sensitivity to people and a willingness to interpret how the pedagogical dynamic of desire affects learning in the class. Making interpretation an important aspect of pedagogical reflection, of course, requires that teachers come face-to-face with their own alterity, their own Otherness, their own desires in the course of encouraging students to do the same. Like Irigaray's analyst, we need, as teachers and theorists, to reinterpret our own transference as the condition that allows us to become the space-time in and through which we listen, speak, and write to/with our students. It is the space-time through which difference, disparity, and desire emerge together in the articulatory practice, broadly conceived.

The hermeneutical aspect, of course, neither takes place in a social, economic, or cultural vacuum, nor can it presume the utter transparency of desire; what it enables, however, is a way of rethinking pedagogical relations that subjects our interpretations to critical scrutiny, that makes desire less opaque and mysterious—and, perhaps, less frightening. Normalizing desire, so to speak, is not intended to encourage a further eroticization of the classroom but rather to encourage an acceptance of the unpredictable, for it may be a rich source of hope in our struggles against systemic injustice.

NOTES

1. I am using the singular form of "difference" here, despite the fact that there are obviously many articulations of difference. When referring to specific, material examples of difference, I will pluralize the noun; when I refer to its use as a concept, it will remain singular. With respect to the politics of difference and pedagogy, there is an extensive literature devoted to the topic that began to appear in the late 1980s and early 1990s. For a sampling of the issues, see Lawrence Grossberg, "Introduction: Bringing It All Back Home—Pedagogy and Cultural Studies," in *Between Borders: Pedagogy and the Politics of Cultural Studies*, ed. Henry A. Giroux and Peter McLaren (New York: Routledge, 1994), 1–28; Deborah Britzman, Kelvin Santiago-Válles, Gladys Jiménez-Méñoz, and Laura Lamash, "Slips That Show and Tell: Fashioning Multiculture as a Problem of Representation," in *Race, Identity and Representation in Education*, ed. Cameron McCarthy and Warren Crichlow (New York: Routledge, 1993), 188–200; Elizabeth Ellsworth, "Why Doesn't This Feel Empowering? Working through the Repressive Myths of Critical Pedagogy," *Harvard Educational Review* 59, no. 3 (1989), 297–324; Henry Giroux, "Resisting Difference: Cultural Studies and the Discourse of Critical Pedagogy," in *Cultural Studies*, ed. Lawrence Grossberg, Cary Nelson, and Paula Treichler (New York: Routledge, 1992), 199–212; Henry Giroux, *Living Dangerously: Multiculturalism and the Politics of Difference* (New York: Peter Lang, 1993); Fabienne Worth, "Postmodern Pedagogy in the Multicultural Classroom: For Inappropriate Teachers and Imperfect Spectators," *Cultural Critique* 25 (fall 1993), 5–32.
2. Joan Scott critiques this concept in "Multiculturalism and the Politics of Identity," *October* 61 (summer 1992), especially 13–14.
3. See, for instance, Homi Bhabha, "Interview: The Third Space," in *Identity, Community, Culture, Difference*, ed. Jonathan Rutherford (London: Lawrence and Wishart, 1990), 207–21; Homi Bhabha, *The Location of Culture* (New York: Routledge, 1994) (all further references to Bhabha's work are from this book); Stuart Hall, "Cultural Identity and Diaspora," in Rutherford, *Identity, Community, Culture, Difference*, 222–37; Hall, "Ethnicity: Identity and Difference," *Radical America* 13, no. 4 (1991), 9–20; Gayatri Chakravorty Spivak, *The Post-Colonial Critic: Interviews, Strategies, Dialogues*, ed. Sarah Harasym (New York: Routledge, 1990); and Gayatri Spivak, *Outside in the Teaching Machine* (New York: Routledge, 1993).
4. The literature on identity politics is extensive. For a sampling of interesting critiques and summaries of identity politics, see Liz Bondi, "Locating Identity Politics," in *Place and the Politics of Identity*, ed. Michael Keith and Steve Pile (London: Routledge, 1993), 84–101; Stanley Aronowitz, *The Politics of Identity* (New York: Routledge,

1992); Mary Louise Adams, "There's No Place Like Home: On the Place of Identity in Feminist Politics," *Feminist Review* 31 (spring 1989), 22–33; Linda Briskin, "Identity Politics and the Hierarchy of Oppression: A Comment," *Feminist Review* 35 (1990), 102–108; and Lisa Duggan, "Queering the State," *Social Text* 39 (1994), 1–14. For a discussion on how radical pedagogy has failed to take up the issue of desire, see Worth, "Postmodern Pedagogy."

5. Lawrence Grossberg, "Cultural Studies and/in New Worlds," in McCarthy and Crichlow, *Race, Identity, and Representation*, 98.

6. Ibid.

7. Homi Bhabha, Introduction to *The Location of Culture* (New York: Routledge, 1994), 2.

8. Indira Karamcheti has made this latter issue the subject of her essay "Caliban in the Classroom," in *Pedagogy: The Question of Impersonation*, ed. Jane Gallop (Bloomington: Indiana University Press, 1995), 138–46.

9. Bhabha, 2

10. My use of the term "desire" that does not easily fit into any single school of psychoanalysis. It is, rather, a hybrid use that recognizes the Freudian and Lacanian emphasis on desire as being born out of initial entry into the symbolic order, yet it also acknowledges that desire is produced in interactions (spoken and bodily) between people in the here and now. This is more along the lines of Irigaray's thought, as we shall see further on.

11. See Luce Irigaray's discussion of the importance of desire and difference in social transformation in some of her later books, *Je, Tu, Nous: Toward a Culture of Difference*, trans. Alison Martin (New York: Routledge, 1993) and *Thinking the Difference: For a Peaceful Revolution*, trans. Karin Montin (New York: Routledge, 1994). For an account of desire as excess, see her earlier work *Speculum of the Other Woman*, trans. Gillian C. Gill (Ithaca: Cornell University Press, 1985) and *This Sex Which Is Not One*, trans. Catherine Porter with Carolyn Burke (Ithaca: Cornell University Press, 1985).

12. Stuart Hall, "Cultural Identity and Diaspora," 228.

13. From a research point of view, Deborah Britzman writes: "If educational researchers are just beginning to understand that schooling produces not just forms of knowledge and particular relations of inequality along race and gendered divides, but more immediately, must coincidentally produce and organize the racial, cultural, and gendered identities of students, the complexities of these matters in tandem and as social relations are not well theorized." "What Is This Thing Called Love?" *Taboo* 1 (spring, 1995), 66.

14. In a slightly different context, Roger Simon claims "pedagogy is a practice within which one acts with the intent of provoking experience that will *simultaneously organize and disorganize* a variety of understandings of our natural and social world" [my emphasis] *Teaching Against the Grain* (Toronto: OISE Press, 1992), 56. It is this tension that constitutes the "doubling effect" I am alluding to here.

15. "Other" with a capital O is being used to emphasize the symbolic construction of alterity, of difference. Seeing all difference as a creation of Otherness reveals the psychoanalytic reading I am bringing to bear here, in which distinctions between self and Other are always about identity and difference. The counterclaim that we have a great deal in common with those who are marked as Other or that as Other we have a great deal in common with those who have so labeled us only underscores the point that sameness and difference are registered in terms of the self as a point of reference. Of course, this does not mean that we have to accept the social valuation attributed to

these differences as a "fixed phenomenological point opposed to the self" (Bhabha, 51) but that, symbolically speaking, difference is always in relation to a *construction or representation* of identity, of self.

16. Scott, "Multiculturalism," 13.

17. Ibid., 14.

18. Clearly, I do not wish to suggest that the experiential effects of living one's difference do not influence, or cannot result in, different forms of knowledge resistant to dominant and oppressive knowledge claims. The literature on standpoint epistemology, for instance, makes evident the connections between difference and identity in a way that highlights how knowledge is mediated through social relations of power. Moreover, it exposes the delegitimation and devaluation of these particular forms of knowledge in mainstream discourses. In this sense, then, writing from one's experience of difference is a crucial method of subverting the disparity that structures difference. However, my point is that relying too heavily on the way Otherness, alterity, and difference are always an aspect of one's "being" presupposes the very causal link between social difference and individual identity that needs to be exposed and challenged.

19. Gayatri Chakravorty Spivak, "Marginality in the Teaching Machine," in *Outside in the Teaching Machine* (New York: Routledge, 1993), 54. Interestingly, Grossberg's phrase "logic of difference" becomes the flip side of the "logic of identitarianism," underlining how easily we recognize difference as being one's identity.

20. I am using the term "symbolic" in a rather broad sense here, to refer to the general use of language, visual images, and sounds for communicative purposes rather than to specific signs and symbols. Similarly, "articulating" is usually associated with speech; however, as will become more evident further on, "articulating" also suggests the production of these general symbolic forms through gesture as well as spoken discourse.

21. Bhabha, 1 (my emphasis).

22. Ibid., 70.

23. Reiterating this point, Spivak remarks that "for the long haul emancipatory social intervention is not primarily a question of redressing victimage by the assertion of (class- or gender- or ethnocultural) identity. It is a question of developing a vigilance for systemic appropriations of the unacknowledged social production of a *differential* that is one basis of exchange into the networks of the cultural politics of class- or gender-*identification*." *Outside in the Teaching Machine*, 63.

24. Diana Fuss, "Identification Papers," in *Identification Papers* (New York: Routledge, 1995), 47.

25. See Michael Eric Dyson, "Be Like Mike? Michael Jordan and the Pedagogy of Desire," in *Reflecting Black: African-American Cultural Criticism*, (Minneapolis: University of Minnesota Press, 1993), 64–75.

26. Both Bhabha and Fuss emphasize the significance of interpretation in "reading" identifications and desires. See especially, Bhabha, 52; and Fuss, "Identification Papers," 32.

27. Bhabha, 52.

28. Henry Giroux, *Disturbing Pleasures* (New York: Routledge, 1994), 19.

29. "Mimetic" is used in a conventional sense here, and not in the sense that Judith Butler and Irigaray use it to denote a citational (and potentially subversive) practice. See, for instance, Butler's discussion of Irigaray and Plato in *Bodies That Matter* (New York: Routledge, 1993), 36–55.

30. Roger Simon, "Face-to-Face with Alterity: Postmodern Jewish Identity and the Eros of Pedagogy," in Gallop, *Pedagogy*, 90–105.

31. Simon qualifies his discussion by noting that he is writing about his own experience and not all educational experience.

32. I wish to emphasize here that teaching through one's identity can be the result of a number of desires that cannot simply be read off from an article or even from performance. Although psychoanalytic interpretation is concerned with discourse and texts, the presumption that an individual's desires are transparent or amenable to decontextualized readings eclipses the radical *specificity* of analysis, in my view.

33. It seems the stakes are high for all educators, and not only for those who consciously assert their own identities in class or who do so through "articulating Otherness." However, it is outside the scope of this essay to deal with this assertion in full.

34. See for example, Karamcheti, "Caliban," in Gallop; Peter McLaren "Schooling the Postmodern Body: Critical Pedagogy and the Politics of Enfleshment," in *Postmodernism, Feminism, and Cultural Politics*, ed. Henry Giroux (New York: SUNY Press, 1991), 144–73; and bell hooks, *Teaching to Transgress* (New York: Routledge, 1994), esp. 135–41.

35. I am particularly indebted to Elizabeth Hirsh's phrase "geography of analysis" and her thorough discussion on transference and the theory-practice relationship that Irigaray proposes. My own reading differs from hers in minor respects, especially in the emphasis I place on gesture here. See "Back in Analysis: How To Do Things with Irigaray," in *Engaging with Irigaray: Feminist Philosophy and Modern European Thought*, ed. Carolyn Burke, Naomi Schor, and Margaret Whitford (New York: Columbia University Press, 1994), 285–315.

36. Luce Irigaray, "The Gesture in Psychoanalysis," in *Between Feminism and Psychoanalysis*, ed. Teresa Brennan (London: Routledge, 1989), 127.

37. The term "transference" is far more contentious and difficult to pinpoint than I am suggesting here. Freud discusses transference in the case of Dora ("A Fragment of an Analysis of a Case of Hysteria," in vol. 7 of *The Standard Edition of the Complete Psychological Works of Sigmund Freud*, ed. James Strachey (London: Hogarth Press, 1953, 3–112), and in a lecture entitled "Transference," *SE* 16, 431–47. Here, the analysand repeats, through displacement onto the analyst, the repressed material that is the source of his or her neurosis. Lacan's reading of Freud suggests that transference really begins as soon as there is a "subject-supposed-to-know"; it is this imaginary attribution that sets off a transferential relationship on the part of the analysand, entwining feelings of love with feelings of authority. See especially, Jacques Lacan, *Four Fundamental Concepts of Psycho-Analysis*, trans. Alan Sheridan (New York: W. W. Norton, 1981), especially chap. 17–19. It is Lacan's notion of transference that has been taken up over the last ten or fifteen years by many who write on psychoanalysis and pedagogy. Irigaray, as we shall see, chooses to locate the transference in the fluid interaction between analyst and analysand. In this sense, she sees transference (and not countertransference) as an issue as much for the analyst as for the analysand.

38. Luce Irigaray, "Le praticable de la scène," in *Parler n'est jamais neutre* (Paris: Minuit, 1985), 242.

39. Irigaray, "Gesture," 128.

40. Ibid., 129. She acknowledges the Heideggerian reference here.

41. Ibid., 127.

42. Irigaray, "Le praticable," 240.

43. Irigaray, "Gesture," 129.

44. Ibid.

45. Hirsh, throughout her essay, gives much theoretical weight to the *hic et nunc* of Irigaray's reconception of the *praticable*.

46. Irigaray, "La limite du transfert," in *Parler n'est jamais neutre*, 302; for an English translation see "The Limits of the Transference," in *The Irigaray Reader*, ed. Margaret Whitford (Oxford: Basil Blackwell, 1991), 113.

47. For instance, Irigaray writes: "Fluid always subsists *between* solid substances to join them, to re-unite them. Without the intervention of fluids, no discourse would hold together." "Le langage de l'homme," in *Parler n'est jamais neutre*, 289. This article is also translated into English as "The Language of Man," *Cultural Critique* (fall 1989), 191–202.

48. Irigaray, "La limite," 304; "The Limits," 116.

Contributors

Derek Briton is a Social Sciences and Humanities Research Council of Canada Doctoral Fellow in the Department of Educational Policy Studies at the University of Alberta. His research focuses on the psychoanalysis of society and culture, particularly the application of psychoanalytic principles to pedagogy. Most recently, he is author of *The Modern Practice of Adult Education: A Postmodern Critique* (SUNY Press, 1996) and of essays in *Action Research as a Living Practice*, ed. Terrance Carson and Dennis Sumara (Garland, forthcoming) and in *JCT: An Interdisciplinary Journal of Curriculum Studies*

Shoshana Felman is Thomas E. Donnelly Professor of French and Comparative Literature, Yale University. She is the author of numerous books, among them *Jacques Lacan and the Adventure of Insight* (Harvard University Press, 1987), *What Does Woman Want? Reading and Sexual Difference* (Johns Hopkins University Press, 1993), and, with Dori Laub, *Testimony: The Crisis of Witnessing* (Routledge, 1992).

Laurie Finke is professor of Women's and Gender Studies at Kenyon College. She is author of *Feminist Theory, Women's Writing* (Cornell University Press, 1992), has coedited, with Martin Shichtman, *Medieval Texts and Contemporary Readers* (Cornell University Press, 1987) and, with Robert Con Davis, *Contemporary Criticism and Theory* (Longman, 1989), and has written several articles on feminist theory, pedagogy, and medieval studies.

Helen Harper is assistant professor in the Curriculum Division, Faculty of Education, University of Western Ontario. Her work focuses on issues of identity formation in relation to school contexts. Her book *Dangerous Desires: High School Girls and Feminist Writing Practices* is forthcoming from Peter Lang Press.

Kaarina Kailo is associate professor of women's studies and Acting Principal at the Simone de Beauvoir Institute, Concordia University. She has published widely in feminist journals both in North America and in Finland. She is active in various Finnish-Canadian associations, and her current research is focused on a comparative study of circumpolar women's literary and spiritual traditions.

Gae Mackwood is a Ph.D. candidate at the University of Alberta. Her research focuses on the intersection of writings by Jacques Derrida and contemporary curriculum theorizing. Her current interests include mind-body antimonies in curriculum theory, educational research methods, and school practices.

Rebecca A. Martusewicz is associate professor in the Teacher Education Department and director of Women's Studies at Eastern Michigan University. She is coeditor, with William Reynolds, of *Inside/Out: Contemporary Critical Perspectives in Education* (St. Martin's Press, 1994) and author of several book chapters and articles that draw upon post-structuralist philosophy to analyze the dynamics of educational relations.

Erica McWilliam is senior lecturer in the School of Culture and Policy Studies (Faculty of Education) at the Queensland University of Technology in Australia. She received a Ph.D. from the University of Queensland and has published internationally on new feminist pedagogy and research. She is author of *In Broken Images: Feminist Tales for a Different Teacher Education* (Teachers College Press, 1994) and is coeditor of *Pedagogy, Technology, and the Body* (Peter Lang, 1996).

Judith P. Robertson is associate professor of English Language Arts education and women's studies in the Faculty of Education, University of Ottawa. She has published articles in *TABOO, Canadian Journal of Education*, and *Changing English*. Her book *Cinema and the Politics of Desire in Teacher Education* is forthcoming from SUNY Press; she is also editing a volume entitled *Elementary Voices: Teaching About Genocide and Intolerance through Language Arts Education* (NCTE, forthcoming).

Sharon Todd is assistant professor in the Faculty of Education, York University. Her published research focuses on the relationships among psychoanalysis, education, and representation.

Index